The 1940 Cincinnati Reds

The 1940 Cincinnati Reds

A World Championship and
Baseball's Only In-Season Suicide

BRIAN MULLIGAN

McFarland & Company, Inc., Publishers
Jefferson, North Carolina, and London

Photographs on pages 16, 22, and 119 are provided by the National Baseball Hall of Fame and Library, Cooperstown, N.Y. All others courtesy of the Cincinnati Reds.

LIBRARY OF CONGRESS CATALOGUING-IN-PUBLICATION DATA

Mulligan, Brian, 1963–
    The 1940 Cincinnati Reds : a world championship and baseball's only in-season suicide / Brian Mulligan.
      p.   cm.
    Includes bibliographical references and index.

    ISBN 0-7864-2090-1 (softcover : 50# alkaline paper) ∞

    1. Cincinnati Reds (Baseball team)—History—20th century.
2. World Series (Baseball) (1940).   3. Hershberger, Willard,
1910–1940.   4. Baseball players—Suicidal behavior—United
States.   I. Title.
GV875.C65M85   2005
796.357'64'0977178 — dc22   2004030531

British Library cataloguing data are available

Cover photograph: Reserve catcher Willard Hershberger (National Baseball Hall of Fame and Library, Cooperstown, N.Y.)

Manufactured in the United States of America

McFarland & Company, Inc., Publishers
  Box 611, Jefferson, North Carolina 28640
  www.mcfarlandpub.com

For the people who have been so very good to me —
Mary, Katelyn, Jack,
and
my mother and father

Acknowledgments

When a thing is worth doing and is followed through to completion, there's usually a team of very selfless people behind it. This book was no different. I am dedicated to many people, both known and unknown to me, without whose contributions I would not have been able to complete this story.

I am indebted to the Cincinnati Reds organization, especially Jarrod Rollins, whose contributions of photographs and willingness to help with this project made such a difference. No matter how the Reds finish in the standings, they are truly world champions and a first-class organization. My thanks also go out to former players from the 1940 team, Gene "Junior" Thompson and Eddie Joost, who shared their recollections with me in separate phone interviews.

I am grateful to the staffs of the South Huntington Public Library; the New York Public Library; the Research Library at the National Baseball Hall of Fame in Cooperstown, New York (especially Bill Burdick); and the Society of American Baseball Research (SABR), all of whom provided valuable resources that enabled me to complete the research for this project.

On the friends and family team, thank you to Dennis Heffernan, Steve Sufrin, and Steve Lysohir for their counsel and friendship; my mother, who in giving me a book of old baseball photographs spurred my interest in Willard Hershberger and the rest of the 1940 Reds; my brother, Paul, who shared my love of baseball growing up and continues to share it today; and my father, who brought a love of baseball and writing into my life. He died before this book was completed, but I know he would have enjoyed seeing it in print.

Finally, anyone who has ever played baseball at any level knows that there is a tremendous amount of joy and a sense of accomplishment when you finally make it home. I'm one of the lucky ones who gets to feel like that every time I make it home and walk through the front door. Big hugs and kisses go out to my family. To Katelyn and Jack, who were always interested in the work I was doing and were excited to see it completed, and, most important, to my wife, Mary, who not only helped me with editing and rewriting the manuscript but also showed a tremendous amount of love, support, and patience through the long hours spent writing, researching, and driving on the multiple trips to Cooperstown. There's no one else I'd rather have by my side.

Table of Contents

Preface

It breaks your heart. It is designed to break your heart. The game begins in the spring, when everything else begins again and it blossoms in the summer, filling the afternoons and evenings, and then as soon as the chill rains come, it stops and leaves you to face the fall alone.
— A. Bartlett Giamatti

The story of the 1940 Cincinnati Reds is, of course, a story about the baseball team and its successful run to a world title, but this book is not so much about the team collectively, as it is about individual players who comprised that championship squad.

Regrettably, most of those players are dead and gone now. Yet as I researched their story both on and beyond the diamond, it came alive with a resonance that is as important today as it was then. It is a story about greatness and achievement, about fragility, cruelty, and compassion — ultimately about the tragedy and triumph of baseball and of life.

The beginning of my interest in this Reds team came to me quite accidentally, while I was thumbing through a coffee-table book of old baseball photographs by Charles Conlon. There, among the more than 100 intimate portraits of baseball giants such as Ruth, Gehrig, Cobb and Mathewson, was a haunting photograph of a little-known, 28-year-old reserve catcher for the Reds named Willard Hershberger, who seemed uncomfortable, looking askance at the camera. The caption underneath read in part, "The only player to ever commit suicide during a major league season."

From that moment on my interest began to manifest itself into something more than just passing (some would say morbid) curiosity. As I learned more about the 1940 season, I wondered how a player who was fulfilling the dream of a million or more American boys and was playing for a pennant-winning team would so suddenly and violently destroy himself. What effect would such a horrific act have on his teammates?

I took greater notice of the players of my own generation who for one reason or another had failed during an important moment of an important game. There was former Phillies pitcher Mitch Williams, who gave up a series-ending home run to Joe Carter of the Toronto Blue Jays in the 1991 series and was harassed and threatened at his home until he was forced to move on (both physically and literally) with his life. I also read Thomas Sowell's excellent report of the 1986 playoffs and World Series, *One Pitch Away*, which detailed the triumphs and tragedies of the players on the 1986 division winners. There was the suicide of California Angels pitcher Donnie Moore, who like Williams had served up a series-ending home run, only to later take his life; and of course, Bill Buckner, the "goat" of the 1986 series, who was mercilessly taunted throughout New England years after his costly error cost the Red Sox Game 6 of the World Series. Buckner, who to that point had a successful Major League career, eventually packed his bags for obscurity in Idaho.

What did it mean to perform under such tremendous pressure and to fail so publicly under the weight of that pressure?

With that as background, I delved deeper into Hershberger's story and by extension the stories of some of his teammates. What I found was a tale both tragic and triumphant and one that is truly American.

I did not set out to write about a baseball season, although many of the important games and performances of that season, culminating in the drama of a seven-game World Series, are chronicled here. What was of greater interest to me was the human side of the story, the people who are often deified or demonized based on their ability to play a child's game — a game that, Giamatti so poignantly wrote, was designed to break your heart.

1

◆ ◆ ◆ ◆

Damn Yankees

It may be an exaggeration to say that every baseball story begins or ends with the sport's most celebrated franchise from the Bronx. Yet despite all efforts to avoid such a predictable opening, this baseball story also starts with the men in pinstripes. As we begin, it is the middle of a sweltering Indian summer, October 1939, the last game of the season at Crosley Field in Cincinnati. The hometown Reds carry a 4–2 lead into the top of the ninth inning and need a win to prolong their season and avoid being swept in the World Series by the New York Yankees.

The Reds have had a remarkable season and are making their first trip to the Fall Classic since their tainted 1919 championship (where they bested the infamous Chicago "Black" Sox). In the 1939 campaign, the Reds posted a 97–57 mark, finishing four and a half games in front of the second-place Cardinals. Their opponents, the AL champion Yankees, have had an even more remarkable season, going 106–45 for a .702 winning percentage, despite a season full of distractions centering around one of the game's all-time great players.

Earlier in the season, New York witnessed the sudden and emotional retirement of their captain, Lou Gehrig, who along with Babe Ruth anchored one of the most feared lineups in major league history, the legendary Murderers' Row. Though Gehrig remained on the bench and on the roster as the season wore on, he eventually became too weak to even bring out the lineup card.[1] The Iron Horse's departure from the playing field, though devastating to the team from both an emotional and production standpoint (he had hit a respectable .295, 29 HRs, and 114 RBIs in 1938), hardly seemed to slow the powerhouse team in pinstripes.

If there was another team in baseball that could withstand the loss of one of the most productive hitters of all time and proceed almost effortlessly to the pennant (winning the league by a full 17 games over the second-place Boston Red Sox), they certainly could not be found in any major

3

league city but New York in 1939. To be sure, the Yankees were also the only team who could watch a player of Gehrig's stature leave so suddenly from their lineup and have a future baseball immortal, such as Joe DiMaggio, already in place to pick up the slack. At the close of the decade, they were about to lose the undisputed heart of their team, yet they had won three consecutive World Series titles, had a prolific scouting and farm system, and were the envy of most every team in baseball.

The Luckiest Man

Even for a franchise as committed and used to excellence as the Yankees, 1939 was all the more extraordinary because of the emotional roller coaster the team endured with Gehrig's departure from the lineup.

In Yankee Stadium on April 30, Lou Gehrig played his 2,130th consecutive game against the Washington Senators, and he knew he was through. "I just can't seem to get going," he told manager Joe McCarthy. "Nobody has to tell me how bad I've been." On May 2, the very next game in Detroit, Gehrig voluntarily benched himself. Teammates averted their eyes as the man known as the Iron Horse sat down on the bench, ending his consecutive game streak, and for all intents and purposes, his Hall of Fame career.

A little more than a month later, on June 21, two days after Gehrig's 36th birthday, Yankee president Ed Barrow told the world what was happening to his stalwart first baseman. The statement from the Mayo Clinic explained, "Lou Gehrig is suffering from amyotrophic lateral sclerosis. This type of illness involves the motor pathway and cells of the central nervous system and in lay terms is known as a chronic form of poliomyelitis (infantile paralysis).... The nature of this trouble makes it such that Mr. Gehrig will be unable to continue his active participation as a baseball player."

Hardly anyone knew what to make of amyotrophic lateral sclerosis (ALS) in 1939, but soon the world would know, as it became clear that Gehrig was not just retiring, he was dying. Not even three weeks after the statement, the Yankees held Lou Gehrig Day at the stadium. It was July 4, and in between games of a doubleheader against the Senators, Gehrig was honored by his 1927 teammates and those from his current squad. In front of the 61,808 fans who packed the ballpark in the Bronx and the many newsreel cameras waiting to bring his story to the nation, Gehrig uttered the most famous lines in baseball history. "Fans," he said. "For the past two weeks you have been reading about a bad break I got. Yet today, I consider myself the luckiest man on the face of the Earth."

Gehrig's simple, graceful speech ended with the words, "So I close in saying that I might have had a bad break. But I have an awful lot to live for."[2]

It was the last time he took the field, spending the rest of the Yankees' fourth consecutive championship season in the dugout, losing weight to the illness that was destroying him. It was sad irony that just as the man who anchored the Yankees and epitomized their strength and consistency grew weaker, the powerhouse team from New York was growing stronger than ever before. Gehrig's was a tragic, unjust fate. Yet as heart-wrenching as his predicament was, if you were not from New York (and even if you were and preferred the Dodgers or baseball Giants), the Yankees were a tough bunch to root for—simply because they won so often. They sported a lineup where not a single player on the team had ever played on a team that had lost a World Series.[3] Admire them? Yes. Root for them? Not likely. Teams playing .700 baseball receive precious little sympathy.

Living Up to the Billing

Although they were facing a very good Reds team in the series, a team that had won 95 games and sported the two winningest hurlers in the game, the Yankees were installed as heavy favorites.

They lived up to the billing.

Game 1 of the 1939 Fall Classic was a nip-and-tuck affair, a pitcher's duel between the Reds' righthander, 25-game winner Paul Derringer, and Yankee ace and future Hall of Famer Red Ruffing. Ruffing had not pitched in 17 days due to a sore arm and matched Derringer in throwing blanks for the first three frames.

In the fourth, Cincinnati broke through and got to the Yankee ace. Right fielder Ival Goodman walked and then stole second. Frank McCormick followed Goodman and collected his second hit of the game, driving Goodman home to give the Reds the early lead at 1–0. The Yankees tied the game in the bottom of the fifth on a mental error made by Reds left fielder Wally Berger.[4]

Berger was playing with an injured and badly infected toe that had resulted from smacking a ball off his foot.[5] After the injury, he played with a hole cut in the top of his shoe because the tightness of the spikes caused him intense pain. As the Yankees batted in the fifth, Joe Gordon singled, and Babe Dahlgren followed with a shot to Berger in left. Whether from the pain in his toe or perhaps because he had just blanked out on the play, Berger forgot about the lead runner. He completely ignored the tying run in Gordon and, surprisingly, threw the ball into second baseman Lonnie Frey, giving the Yankees an opportunity to score. Yankee third base coach Art Fletcher watched the play unfold and, taking advantage of Berger's miscue, waved Gordon around third.

Frey tried to react quickly and threw the ball home to Lombardi, but the throw was off-line and late. Gordon scored and the game was tied at one, much to the delight of the Yankee Stadium crowd.

For the next three and a half innings, the game remained tied. In the bottom of the ninth, Charlie Keller launched a Derringer offering deep into right center field. Goodman and center fielder Harry Craft both ran toward the ball, but for a split second seemed undecided as to who should make a grab for it. Goodman lunged and got his glove on it but couldn't hold the ball. By the time he recovered, Keller had arrived safely at third.[6]

That moment of indecision in the bottom half of the final frame proved costly.

Joe DiMaggio was due up next. Though he had come through with a weak infield hit in the fourth, the Yankee Clipper had been slumping for weeks. Slump or no slump, DiMaggio had a remarkable season. He led the league in 1939 with a .381 average, and there was no way manager Bill McKechnie was going to let him beat the Reds. He ordered Derringer to walk him, putting runners on first and third.

For the Reds skipper it was a matter of choosing his poison. After issuing an intentional pass to DiMaggio, McKechnie now had to decide whether to walk Bill Dickey, load the bases, set up a force all around, and pitch to George Selkirk or try his luck with Dickey. He decided to try and have Derringer get Dickey. It didn't work. Dickey singled up the middle, giving the Yanks the 2–1 Series opening win. Though his decision proved wrong, McKechnie's reasoning for the move was sound.

> Look, If I had walked Dickey and pitched to Selkirk, the infield would have been drawn in to make the force at the plate, and I would have had to pitch low to Selkirk to make him hit the ball on the ground. But Selkirk is a low-ball hitter. That is his strength. It would have been murder to pitch to his strength. Now Dickey, though a wonderful hitter is a slow runner. With the infield halfway, I could get him to hit the ball on the ground and the infielder would have the option of throwing to the plate or trying for a double play.[7]

Reds first baseman Frank McCormick said the 2–1 loss "took the heart out of us," and tempers flared in the closed-door clubhouse after the game. Derringer was furious. He screamed at Goodman for failing to catch Keller's drive in the ninth. Goodman reacted by punching Derringer in the jaw.

Apparently Goodman's punch to the face wasn't able to send a loud enough message to the still angry Derringer, who continued to run his mouth and told reporters when the clubhouse doors opened, "Big League outfielders should catch fly balls."[8]

McCormick may have been right. Maybe the Reds lost their heart after their Game 1 defeat because Games 2 and 3 were handily won by New York. In Game 2, slender righthander Monte Pearson drove a crowd of 59,791 wild with expectation as he pitched into the eighth without allowing a hit. The Yanks put up a three-run third when first baseman Babe Dahlgren doubled to open the inning, was sacrificed to third, and scored as Cincinnati shortstop Billy Myers fumbled Frank Crosetti's grounder, preventing a play on Dahlgren, who raced home with the game's first run. Though Myers recovered in time to retire Crosetti, leaving two on and nobody out, Reds 27-game winner Bucky Walters couldn't shut the door.

Red Rolfe singled to right, and Charlie Keller looped a liner down the left field line that Wally Berger, who was still playing with a sore toe and the top half of his shoe cut out, couldn't hold. That allowed Rolfe to score and saw Keller pull into second with a double. Bill Dickey knocked in Keller, giving the Yanks a three-run lead. Dahlgren hit a solo homer in the next inning to push the margin to 4–0. From then on, the Reds went meekly. A single by Lombardi with one out in the eighth and one by Billy Werber, with two out in the ninth, were all the offense the Reds could muster as they went down to defeat.[9]

At the time, it was the second shortest game in World Series history, clocking in at a brisk 1 hour and 27 minutes, 2 minutes longer than the record-holder between Detroit and Chicago in 1908.[10] The no-hitter by Pearson through seven and a third innings tied a World Series mark that was set in the third game of the 1927 contest by Herb Pennock. In the first two games, the Reds offense was woeful — one run in 18 innings and a .107 team batting average — certainly not the stuff of which world champions were made.[11]

Back in Cincy

The Reds hoped returning home would help stymie the Yankee onslaught after an off day for travel. A bright blue, nearly cloudless sky welcomed a packed crowd to a soupy, upper 80s temperature at Crosley Field that made it feel more like August than early October. But October it was — a month the Yankees owned and despite the fact that the Reds had come home, the outcome in Game 3 proved to be no different than the previous two contests.

The Bombers jumped on ineffective rookie Junior Thompson early, smacking him around for seven runs in four and two-thirds innings in the first World Series game at Crosley Field (since it was known as Red-land Field) in 20 years. In fact, the word *home* more aptly described the home runs that paced the Yankee attack than it did any kind of home field advantage for the Reds.

In the first, with the Cincinnati crowd eager with anticipation and a rookie hurler on the hill, the Yankees started their assault almost imme-diately. Crosetti started with a lead-off walk off of the obviously nervous Thompson. He moved to second when the next hitter, third baseman Red Rolfe, grounded out to McCormick at first. Keller then smacked Thomp-son's next offering into the right field bleachers, giving the Yankees the lead. Thompson escaped without further damage in the first, but the Reds were already in a 2–0 hole.[12]

Cincinnati mounted a mini-two-out rally of their own in the bottom of the first when Goodman, McCormick, and Lombardi strung together back-to-back-to-back singles off Lefty Gomez to make the score 3–1. The next inning, Thompson appeared to be over his first-inning jitters as he succinctly dispatched the bottom of the Yankee order. Gomez, who had strained a stomach muscle trying to corral Goodman's single in the first, was the third Yankee hitter in the inning, and when he winced in pain after a swinging strike three, McCarthy had no choice but to pull his Game 3 starter from the contest.

McCarthy inserted Bump Hadley into the game to take Gomez's place on the hill, and like Gomez before him, Hadley gave up a string of sin-gles — this time four of them — to Myers, Thompson, Werber, and Good-man. The Reds scored twice to take a 3–2 lead, but the Yankees hadn't quite finished with Junior Thompson.[13]

In the third, Thompson seemed to be cruising along well enough, getting Crosetti and Rolfe each to foul out. But then with two out and nobody on, Charlie Keller drew a walk, and DiMaggio followed with a drive that cleared the center field fence and put the Yankees back in the lead, 4–3.

Hadley began to find his rhythm and moved through the third and fourth frames, allowing only a single hit. As the game moved into the fifth, Thompson began to unravel. Rolfe singled with one out, and Keller knocked his second homer of the afternoon into the right field stands. Bill Dickey followed with another homer later in the inning to put the Yan-kees in firm control. The 22-year-old Thompson was lifted, the four

Yankee homers sending him to the showers. The rout was on, and the Yankees took Game 3 by a 7–3 score.[14]

The next day, as the Reds dug in preparing to stave off elimination in Game 4, there was little doubt as to the eventual outcome. Yet McKechnie's squad still had fight in them. The early October heat wave persisted, and a heavy humidity hung in the air once again as the Reds took to the field.

The Crosley Field faithful cheered wildly to inspire their team at the game's outset, though aside from the temperature there was little heat generated by either offense in the opening innings. The game proceeded much the way Game 1 had, settling into a methodical scoreless rhythm, only this time it was Derringer and Oral Hildebrand in the pitcher's duel. The game remained knotted into the seventh, as the increasing tension played havoc with the nerves of the Cincinnati fans.

And then it all changed.

When the Yankees scored two runs on solo homers by Charlie Keller and Bill Dickey to untie the score in the top half of the inning, it seemed that whatever air was keeping the Reds balloon afloat had suddenly burst, and the hope for avoiding a sweep was all but lost.

But the Reds didn't quit. In the bottom of the inning, aided by a Red Rolfe error at third, a walk, and singles by pinch-hitter Willard Hershberger, Billy Werber, and a double by veteran Al Simmons off Yankee reliever Steve Sundra, the Reds moved ahead 3–2, to the delight of the Crosley fans. Bucky Walters, who along with Derringer was co-ace of the Reds staff, relieved the Big Rightie in the eighth, and set the Yankees down without a run.

In the Reds half of the eighth, Yankee reliever Johnny Murphy, who had spelled Sundra in the seventh and prevented the Reds from doing further damage, gave up a run when Cincy right fielder Ival Goodman doubled and catcher Ernie Lombardi singled him home, driving the now frenetic crowd wild, as the Reds padded their lead to 4–2, heading into the top of the ninth.

As the game moved to the ninth, Reds fans had good reason to believe that at the very least, these Yankees (no matter how good they were) would not take the series in four straight from their beloved National League champs. Though even the most ardent Reds fan would have probably conceded their team would not come back from three games down to topple the mighty Yankees, they would also have similarly believed that a two-run lead in the ninth was fairly safe in the hands of their team's quality pitching staff, especially with 27-game winner and National League MVP Bucky Walters now on the hill.[15]

Bucky Walters (l) and Paul Derringer (r) won a combined 52 games in 1939, accounting for more than half of the Reds victories. They were a combined 0–3 in that year's World Series against the Yankees.

The Reds and their fans soon discovered otherwise.

A two-run deficit in the final frame, even on the road with the opposition's best pitcher on the hill, was hardly insurmountable for a veteran and tested Yankee squad. What appeared to be a likely victory for the Reds came into doubt when Charlie Keller and Joe DiMaggio preserved New York's hope for a sweep by stringing together back-to-back singles to start the ninth.

With Keller on third and DiMaggio on first and nobody out, Yankee catcher Bill Dickey stepped to the plate. Reds manager, 53-year-old Bill McKechnie, paced in the dugout, reviewing his options and ordered the infield back to double-play depth. Dickey hit a slow-roller to Reds second baseman Lonnie Frey that looked like a sure-fire double-play ball. But shortstop Billy Myers dropped the throw as he covered second, and when the dust settled, everybody was safe. Keller scored, slicing the lead to one, and the momentum began to shift to the Yankees.

The next hitter in the New York lineup, George Selkirk, flied out, which would have ended the game if the Reds hadn't botched the double play.

But a Reds victory was not to be.

DiMaggio moved to third on Selkirk's sacrifice fly, and Joe Gordon stepped into the batter's box and smacked a Walters offering — on a line to Bill Werber at third. Werber's throw was too late to get DiMaggio at the plate, and the game was tied. The Reds retired Babe Dahlgren, and pitcher Johnny Murphy to prevent Joe McCarthy's team from taking the lead, but then went quietly in the bottom half of the ninth, the confidence with which they began the inning all but gone.[16]

The Tenth Inning

As the teams headed into the extra session, any remote thoughts of making it a series seemed to disappear. Bucky Walters, pitching his third inning in relief, faced the top of the Yankee lineup and walked Frankie Crosetti to start the inning. Red Rolfe sacrificed Crosetti to second, bringing Keller to the plate. Keller, who was swinging a hot bat, grounded the ball to Myers who, feeling the jitters and perhaps thinking about the botched play in the ninth, fumbled it, allowing Crosetti to advance to third and Keller to be safe at first. As Reds fans began to get that sinking feeling, Joe DiMaggio stepped into the batter's box. DiMaggio—who with Keller were the only Yankees hitting above the .300 mark for the series—got his pitch and drove it into right, where Goodman bobbled the ball and made a long throw to the plate. Crosetti had already scored to put the Yanks ahead, but as Cincinnati backstop Ernie Lombardi reached to grab Goodman's throw, Keller, who was 40 pounds lighter and several inches shorter, crashed into him, looking like a defensive back in football who hits a wide receiver at the moment the ball arrives.

Both men fell to the ground, along with the ball.

Keller recovered quickly and got up to touch home, but the 6'3", 230-pound Lombardi lay motionless with the ball a couple of feet away. He was unable to move or clear his head and get back in the game.

The 32,000-plus crowd at Crosley Field began to scream and yell, pleading for Lombardi to get up. The yelling grew louder, but Lombardi was unable to move and DiMaggio, to his credit, never stopped running. As Joltin' Joe saw the scene unfold at the plate, he continued racing around the base paths— sliding across home with the final run of the series. As he scored, a crescendo of boos and mocking taunts cascaded down from the stands at Lombardi, who continued to lie on the ground like a wounded horse. It was painfully obvious to the fans that there would be no come-back and no salvaging of Cincinnati pride by avoiding a sweep.[17]

The Reds took their turn at bat in the bottom of the tenth, but it proved to be merely a formality, as they failed to answer the Yankees with a rally of their own. Soon, the jeering of Lombardi stopped, and the dejected Crosley faithful exited quietly from the ball park to face a winter to recover from the nightmare of the tenth inning. Veteran writer Fred Lieb later recalled that he "never saw a more disgusted crowd than the Reds' fans as they filed sorrowfully out of the Crosley Field in that warm October Sunday afternoon."[18]

Dominance and Heartbreak

The quiet Cincinnati clubhouse took no solace in the belief that there was little shame in losing to the Yankees, whose 1939 club was among New York's best ever. This championship, their fourth in a row and fifth title under Joe McCarthy, earned McCarthy a tie (at the time), with Connie Mack for the most World Series victories by a manager. Even more telling of the Yankee dominance was that in their last seven World Series appearances, dating back to the Miller Huggins–managed Murderer's Row teams of 1927 and 1928 and McCarthy's first title in 1932, the Yankees had lost a total of three games— all to their cross-town rivals, the New York Giants.

So dominating were these Yankees that a *New York Times* editorial succinctly summarized their greatness at the conclusion of the 1939 series

Ernie Lombardi's "snooze" behind the plate in Game 4 haunted him throughout his life. Unfairly branded a goat for losing the series, Lombardi had been
knocked nearly unconscious from a collision at the plate.

by saying that though the series lacked excitement, seemed monotonously
one-sided, and had to compete with a world war, "It managed, neverthe-
less to maintain its hold on the front page."[19]

 Those in the heartland had a decidedly different view. For Reds fans,
it was a heartbreaking way to end a season of promise. It had been 20 long

years since Cincinnati had been to the World Series, and although they had won their first World Championship against the White Sox the last time out, the underdog Reds title team of 1919 had an asterisk permanently attached to it. The lifetime expulsion of eight players from the Black Sox for fixing to lose the 1919 series left even the most diehard Reds fan unable to believe that series had been won by the Reds and not thrown by the Sox. World champions they were, but through no fault of their own, there was never a more circumspect champion in the entire history of professional sports.

Two decades later, with the 1919 championship all but ancient history, Reds fans, happy with a return to the series, were surprised by a sweep of their team at the hands of the mighty Yankees. The fans dejectedly exited the turnstiles at Crosley Field after their team's disheartening collapse in Game 4, but no one's heart was hurt more or will break more silently over the years than the object of their ire, Ernie Lombardi. The play in the tenth inning haunted him for the remainder of his life.

As the 1939 season ended, the Reds and their fans were left hoping that it wouldn't be 20 more years before they got another shot at the World Series.

They would have little to worry about.

The very next season, the year before America entered World War II, the Reds again returned to the World Series. The story of that season is one that does not end with the sipping of champagne after the final out in Game 7 in 1940; nor begin, as one might naturally expect, with the final out in October 1939. The story of the 1940 Reds team begins instead with the firing of a shotgun in the bathroom of a small house in a southern California town, nearly 12 full years before the franchise from Cincinnati finally earned the right to call itself the best team in the world.

2

◆ ◆ ◆ ◆

The Best Little Catcher

Twenty-two miles southeast of Los Angeles, in the heart of southern California, lies the city of Fullerton, a community that balances a mix of residential, commercial, industrial, and cultural concerns. Due to its proximity to tourist attractions such as Disneyland, Knotts Berry Farm, and other family amusements, the area attracts hundreds of thousands of tourists annually. It is far different today than in the pre–Mickey Mouse days of the early 1900s, when the area was laying the groundwork for the mini-metropolis it later became. Yet even in those early days, Fullerton was a city making an impact. Though Major League Baseball didn't make its presence felt out West until the late 1950s, there was no shortage of talent in the Golden State. The area's premiere high school, Fullerton Union, which today is a typical southern California high school distinguished by the notable number of award-winning scholars, athletes, and business-people that have graced its halls, was back then considered a mecca for high school athletics.[1]

A High School Star

Hall-of-fame baseball players, such as Washington Senator fireballer Walter "Big Train" Johnson (class of 1905) and Pirate standout Floyd "Arky" Vaughan (1930), are among the school's roster of esteemed alumni that also includes the 37th president of the United States, Richard Milhous Nixon (1927), and, far less notably, a scrawny-looking, quick-footed catcher, who attended Union at the same time as the future president, named Willard Hershberger.[2] Hershberger's name is unlikely to appear among the school's annals of prestigious alumni and the name of the former catcher would be hard pressed to earn a glint of recognition in the eyes of anyone other than a baseball trivia expert or the most diehard fan

Hershberger had a life other high school boys would have envied — a standout in three sports, popular among his peers, and president of his class. He was a young man destined for success until his father committed suicide in 1928.

of the Cincinnati Reds, the team for which he played. But back in 1926, it seemed if anyone from Fullerton was going to make a mark on society and be destined for greatness, the wiry catcher from Lemon Cove was as likely a candidate as any.

In the mid–1920s, Willard Hershberger had earned and deserved his reputation as Fullerton's star athlete. He started as a ninth-grader on a 1926 varsity team,[3] that the school, even 75 years later, ranked as one of its 10 greatest teams of all time in any sport (a significant milestone, given the number of sports the school sponsored and the fact that the school has been turning out quality athletes for over a century). Fullerton's 1926 yearbook spoke of him as "the best little catcher to wear a Fullerton high school suit,"[4] and if anything, the statement belied just how versatile an individual he was.

Like most gifted athletes, Hershberger garnered a great deal of attention on his high school campus. A talented and versatile three-sport athlete — competing in basketball, football, and of course baseball — on a campus that valued athletics, Hershberger's high school experience was idyllic. A celebrated athlete at Union, he was far more than the stereotypical high school jock. Off the field, he was a well-rounded student and leader who performed well academically. As a junior, he was president of both his class and a group known as the Varsity Club, an organization comprised of seniors with the sole exception of himself — a testament to his popularity, even as an underclassmen. Yet despite his academic and social successes, Hershberger remained a sportsman at his core, with interests ranging from high school team sports to more individual pursuits, such as hunting and shooting.[5]

Breaking a Brooding Silence

It seemed to be a life other high school boys envied — class president, a standout in three sports, and by all appearances one of the most popular and pleasant members of his class. For all anyone could tell, he was a young man destined for success. Until it all came crashing down on November 21, 1928.

On that night, after an early evening hunt, 17-year-old Willard Hershberger left his shotgun leaning against a wall in the downstairs hallway of his two-story house. He left the gun in the hall instead of putting it away in the upstairs closet where it belonged, a mistake for which he never forgave himself. In the early morning hours, his father, Claude, who had recently been demoted at the oil company where he worked and was silently consumed with financial worries for weeks, decided to break his brooding silence in a most dramatic and violent fashion. At around 2:30, unable to sleep, Claude rose from his bed and wandered through the dark, still halls of the house at 222 North Yale Avenue.[6] He picked up the shotgun his son left resting against the wall in the downstairs hall and pulled a walking cane from a nearby canister. With the gun in one hand and the cane in the other, he made his way to the bathroom. Once inside, he sat down on the edge of the tub, pointed the shotgun at his chest, and using the cane to help reach the trigger, pulled the trigger, causing a blast the force of which blew the 54-year-old father of two into the tub. Young Willard, whose bedroom was directly above the bathroom, woke to the thunderous blast and ran downstairs to find his father. His 15-year-old sister, Lois, and their mother arrived immediately after Willard, and they stood there crying, holding each other for comfort.[7]

As Lois told *Sports Illustrated* in 1991, Willard blamed himself for not putting the gun where it belonged. "We were both so upset ... we absolutely never spoke a word about it for the rest of our lives."[8]

Although they never spoke of it again, the event left an indelible mark on the young man. In the instant that he heard the sound of the gunshot that took his father's life, Willard went from the best little catcher in high school to the man of the family — becoming the sole provider for a widowed mother who worshiped him. She became the most important and only woman in his life. It was a tragedy that not unexpectedly fractured the family.

After the suicide, Lois seemed to adjust as best as could be expected, but Willard did not. Hershberger's personal demons surfaced slowly after the incident. No longer was he the popular, outgoing star with the cackling laugh his friends at Fullerton High had known. Instead, he withdrew, becoming more painfully introverted. The death of his father and the role he believed he played in it ate away at him, changing his life forever.[9]

The outward signs showed Hershberger to be a different person following the suicide. He was now a young man, who in addition to blaming himself for his father's death suddenly had the weight of providing for his mother and his little sister thrust on his shoulders. Yet through the difficult times he endured, the one area in his life that seemed to remain unaffected was baseball.

Baseball Grounds Him

Fortunately, his stellar play on the Fullerton diamond made the scouts take notice and professional baseball came calling in 1929, offering a diversion and an opportunity at an income to help with the financial problems at home. Hershberger embraced the opportunity and adjusted his game to come out from behind the plate and play second base for the Tucson-based minor league club that signed him.[10] The move to second was short-lived, however, when early in his first year as a pro, Tucson's regular catcher scuffled with a reporter and broke his finger in the fight, prematurely ending his season. In a similar twist of fate, Tucson's second-string catcher wound up on the disabled list as well and Hershberger, the newly converted infielder, was enlisted as a temporary emergency replacement at the position where he excelled in high school. It was a move that turned out to be permanent as he stayed behind the plate for the rest of his career.[11]

Hershberger soon discovered that life in professional baseball was anything but stable as he was released by Tucson in the middle of his first season. He remained committed to the game, however, and continued to pursue the one thing in life that grounded him. He caught on with El Paso the following year and hit a stellar .356, beginning an impressive seven-year minor league streak, where he played for several teams and hit better than .300 six times.[12] He capped his minor league career with an impressive final season as catcher for the 1937 Junior World Series Champion Newark Bears, then the New York Yankees' top affiliate, perhaps the greatest minor league team in history. For the Bears, Willard hit .328, knocking in 66 runs in 311 at-bats, striking out a measly 6 times. It was a season good enough to earn him International League Catcher of the Year honors.[13]

An Odd Person in Many Ways

The 1937 Junior World Series Championship was the crowning achievement of an impressive minor league career that up until that time had brought the trusty backstop his own fair share of baseball notoriety in addition to a ticket to the big leagues. When the Cincinnati Reds bought Hershberger's contract from the Bears toward the end of the 1937 season, the biographical release announced the acquisition by speaking of the novel record he held in professional baseball, a record that today is broken by every player on the Major League roster.

> He is the first player to have performed on both the Atlantic and Pacific coasts within a period of 48 hours. In 1936, he played in a Sunday game in Newark. The next day the Oakland club of the Pacific Coast [League] wired it was in desperate need of a catcher. At the time, the Bears had three receivers and Hershie was selected to make the trip to Oakland. The catcher boarded an airplane at the Newark Airport, Monday afternoon and the next day arrived in Oakland in time to catch for the Oaks.[14]

The same release eerily touched on the young receiver's fascination and expertise with shotguns, calling Hershberger a "crack shot with a rifle," saying in part: "This spring he demonstrated his ability with the rifle while at the Bears' training camp in Sebring, Florida. With some of his pals, he visited a shooting gallery and almost walked away with all the prizes in the place. After that, the gallery owner refused to allow Hershie to shoot for any of the prizes."[15]

It is strange, given the manner of his father's death, that Hershberger's love affair with guns continued to be such a prominent part of his life that it was mentioned in the team's press release. It is odder still that his cousin Blanche McKee Maloy recalled in an interview with *Sports Illustrated* that he was shaken so badly by the tragedy of his father's suicide that to her knowledge, he "never took a bath again, only showers."[16] Shaken by the prospect of the bath but not the shotgun?

"He was an odd person in many ways," Jack Fallon, a pitcher and teammate of Hershberger on the 1937 Bears, remembered. He explained that Hershberger had built a huge collection of guns, "He carried one in his suitcase and usually bought a new one in every city." Fallon told *Sports Illustrated* of a time Hershberger took target practice in a Binghamton hotel room. "The hotel-room was papered in a daisy pattern. Hershie had this pump gun, an air rifle that shot .22 caliber pellets. He shot the center out of every daisy on that wall. He set bottle caps on the edge of the tub and from his bed across the room ... shot the caps off the tub."[17]

A Simple Twist of Fate

Even with all his idiosyncrasies, there was little doubt that Hershberger could play the game of baseball and play it well. One of the curiosities, in a life filled with strange twists of fate, was that Hershberger hadn't made it to the Major League sooner.

In his years in the minors, Hershberger as a backstop hit better than .300 consistently, something most teams in the majors were unable to replicate behind the plate.[18] With the sole exception of the Yankees, whose perennial all-star Bill Dickey also had six of seven .300-plus seasons, in the period between 1930–37, no other team in the majors had the *position* hit better than .300 for more than four seasons (the exceptions being Cincinnati's Ernie Lombardi, who had four years of .300-plus ball, and the Phillies' Spud Davis), let alone a single player. The remaining teams in the league had a catcher hit better than .300 for a season or two, but there was little consistency above the .300 line for most teams. Several teams (the Washington Senators, Cleveland Indians, and Chicago White Sox in the American League and the Boston Bees and Pittsburgh Pirates in the Senior Circuit) were particularly woeful behind the plate, with none of the teams having the position cross the .300 barrier more than twice in a seven-year stretch. The Sox, Pirates, and Senators settled for a single .300 season each. Hershberger's minor league record is detailed below.[19]

Year	Team	G	AB	H	2B	3B	HR	RBI	Avg
1931	El Paso	115	432	134	28	8	4	Not listed	.356
1932	Hollywood	—	No	record	—				
1932	Erie	94	333	113	18	11	2	Not listed	.339
1932	Newark	11	33	7	1	1	0	7	.212
1933	Binghamton	103	345	105	18	3	2	58	.304
1934	Hollywood	114	332	102	18	1	3	46	.307
1935	Newark	107	313	97	6	4	6	49	.310
1936	Newark	16	54	14	3	2	1	5	.259
1936	Oakland	89	259	68	6	4	1	40	.263
1937	Newark	95	311	102	15	3	5	66	.328

Hershberger's luck (or lack of it) had him in the Yankee system playing behind Dickey by virtue of a strange episode that saw two scouts come away from a California scouting trip with decidedly different results than their initial agendas called for, forever altering the destinies of Hershberger and Fullerton teammate and future Hall of Famer Arky Vaughan.

Both youngsters were garnering a fair amount of attention from Major League scouts in the East. So impressive were the reports on the teammates that Pirate scout Art Griggs journeyed to California to see Hershberger, and Yankee scout Bill Essick left at about the same time to see Vaughan. Essick sidetracked his trip to Fullerton to see another player in Long Beach. At about the time Essick arrived in Long Beach, Griggs landed in Fullerton. While in Fullerton, it was Vaughan that caught Griggs's eye, making the scout forget all about the express purpose of his trip — to scout Hershberger. Several days later, Essick arrived. With Vaughan having been snapped up by the Pirates, Essick focused his attention behind the plate and was impressed enough to sign Hershberger instead. As *Sports Illustrated* recounted, it was a strange twist of fate that left Hershberger the property of a team with one of the all-time great catchers (Hall of Famer Bill Dickey) underneath a glass ceiling, when if Essick had not gone to Long Beach, the Yankees surely would have inked another in their impressive array of Hall of Famers in Vaughan. Hershberger most likely would have landed with the Pirates, a team that changed catchers five times in seven years, almost certainly being called up before his eventual first year in the big leagues, 1938.[20]

Hershberger earned a title with the Newark Bears in 1937. At the end of that year, Bill McKechnie acquired him to back up Ernie Lombardi. He did not live to see the Reds championship in 1940.

From Newark to Cincinnati

As a member of the Yankee farm system, Hershberger bounced from affiliate to affiliate. In 1932, he traveled across the country, making the rounds from Hollywood to Newark, spending the majority of the season with Erie of the Central League, where he hit .348, and made the all-star team. In 1933, he began spring training with Newark but failed to make the cut. He was shipped to Binghamton, made another all-star team, and ended the season with a .305 average. Over the next few years, he saw time in Hollywood, Oakland, and again with the Yankees' top affiliate, the Newark Bears. In 1937, Hershberger and Buddy Rosar split backstop duties on a Bears team that was among the greatest teams in all minor league history—finishing at 109–43, a lofty 25.5 games ahead of the second-place Montreal Royals. Both catchers played well enough to be named to the league's all-star team. The Bears swept four games from the Syracuse Chiefs in the semifinals and did the same to Baltimore in the International League finals. In the Little World Series, where the IL champion faced off against the American Association champ, the Bears fell behind three games to none, before storming back to win four straight against the Columbus Red Birds.[21]

For Hershberger, the title he earned with Newark was the last world championship he saw. At the end of the 1937 season, with the Reds in retooling mode, new skipper Bill McKechnie acquired Hershberger in a trade. The young receiver served as a capable understudy for Ernie Lombardi and played in the 1939 World Series but did not live to see the Reds World Championship the following season.[22]

3

♦ ♦ ♦ ♦

"One of the
Greatest Individuals"

On October 8, 1939, the man they called the Deacon dressed in the sullen home clubhouse of Crosley Field and in characteristic soft-spoken fashion told his team their four game sweep at the hands of the Yankees was "tough luck." "See you in the spring," the manager said.[1] He hadn't even asked Lombardi what had happened on the play that left him sprawled and unable to stop the Yankees from pouring it on. It didn't really matter why it happened. It happened.

In the visitors' clubhouse, the Yankees celebrated. A joyous refrain of "East Side, West Side," followed by Yankee skipper Joe McCarthy merrily chortling "Roll Out the Barrel" offered a stark contrast to the ghostly quiet that permeated through the soon-to-be-deserted Crosley Field. Slapping congratulations on the backs of one another, the New Yorkers savored the miraculous Game 4 comeback in a style fit for world champions. In the din of the celebration, an ailing Lou Gehrig, who had accompanied the team to Cincinnati even though he was no longer on the active roster, called it the greatest finish he had ever seen.

"Don't forget, it's nine straight!" a jubilant McCarthy yelled to the writers assembled in the clubhouse, adding an exclamation point to the Yankees' achievements, though one was hardly needed.[2] If two consecutive sweeps of the World Series didn't give the Yankees complete invincibility, it sure made it seem like they were unbeatable on baseball's greatest stage.

Meanwhile, a decidedly different summation was being offered in the quiet home locker room, where the downcast National League champs were left muttering to themselves as they dressed for the long winter ahead.

McKechnie went to the manager's office sat in his swivel chair, put his feet up on a window ledge, and stared off in silence, collecting his thoughts. It was only a matter of minutes before the reporters entered the office and fired their questions at him. "They're not as good as all that,"[3] he said, without a trace of being a sore loser, to the writers waiting for his observations following the defeat. McKechnie was tired and disappointed, and it came across. He meant the New Yorkers no disrespect, but he truly believed his club, even in defeat, could have been the world champions. It was a remarkable thought in itself, because the Reds hadn't beaten the Bronx Bombers in a single game.

The questions about players' costly mistakes and what went wrong in the late innings came as McKechnie knew they would, and he deflected them with the skill and diplomacy of a seasoned big league skipper.

"We never discuss those things," McKechnie replied, refusing to criticize his team for the press corps. "You can't explain that tenth inning and that play with Lombardi. It's just one of those things."[4] He made the rounds, shaking hands with his players, thanking them for their effort and a championship season.

While the celebration continued for the New Yorkers, McKechnie dressed and left the ballpark. He got into a cab with his coaches, Hank Gowdy and Jimmie Wilson, and lit a cigarette. "I don't care if they are the greatest team in baseball; we should have beat 'em and if we ever get another crack at 'em we will," he told his coaches.[5] He looked at the missed chances, especially in Game 1, where the Reds lost 2–1, due to a misplay by second baseman Lonnie Frey, wasting a strong outing from Paul Derringer. He also lamented the Game 4 mistakes—the missed double play and later the Lombardi-Keller collision that cost his team. They were games he felt his club could have won. If those games had swung to the Reds, the series would have been tied at two games apiece. McKechnie believed the Reds would have had the advantage after that because he said Yankees Game 1 Starter Red Ruffing was spent. "We would have had more pitching left," he said. "They couldn't have used Ruffing again. He was through."[6]

Whether Ruffing would have had similar success had the series gone further is a matter of conjecture. Whether even an ineffective Ruffing would have somehow swung the series in favor of the Reds is also open to debate. These were the Yankees, after all. Even if they hadn't been on a record-setting pace for consecutive World Series victories, they may have gone on to beat the Reds anyway—just so they could continue to torment their second-year manager who seemed to have little luck in his dealings with the New York franchise.

The loss in the 1939 series aside, the Yankees provided an interesting thread through the long and winding baseball career of Bill McKechnie.

So much so that if fact could imitate fiction and a real-life character could be put in the position of Joe Hardy and sell his soul to the devil for a chance to beat the New Yorkers, McKechnie's name might wind up somewhere near the top of the list. That's because the man they called the Deacon had little success in his previous dealings, on an even indirect basis, with the men in pinstripes.

Logging His Baseball Miles

Bill McKechnie logged his baseball miles the hard way, playing as a semi-pro, bush leaguer, and even with the renegade Federal League from 1914 to 1915. For the most part, his playing career was nondescript, and he served mainly as a utility man over the course of 11 years. The Pittsburgh Pirates brought him up in 1907 as a third baseman from the Pennsylvania-Ohio-Maryland League, and he saw stints with the Pirates twice, the Giants, Highlanders (New York's predecessor to the Yankees), the Boston Nationals, and the Reds. He never batted as high as .260 in the majors and was even known as ".158 McKechnie"[7] when he played for Frank Chance's New York squad. When questioned by baseball writer Fred Lieb as to why he would keep such a weak hitter on his team, Chance didn't hesitate: "Because Bill McKechnie has more brains than the rest of this dumb club put together."

It was his ability to absorb the game as a player and study under what he called "some pretty good managers" where the value of McKechnie's Major League playing career had its greatest impact. In his short time with the New York club that eventually

Mild-mannered with sad eyes sunk into a kind, grandfatherly face, McKechnie "was one of the greatest individuals I ever met, pure and simple," said Gene Thompson.

became the Yankees, McKechnie remembered that Chance "taught me a lesson, I'll never forget. It has to do with fining ballplayers."

"We were playing Washington," McKechnie said. "I was [playing] second base and Bert Daniels was in right field. A short looping liner was hit out there. Daniels came in for the ball and I went back for it. There had been a shower and little pools of water had formed in the outfield. I heard Daniels sloshing through the water and stopped to avoid a collision."

As it turned out, Daniels wasn't able to reach the ball. When the ball fell in for a hit, McKechnie said Chance blamed him for not getting to it. "Chance said it was my play, slapped a fine on me and shipped me to Buffalo that night," McKechnie recalled. "I felt bitter and sick all over. In my mind I had done the right thing."[8]

The fining and demotion Chance levied against him had a scarring effect on McKechnie but helped him later on in how he dealt with the players he managed. McKechnie's policy became never to fine players for misplays in the field.

"I played for some pretty good managers but even then I thought they would have been better if they had been a little more thoughtful in the treatment of their players," the Reds' skipper told *Look Magazine*. "There is no secret to having a bunch of ballplayers hustling for you. Just treat them they way you would like to be treated. When they make a mistake, tell 'em about it, but don't abuse 'em. When they do well, tell 'em about that too. Remember they're not all alike, and judge every man the way he's entitled to be judged — as an individual."[9]

Thomas Swope wrote in a profile of the Cincinnati skipper that players who played for McKechnie never told tales about how their manager treated them unfairly or double-crossed them, saying they were more likely to look at him as a father figure than a boss. He was a man who was able to treat players just and fair and bring out their best as ballplayers, while at the same time, earning their respect away from the field.

> Without any iron discipline [McKechnie] curbs their taste for improper actions on or off the ball field. Players who think nothing of straying from the straight and narrow under other managers seldom do so when playing for McKechnie. And not because he employs any honor system or fines them…. They just don't want Bill to know they are not doing right by him and the rest of the players on the team.[10]

The Deacon

A churchgoer and family man, who as a boy sang in the choir of the Miflin Avenue Church in Wilkinsburg, Pennsylvania, McKechnie earned

the nickname Deacon, for being a 33rd degree Mason and for the princi-
pled life he led in his community. The Freemason principles of duty,
fidelity, integrity, and trustworthiness were ones the likable manager took
quite seriously and were among the traits that most endeared him to his
players. Yet not everyone agreed that those traits translated to success in
the dugout. Defined by many owners as a "player's manager," who wasn't
given to explosive exhortations, some regarded McKechnie as soft. Many
of the owners, who were accustomed to fiery managers, thought McK-
echnie's approach far too laid-back to be successful. In short, they thought,
he was too likable to be a winner. As it turned out, they couldn't have been
more wrong.

Although mild-mannered with sad eyes sunk into a kind, grandfatherly face, McKechnie, who stood 5' 10", could be moved quickly to anger
by a player who wasn't giving his all or when an umpire blew a call. As
sportswriter Frank Graham wrote, "In such moments he can curl the
offender's hair and blister his ears with language he never learned in the
choir loft on Mifflin Avenue. And once he is convinced a player hasn't
been fair with him, he can get rid of him so quickly, the culprit will still
be in a daze as he makes his departure."[11]

Among McKechnie's many virtues were a sense of fairness and
patience — attributes that are tested numerous times throughout his Hall
of Fame managerial career. Two instances, both involving the pinstripers,
who seemed destined to pester the affable McKechnie, stand out. The first
involved his unceremonious firing after winning the pennant for St. Louis
in 1928 (but losing to the Yankees in the World Series, four games to none);
the second centered around the man who was synonymous with the Yankees himself, Babe Ruth.

Prior to signing on to manage in St. Louis, McKechnie had proven
himself a savvy field general in the big leagues. Though Edwin Pope wrote
that he was more "nurse than boss," there was little arguing with the Deacon's success.[12] He managed for six seasons (five in the National League
and one in the Federal League), where he finished above .500 every year
and took the Pittsburgh Pirates to the World Series, winning a championship. In 1925, McKechnie's Bucs finished with a .621 winning percentage and won a seven-game series over Washington.

The following year, the team slipped to third, only four games off the
pace, but McKechnie, in a move that stunned him, was fired by club owner
Barney Dreyfuss.[13] The firing, coming merely a year after winning the
World Series, floored the genial manager. It was the second time a trigger-
happy owner decided his fate, and McKechnie, whose sense of fairness
was essential to his personality, realized that fairness had little to do with

job security in the big leagues. Anything less than a world championship can, and in his experience did, result in dismissal — especially when working for an impulsive owner.

After being dismissed by the Bucs, McKechnie was offered a coaching position with the St. Louis Cardinals the next season. The irony of the hiring — for it was the Cardinals who cost McKechnie his manager job in the Steel City when they bested McKechnie's Pirates for the 1926 pennant — was not lost on the Deacon.

With a family to feed and a love for the game in his blood, McKechnie didn't dwell on his unceremonious Pittsburgh departure for long, and he accepted the Cardinals coaching position. He didn't serve long in

McKechnie had an uncommon amount of patience and tried to live his life according to a moral code. Thompson said, "There was just a genuine goodness about him."

the role, though. Eventually, he was promoted to take over the managerial reins when another impatient owner, this time the Cardinals' Sam Breadon, fired St. Louis skipper Bob O'Farrell for failing to win the pennant.[14]

In similar circumstances to McKechnie's firing in Pittsburgh, O'Farrell had won a seven-game World Series (this time over the Yankees), but like McKechnie failed to win the pennant the following year (1927), when he trailed the Deacon's old team, the Pirates, by a single game in the National League standings. That single game that separated the world champs from consecutive pennants was apparently enough for Breadon to make the change.

As the 1928 season began, McKechnie found himself at the helm of the Redbirds. His former team, the Pirates, had captured the National League flag from St. Louis in the 1927 season and although he had little to prove, McKechnie would have liked nothing better than to steal the pennant back from Pittsburgh. During the 1928 campaign, McKechnie did just that. He guided St. Louis with skill, capturing the National League flag, and earned the right to once again face his own personal nemesis— the New York Yankees—in the World Series.

And just as they had in the past, the Yankees again managed to serve as a catalyst to disrupt the equilibrium of McKechnie's baseball life.

By all accounts (witness Bob O'Farrell's firing), Sam Breadon is an impetuous owner. He was so incensed after the McKechnie-led Cardinals lost four straight to the Yankees in the World Series that he took his frustrations out on McKechnie, demoting him the season after he won the pennant to manage Rochester of the International League. It was a move that stunned McKechnie as much as the demotion by Chance had in his playing days and even more than his firing by Dreyfuss in Pittsburgh. He began to seriously question his future and consider a life outside of baseball.

I Coulda Been a Tax Collector

Determined to leave the game for a profession with more job security, McKechnie looked for opportunities off the diamond. But because he was not exactly sure of what a life outside of baseball would entail, he returned to the dugout to begin the 1929 season managing in the International League, switching positions with Rochester manager Billy Southworth, who was tapped to manage the parent club. McKechnie remained a solid field general and did the same stellar job in the minor league dugout as he had in the majors, putting Rochester way ahead in the International League standings. But his success at a lower level of ball offered McKechnie little solace.

With a family to support and working in an occupation where even pennant-winning managers can be fired, the pragmatic McKechnie began to sour on the prospects of any long-term future in the game. He figured the other owners were going to wonder what was wrong with a manager who kept getting fired—even after his teams won. He began to wonder himself and decided to leave baseball for good.[15]

The reckless Breadon tried to dissuade him. Realizing he made a mistake in dismissing McKechnie, Breadon called Rochester GM Warren Giles halfway through the 1929 campaign to confess he made a terrible error and wanted McKechnie sent back to the Cardinals, who were languishing out of the pennant chase. McKechnie dutifully reported back to the parent club but was not moved to change his way of thinking. He steered the Cardinals to a 34–29 mark during the second half of the season, but the Redbirds, who faded early from the race under Southworth, couldn't make up enough ground to contend.[16]

McKechnie had made up his mind that he was through with baseball, and he made a strange choice in seeking job security when he decided on a career with an even shorter lifespan than that of a big league manager — aspiring politician. It may have been his natural instinct to lead that inspired the Deacon to seek the tax collector office from his hometown of Wilkinsburg, but winning in the political arena proved to be more difficult than winning the World Series. Although he was determined to devote all of his energies to being tax collector, McKechnie never got the chance to leave the dugout because he lost the election.

"It was his own fault he got licked," one of his friends told *Look Magazine*. "We think so well of him in Wilkinsburg that he could have had any office he wanted if he tried hard enough for it. But you just couldn't get him to go out and blow his own horn."[17]

Although campaigning clearly was not his strong suit, McKechnie seemed to be at a crossroads. There was no baseball job to return to or political position to accept. But almost as quickly as McKechnie had closed the door on the game, baseball opportunity knocked again.

Ironically, opportunity's name in this instance was the ever-impulsive Sam Breadon, who caused McKechnie to reconsider his future in baseball in the first place. Breadon publicly apologized for dismissing McKechnie after he had won the pennant. After Breadon brought the Deacon back to manage the second half of the 1929 season, the Cards owner was impressed enough with McKechnie's performance that he decided he wanted him to manage the following season and the season after that. McKechnie resisted the overture, but Breadon was both apologetic and persistent, and it soon seemed like the manager was seriously considering reupping with the Cardinals.

Breadon's mea culpa was extraordinary for an owner. "I want you all to know I was dead wrong in letting McKechnie go," Breadon said to a country club gathering of the St. Louis elite, including the press corps. "I pulled a prize boner. He's the best manager in baseball and if any of you want to come over here and give me a good swift kick, I'll take it."[18]

The Cardinals were not Deacon Bill's only suitor, however. When Judge Emil Fuchs, the new owner of Boston's National League franchise, offered McKechnie an eight-year deal as opposed to the two-year deal being dangled by Breadon and the Cardinals, even Breadon conceded. "Bill, it's more than I can do for you. You'd better take it."[19]

Eventually, McKechnie did take the Boston job, which led to the uncomfortable situation with the Babe.

The Sultan of Swat

McKechnie began his eight-year tenure with Boston in 1930 and did his best with the traditionally woeful franchise. But even he couldn't work miracles. His first year at the helm was his first losing season as a manager, and although he did bring winning baseball to the Braves, including three consecutive seasons of better than .500 baseball and four overall during the eight-year span, the team never finished higher than fourth.

In the middle of his tour with Boston, McKechnie unwittingly found himself as the legendary Babe Ruth's final manager. The year was 1935 and it turned out to be the worst year of McKechnie's managerial career — both on the field, managing one of the worst teams in the entire history of the sport, and from an emotional standpoint. The finances of the Boston club were shaky, and the play was worse. The club finished a dreadful 38–115 for a .248 winning percentage, making fans who watched the daily massacre the only thing scarcer than wins in Boston.

In an effort to bring more people to the ballpark, Judge Fuchs decided to bring in the legendary Bambino, who was at the end his playing career. Fuchs offered the Babe a slew of titles and promised him a role in shaping the club. For his part, Ruth had quit the Yankees the year before when he was denied a similar role with New York. Fuchs guessed that Braves fans would interpret the move as a way of bringing Ruth back to Boston, righting the disastrous wrong inflicted on the city by the Red Sox who had traded him to the Yankees. Fuchs didn't for a moment believe that an aging Ruth would turn around the fortunes of his moribund club, but he did think Ruth's presence would bring fans to the park to witness the final year of the game's greatest player. The Babe believed he would either manage or fulfill a role as player-manager for the Braves.[20]

Fuchs, though, never had any intention of putting Ruth in charge. He also never informed his manager, McKechnie, that he was bringing Ruth on board or exactly what his thinking was. In fact, McKechnie found out about the Ruth signing not from anyone associated with the team but from the Boston beat writers. The conservative and well-mannered McKechnie was stoic for the media, playing it as if he had been consulted all along and publicly said Ruth will help the Braves. The constant losing and the difficulty in dealing with not only one of the game's greats but also a giant of American society who was impatiently waiting to take his chair made for McKechnie's most unpleasant season in the big leagues.

By mid–June, Ruth realized Fuchs was stringing him along and had no intention of allowing him to run the club. So the Sultan of Swat called the Boston media together in the clubhouse as McKechnie and his players were getting dressed for a game. He announced his bitter intention of "getting the hell out of this dump," to the media, in earshot of McKechnie and all his players.[21]

It was an awkward moment for McKechnie, as was most of Ruth's short tenure in Boston, yet despite the strangeness of the situation and the continual losing, McKechnie recalled the more positive aspects of the ordeal to the *Saturday Evening Post*, which reported the situation following the hastily called press conference as follows.

> There was a period of painful silence. Finally, one of the players reached in his locker, drew out a baseball and took it over to the Babe. "Sign this for me, will you Babe? I want to take it home and keep it." One by one all the players took balls to the Babe for his signature. These weren't bug-eyed fans, they were hardened ballplayers, yet they wanted something to show they had played on the same team with the great man. McKechnie says it was the most impressive manifestation of honest admiration he ever saw.[22]

The Deacon stayed on in Beantown for two more seasons, righting the ship somewhat and finishing his last season much as he began his first, bringing the team back above .500. After Boston, where he even managed to win a Manager of the Year Award from the *Sporting News* for taking a perennial loser into the first division, Deacon Bill McKechnie was a wanted man. *The Saturday Evening Post* explained, "He didn't win any pennants in Boston, but the manner in which he handled mediocre players stamped him as an unusually competent manager. He attracted more national attention with losing Boston teams than he ever did with pennant-winning teams in Pittsburgh and St. Louis."

A New Man in Cincinnati

McKechnie had four job offers when his Boston deal expired in 1938 and selected Cincinnati and Warren Giles, a familiar face from his Rochester days, who was now in charge of the Reds front office.

The Reds, like Boston before McKechnie took over, had been on a miserable tear of their own. From 1929 through 1937, the once-proud Queen

City franchise had not posted a single winning season. In 1937, they were virtual laughing stocks, finishing dead last in the Senior Circuit, a full 40 games behind the first-place New York Giants. But the team McKechnie managed in 1938 was remade from the last-place finishers of the prior year. Five pitchers and 17 hitters who saw duty for the Reds in 1937 were sent packing and were no longer playing with the club the following season. The turnaround McKechnie orchestrated that year was more than a little remarkable. The Deacon gave the Reds their first winning season since 1928 and moved the club into the first division. They finished six games off the pace — a full 34-game improvement in the standings, with a record of 82–68.

The addition of Bucky Walters to the Reds staff was a key acquisition. But what was most indicative of McKechnie's managing abilities was the way he took players who were failures or quasi-failures on other teams and made them valuable members of his team.

> Examples are Lonnie Frey, previously shuffled around the league; Paul Derringer who lost 27 games in one season; [and] Bill Werber, the despair of many an American League manager.... Earlier, while McKechnie was with the Boston Bees, Jim Turner and Lou Fette were brought up to the majors and made stars at an age when most pitchers were considered through.[23]

Even more remarkable than the 34-game turnaround was that the Reds could have conceivably gone from worst to first. As *Look Magazine* reported, McKechnie probably would have won the 1938 pennant if pitcher Lee Grissom hadn't broken an ankle trying to steal second in a game the Reds already had won. The loss of Grissom's services cost Cincinnati valuable games.[24] Whether Grissom would have turned the tide is pure (and not necessarily reliable) conjecture. Yet McKechnie, who did have his club firing on all cylinders and was an excellent handler of pitchers, might have worked his magic with a healthy Grissom.

Though he fell short in 1938, the next year brought McKechnie back to within sight of the championship. The Yankees were waiting for him again, and though they denied the Reds the title in four straight games, the on-field accomplishments of McKechnie's squad in those first two years at the helm of the Reds gave the fans hope.

An accomplishment that was perhaps even greater than the Deacon's on-field achievement was the respect his players had for him in the short time he managed the ball club. It was every bit the equal of the respect the Boston players had shown for Ruth in the down-beaten Braves clubhouse during McKechnie's previous managerial post.

As pitcher Gene Thompson, a rookie on the pennant-winning squad of 1939 and a staple on the 1940 squad, recalled,

> Bill was one of the greatest individuals I ever met, pure and simple. He was like a father figure to all of us and we all respected him like a father. People now have six coaches, laptops and computer readouts and all this stuff, I never once saw him take a piece of paper or note card out of his pocket or rely on his coaches … he just managed. He was very good with pitchers and was more instrumental to me than anyone else. There was just a genuine goodness about him."[25]

McKechnie had great reserves of patience and apparently tried to live his life according to a moral code. His players seemed to recognize the code that he lived by made up the essence of the man. That code helped them through the dog days of the 1940 season when he and his players were severely tested as they set their sights on baseball's ultimate prize.

4

◆ ◆ ◆ ◆

The Jungle Cats

At the beginning of the 1940 season, the Reds infield was a solid defensive corps, unspectacular offensively, except for MVP first baseman Frank McCormick. It was sound defensively because that is precisely how manager Bill McKechnie wanted it. He believed that pitching and defense won pennants. And who could argue? At the conclusion of the 1940 campaign, his third full year as manager of the Reds, McKechnie had contended for a pennant and won two NL flags and a world championship. Not bad for a team that until his arrival had been mired in the second division.

The Deacon achieved his success behind the National League's two top pitchers and an infield defensive unit that seldom betrayed its hurlers. The Reds fielders didn't just lead the league at the end of 1940 season with a .981 fielding percentage, they led every team that had ever played in the history of Major League baseball by committing only 117 errors in 156 games.[1]

They called themselves the Jungle Cats in the 1939–40 pennant-winning era. They attacked opponents with a defensive ferocity that all but made up for their offensive shortcomings. Around the horn it was the New York–born and bred Frank McCormick (Wildcat) at first; Lonnie (Leopard) Frey at second; Billy "the Jaguar" Myers at shortstop; and Billy Werber, "the Tiger," at third. They took to yelling these names at each other during infield practice as a way of psyching themselves up.[2]

The creation of the Jungle Cats was the brainchild of Billy Werber, and it was designed as a way of challenging what he thought was an uninspired bunch of infielders. Werber recalled that when he signed with Cincinnati, "I didn't get down there until the day before they broke camp.... Well, it didn't take me long to determine in my own mind that the ball club was a little dead ass. And after a bit, when I got to know the guys in the infield a little better, I'd say, 'Bounce around on the balls of your feet! Fire that ball!' I'd say, 'Be a jungle cat!'"[3]

It was dime-store psychology to be sure, but the infield, which had a history of being erratic up the middle, began to gel as a unit. It's hard to imagine that having a nickname could inspire a player to better performance in the field, but in Werber's view, earning the imprimatur of a jungle cat contributed in no small part to the infield's success. It was especially true when it came to the first sacker, Frank McCormick, who was playing in his first full season. As Werber explained:

> I got 'em to bouncing ... [Lonnie] Frey had these liver spots all over his body ... you know part of his body'd be white and next to that'd be a big red spot. So I got to calling him the Leopard, because he was spotted all over. And then [with] [Billy] Myers, the shortstop ... I said we're gonna call you the Jaguar." And he said, "Who are you?" I said, "I'm the Tiger!" ...And I got these guys fired up.[4]

McCormick, the rookie first baseman, was the last to join the Jungle Cats. Not because he didn't want in, but because Werber wouldn't let him in. It was, to Weber's thinking, a way of getting big Frank to hustle more. As Werber told the story, when the others had been given their jungle nicknames, McCormick approached Werber to ask what his name was. He was obviously expecting a name from the animal kingdom like the ones given to his fellow infielders, but instead Werber's caustic reply was, "You're a lead ass. All you wanna do is loaf." The prickly Werber then told the rookie to pay attention to the other aspects of his game, "You hit. All you care about is hitting."

Werber explained that McCormick didn't run hard out of the batter's box when he figured he was going to be thrown out or when a ball was hit to the outfield. Much to Werber's dismay, McCormick seemed satisfied with a single on any ball hit beyond the infield and didn't bust it down the line. This prevented him from taking second base if the outfielder happened to bobble the ball.

Werber chewed McCormick out good and told him to hustle to first so he could end up at second on an outfielder's misplay. McCormick was still a green rookie who wanted desperately to belong and he tried to strike a deal with the hard-as-nails third baseman. McCormick wanted to know if he would be brought into the Jungle Club if he hustled more. Werber, still playing the wily old veteran to the impressionable rookie, held out. "We're not gonna promise you anything," Werber told McCormick. "You get out there and show us something."

McCormick started hustling and hitting, and he approached Werber again one night when all the infielders were having a postgame drink in the hotel bar on one of the team's road trips. "Take me into the Jungle

Club," McCormick said. Werber told him he'd have to buy them all a beer first and McCormick dutifully obliged. "Am I in?" McCormick asked after the round had been bought. "You're in," Werber told him. "You're the Hippopotamus."

"No, no," McCormick objected, telling Werber he didn't want to be the hippopotamus. "Okay," Bill said, finally relenting. "You're the Wild-cat."

Years later, Werber told the tale of an excited McCormick:

> He jumped off that stool and ran out in the lobby there in the hotel and ran up to McKechnie and said, "They named me the Wildcat! I'm in the Jungle Club!" [Laughs] And that's what the Jungle Club was. I helped infuse a little life into them and I think it improved their play in games.[5]

Frank "Buck" McCormick

Frank McCormick was "the big city boy who made good in the majors' smallest town."[6] He grew up in the Yorkville section of Manhattan, the same neighborhood that produced his idol, Lou Gehrig.[7] Like Gehrig, he became an Iron Man of sorts, and he actually looked a bit like the Iron Horse.

McCormick was slow to get to the majors due to several injuries he suffered in the minor leagues.[8] When he got to the majors, he was deter-mined to stay there, and he knew that one of the ways to do this was to stay in the lineup when he got the chance. He worked hard to lose the injury-prone label he had earned in the minors, staying in the lineup even when he should have come out. So determined was he to play every day that after Gehrig's streak of 2,130 consecutive games had come to an end, McCormick had the game's next longest consecutive game streak for quite a while, until it ended at 682 games.[9]

The 6' 4", 205-pound first baseman was a 21-year-old playing semi-pro ball in the Washington Heights area of New York when he received a tryout with his hometown New York Giants. After the initial tryout, he didn't get another look with the team from the Polo Grounds. As the story goes, one of the Giant scouts told him, "Son, if you have a good job keep it."[10] It was said of the Reds first baseman that though "he grew up in Yorkville, just a .5-cent fare from three big league yards, he had to travel all around the map to get into any of them through the players' entrance."[11]

McCormick didn't listen to the naysayers. He played baseball and worked a second job to keep his dream of playing professional ball alive.

In 1934, he was an outfielder for the New York Independents, a traveling team managed by George Halpin that had no home park. While playing ball for the Independents, McCormick worked in a shipping department in downtown Manhattan to help make ends meet. When the shipping department job stalled and sputtered, Frank focused his full attention on a career in baseball.[12]

Depending on the source, McCormick either petitioned Reds general manager Larry MacPhail with numerous letters seeking a tryout[13] or a tryout was arranged for him by the Independents manager, Halpin.[14] Whatever the true genesis of his opportunity was, McCormick finally earned a look from a professional team. He traveled to Beckley, West Virginia, a Class C Team in the Mid-Atlantic League, to showcase his talent and even had to borrow $50 from an uncle to make the trip.[15] It may not have been glamorous, but it was a start.

Before he became the National League's Most Valuable Player, it was said of McCormick, "though he grew up in Yorkville, just a five-cent fare from three big league yards, he had to travel all over the map to get into any of them through the player's entrance."

Beginning at the lowest rungs of the minors wasn't the only concession Big Frank had to make. Due to a glut of outfielders at Beckley, McCormick correctly sensed his odds were better at sticking with the club at a position other than the outfield, so he wisely traded his outfield dreams for a first baseman's glove and was able to stick with the team.[16]

McCormick smacked 91 runs across the plate and batted a robust .347, making enough heads turn at the parent club to earn a late season call-up to Cincinnati. He got into 12 games toward the end of the 1934 season, going 5 for 16 and knocking in 5 runs.[17]

As Major League debuts go, it was pretty good, but it didn't change the fact that he was going back to the minors. The following season, he changed his minor league address five times, going from Toronto to Fort Worth to Nashville to Dayton and then to Decatur.[18]

Playing for many different teams in a single season meant managerial and coaching changes as well. Though well-meaning, coaches at each stop along McCormick's well-traveled minor league route made continual adjustments to his batting stance. The many changes had the effect of taking the power out of his hands, and he failed to drive the ball the way it was expected he would as a first baseman.[19]

The following season in 1936, McCormick found himself in Durham, playing for Johnny Gooch's Bulls. Gooch's philosophy was simple. Keep the bat up, be ready, and forget all other adjustments.

It worked wonders. McCormick's season at Durham was phenomenal. He hit .381, compiled 211 hits, 49 doubles, and 138 RBIs, leading the league in each of those categories. The bulk of the next season was again spent in the minors, this time with Syracuse — where he batted .322. His offense was spectacular and his defense equaled his performance at the plate and may have even surpassed it. It was a style of play that fell right into line with the game plan of the new skipper for the Reds in 1938, Bill McKechnie. Subsequently, McCormick was given an opportunity to stick with the Reds. He made the most of it.

In his first full season in the big leagues, McCormick was extraordinary with both the leather and the pine. He posted a .995 fielding average, led the league in hits with 209 (actually both leagues), batted .327, and struck out a measly 17 times in 640 at-bats, the kind of statistics that made him an All Star.[20] McCormick appeared in every inning of every game and at the time was only the eighth player in Major League history to have more than 200 hits in his first full season. Only Rip Collins of the Chicago Cubs had a higher average of chances accepted in the field, making him truly an all-around All Star.[21]

"The big leagues is where the men play," he said in 1938, "and now to find myself a part of it — well the only comparable thrill I can recall is the first time I stepped into a pair of long pants. You know, in my neighborhood, you had to be pretty well grown, 15 or 16 years old, before they allowed you that privilege."[22]

He may have knocked around the minors for a while, but there was no doubt that Frank McCormick belonged in the big leagues. He led the league in hits in his first three full years, from 1938–40. In 1939, he led the league in RBIs with 128, his stick helping lead the Reds to the pennant. Although the Reds as a team had little to show for their World Series effort against the Yankees that year, the same could not be said of McCormick. He hit .400 against the Bombers and set the stage for his MVP campaign the following year.[23]

Three-for-Three

As the Reds moved through their opponents in the National League during 1940, it was clear that they had done so by the slimmest of margins. Though they won the division going away, they had won an extraordinary number of one-run games (41), which at the time, was a record.[24] McCormick was vital to that effort. Though an argument could be made that pitching was more valuable in such close contests, *Sporting News* made the case that a player like McCormick proved to be just as vital as stellar

In 1940, Frank McCormick became the third successive Reds player to win the Most Valuable Player award, following Ernie Lombardi and Bucky Walters.

pitching, if not more valuable. "In order to win, they [the Reds] found it necessary to take advantage of every scoring opening and to maintain a superior defense. Under such circumstances, the most valuable Red was the player who could contribute to the offense and at the same time aid in the defense."[25]

There were players, to be sure, who bested McCormick in any number of hitting categories. He was tops in the league in hits (191) and doubles (44), but he finished behind MVP runner-up, St. Louis's Johnny Mize, in a number of important categories, including homes runs (43 to 19), RBIs (137 to 127), and total bases (368 to 298). McCormick finished seventh in the league in batting, but the individual statistics were hardly the point.[26] McCormick's team had won. It was due in large part to his efforts that they won at all, making him the most valuable player to his team. His hits and runs came when they were needed most.

> Big Frank not only contributed needed runs in close games, but also cut off many potential tallies that might have given victory to the opposition. These special qualities are essential to any club, but to the Reds, who won so many games by the margin of a single run, they were especially vital ... his all-around performance, plus the fact that his work aided in winning the championship are ample evidence that the committee which named him as most valuable did a good job.[27]

McCormick was the third successive Red to earn the MVP award, honors that not coincidentally went hand in hand with the team's rise in the standings. Lombardi proved most valuable in 1938, Walters was selected in 1939, and Big Frank was chosen for the honor in the World Championship year of 1940. His first base counterpart, World Series opponent and fellow New Yorker, Tiger slugger Hank Greenberg earned the honors in the junior circuit,[28] setting up a World Series that matched the most valuable players on each of the league's best teams against one another.

The Hot Corner

In the other corner of the Reds diamond was a player who had earned a reputation as a malcontent, a clubhouse lawyer, and a destroyer of team morale. He had been called a lot of other things, too, and perhaps had "as many bum raps as any ball player in the game." That was the reputation that preceded Billy Werber's arrival in Cincinnati. It seemed that when

Werber guarded the third baseline for a team, he became a lightning rod for negativity and controversy, and there was little denying that the hot corner was aptly named. Strangely though, the negative tags that followed Werber around in the American League seemed to disappear once he vacated the AL for Cincinnati in 1939.[29]

Billy Werber spent the first six years of his big league career in the American League, coming up with the Yankees and playing very little before being traded to the Red Sox.[30] He played in a total of seven games for the Yankees in the 1930 and 1933 seasons, yet he believed that it was that brief experience with the mighty New York franchise that had a lot to do with his reputation as a "bad influence."

"When I was a kid breaking [in] with the Yankees," he told George Kirksey in 1941, "I spoke up if I had anything to say. I was taught by my father not to take any abuse. I never give it to anyone else and I never take it from others. I was independent financially early in my career and didn't have to depend solely on my baseball earnings for a livelihood."[31]

A business-minded player who spoke his mind, writer Lee Allen said of him, that though there "aren't many players who are wasting their time financially by playing big league baseball Bill Werber was one of them."[32] There were sound reasons for Allen's assessment. Werber was fluent in Spanish and French and had plans to go into his uncle's law practice, a firm that among other specialties handled cases brought by the Sioux Indians against the U.S. government. Those law plans never materialized, due to Werber's early devotion to the game. For Werber, baseball was a passion, but not his only one. He possessed a keen business mind that didn't disappear when he became a ballplayer. So while the game may have interrupted his law plans, it didn't stop him from thinking of a life outside of baseball. He always kept one foot in the world of business, serving as a partner in his father's insurance company during the off-season.

The insurance job wasn't an act of charitable nepotism on his father's part, either. Werber was a talented insurance executive and wrote a group insurance plan that had been published in the insurance trade journals. At the time, it was considered one of the best treatises written on the subject.[33]

The truth was that when it came to Billy Werber, he was probably a better businessman than he was a ballplayer. By 1976, after he was long retired from baseball, he made Lee Allen's words more than a little prophetic. Werber had, in fact, become a millionaire outside of the game. He inherited the insurance business from his father, helped it grow, and passed it along to his own son.[34]

Although he may have been better at business than he was at base-

Before he arrived in Cincinnati, Billy Werber had a reputation as a malcontent. Once he moved over from the American League, he was viewed as a positive influence in the clubhouse.

ball, the man who called himself the Tiger was hardly a slouch on the diamond. A graduate of Duke University, who "missed making Phi Beta Kappa by only a point and a half," Billy Werber was still a freshman at the North Carolina school when the Yankees gave the multitalented Blue Devil a $2,500 contract (nearly $850 a year) to play his way through college. On graduation, he was sent by the Yankees to Albany, where he hit .339 in 84 games and was named the Most Valuable Player on the team, an honor that earned him $500 worth of furniture.[35]

There were several stops around Yankee farm towns—places like Toledo and Newark and eventually Buffalo—before it was decided that Werber was ready for the big time.

By the spring of 1933 his time had come. Werber began playing a strong shortstop at the big league level for the Yankees and by his own admission, "thought he had the [Yankee] job sewed up." Then, fate intervened.

In this instance, fate was disguised as the Boston Red Sox. The Sox were in need of a shortstop, and their scout, Jack McAllister, inquired about taking a look at Frank Crosetti, then a Yankee back-up. McAllister was interested in seeing Crosetti in game action for the purpose of making a deal. The Yankees obliged. They sat Werber and began showcasing Crosetti, who in the words of Werber "went on like a house of fire." "He [Crosetti] was so good they [the Yankees] kept him at short and sold me to the Red Sox. I was a little disappointed but went to Boston and finished out the season playing short."[36]

The following year, Boston moved Werber to third, trading his future teammate (and future MVP pitcher on the Reds), then incumbent third baseman Bucky Walters, to the National League's Phillies. While playing third base for Boston in 1934, Werber led the league in steals with 40 and hit over .300 for the only time in his career, batting .321 in 632 at-bats.[37]

A fiery Marylander and a competitive fighter who "flashes brightest when the heat was turned on and there's blood on the moon,"[38] one of Werber's toughest days as a big leaguer, came in his otherwise stellar season of 1934. That day set the course for his outlook on the game and his view of the fans.

> I made four straight errors I think … the fans booed me something awful. I was plenty discouraged when I sat on my stool in front of my locker after the game. But I made a resolution right there that I'd never pay attention to what the fans said about me. They can boo me or cheer me and it doesn't make any difference. It can break the heart of a ballplayer … to be the target of abuse. I've told my children never to boo anybody, regardless of how bad they may seem to be.[39]

Incidents such as that made Werber, a thinking man's ballplayer, question what it meant to be a baseball "lifer," despite how good he felt about being a ballplayer.

"I remember sitting in the dugout.... It's batting practice and we're laughing and giggling and [Boston catcher] Rick Ferrell nudges me in my ribs and we're all chuckling and laughing on the bench and he said, 'Can you imagine getting paid for doing this?' And that's the way most of us felt about being a ballplayer."[40]

But as good as the good times were, the bad times were even more devastating. He knew baseball was not going to be forever, and he learned early on never to be overly impressed by his press clippings nor overly depressed by nitpickers. He thought he should prepare to get out of the game as quickly as he could, due to the stress he saw it put on players, some of which he experienced firsthand.[41]

He told writer Jack Murray that the way fans booed Babe Ruth in his final years, when he no longer could hit the ball like the Sultan of Swat, impacted him more than any other thing he saw as a ballplayer. "If this game can be so unkind to a man who's done so much for it, maybe it's not for me."[42]

To Werber, ballplayers were artists, supremely skilled in their profession, who performed in a veritable goldfish bowl where their slightest mistake was made before the eyes of thousands of people. There were thousands of doctors, dentists, and lawyers throughout the country, he reasoned, yet there were "only 400 men who could meet the standards of big league play in

Werber said of the fans' reaction: "They can boo me or cheer me and it doesn't make any difference. It can break the heart of a ball player ... to be the target of abuse. I've told my children never to boo anybody, regardless of how bad they may seem to be."

this country. Can you imagine a young dentist attempting to extract a wisdom tooth before 50,000 roaring spectators who would boo him unmercifully if he were so much as to chip the enamel with his instrument?"[43]

Werber explained how it was from the vantage point of someone down on the field:

> Few outside the dugout or the locker room understand the terrific pressure under which a ballplayer works. The hours are fine and the pay is wonderful, an envious Joe Fan will tell you. But a player burns up more nervous energy during a game than a stoker feeding a forced draft furnace. I know ace pitchers and league-leading hitters who after years in the game, are still nervous as a cat before the first pitch is made and limp as a damp towel for hours after the last one.... I've heard them say, "This is my last year at this game. You other suckers will never see me back here next year to have more years taken off my life!"[44]

Though he had formed some hard opinions about the dark side of what many viewed as a glamorous profession, Walters played extremely well for the better part of the 1934 season, until a September injury caused him to develop a bone spur. His play fell off the following season.

By 1936, Red Sox manager Joe Cronin began experimenting with Werber in the outfield, and Billy played nearly a third of the games in which he appeared, guarding the Fenway Park fences. Though he hit .275 and stole 23 bases on what was essentially still a bum leg, the situation in Boston wasn't working, and the Red Sox cut Werber at the end of the 1936 season.[45]

Without a baseball job for the following spring, Werber shopped himself and accepted an offer from Philadelphia Athletics president and manager Connie Mack. He played two years for the Athletics, hitting .292 in 1937, leading the league in stolen bases (for the third time) with 35, and then slumped to .259 the following year. He was dealt to the Reds prior to the 1939 season.

A Series of Calls

The deal to the Reds almost didn't happen due to a disagreement over who owed Werber $1,500.

According to Werber, a friend called to inform him that he was packing his bags for Cincinnati. Bill's initial reaction was "great, the Reds are going to win the pennant." The next call came from Reds GM Warren Giles to inform him of the deal, but the two men failed to agree on terms.

He turned to his wife and told her that in the next few minutes Connie Mack would be calling. Sure enough, the phone rang a few minutes later and it was Mack. Werber explained the $1,500 chasm and Mack said he would send Werber the difference once the sale was finalized. Werber refused on principle, saying that if the Reds wanted him they were responsible and should fully compensate the A's for his services.

After he hung up with Mack, the phone rang again. This time it was Bill McKechnie. The Deacon said he'd like to have Werber in Tampa for spring training and told him he would pay his expenses both ways if they failed to come to terms. Werber again declined. And then in what had become quite a busy day for the phone in the Werber household, Giles called again, telling Werber to come to Tampa and the Reds would meet his terms.

Werber said, "That's the last disagreement I've had with them."[46]

Though he was always one to give his best effort on the field, until he came to the Reds, Werber was not well liked by his fellow players. Those problems seemed to disappear once he joined Cincinnati.[47] He roomed with Bucky Walters, and his teammates on the Reds regarded Billy as a "hustler, a team man and a winning ball player ... both on and off the field."[48]

Werber was a catalyst who gave the Reds even greater quickness on the base paths, a solid glove at third, and most of all, an infusion of high intensity.

Reds public relations director Gabe Paul was quick to point out that when the Reds acquired Werber, they were a streamlined outfit with one of the fastest lineups in the major leagues. "At six positions they can show players who are among the speed merchants of the league.... Two years ago the Reds did not possess the speed they have today. They were a slow team. They finished last. Today, they are outstanding in this respect and are rated as contenders."[49]

The years with Cincinnati were among Werber's finest in the big leagues. Whether he had truly been a malcontent or not in his American League days, Werber was a key component of the NL pennant winners in 1939 and 1940, batting .289 and .277, respectively. He led the league in runs scored in the 1939 campaign with 115 and led all third basemen in fielding in 1940.

The Jitter Bugs

When Billy Werber was describing the plight of a player once the fans got on him, he was in part talking about his teammates in the middle of the Reds infield, who had experienced the rough treatment from the game's paying customers firsthand. The fact that Lonnie Frey and Billy Myers had earned the reputation as jittery infielders and were able to improve their play significantly under McKechnie's guidance to shore up the middle of the infield was one of the key ingredients to the club's recipe for success in 1939 and 1940.

Tom Meany, writing in the *World Telegram* in 1939, attributed much of the reason for that year's pennant winner in Cincinnati to the surprise solid infield play of Myers and Frey. Meany explained that McCormick and Werber, both solid fielders at the corners, had played no better or worse than had been expected. It was Frey and Myers who turned heads with their play. "They played far better," Meany wrote, "than anybody, including McKechnie, anticipated they would, and it was the improvement of the jitterbugs which took up the slack."[50]

A Bust in Brooklyn

Linus (or "Lonnie"—depending on the source) Frey got his first big league call-up in 1933 when he was just 23 years old. The Brooklyn Dodgers needed substitute infielders due to a rash of injuries to their starters, and Frey was among the top players on their list. It was a far cry from the regular stenographer's job he had held only two years before, when baseball was still a game he played purely for fun.

A native of St. Louis, Missouri, Lonnie Frey did not plan on a baseball career. For him, the game was primarily a weekend pursuit. Frey had earned his diploma from business college and was happy enough going to his stenographer's job in a St. Louis packing company and playing baseball in his spare time with the Honey Dew team in the Municipal League. One day, on his arrival at the office in 1931, there was a blue envelope with his name on it that said due to a drop in business, his services at the office were no longer required. A similar letter was received by all of the other junior staffers at the company.

With the country in the throes of the Great Depression, finding work was not easy. For Frey, week after week of job hunting proved fruitless, and he eventually decided to see if he could support himself playing the game. It was a baseball career that quite literally grew out of the Depression.[51]

Called "Junie" or "Junior," due to the young age at which he broke into the big leagues, Frey originally tried to land a spot with his hometown Cardinals and reported to Sportsman's Park for an open tryout. He was rated too small by the Cards and sent on his way.

The manager of the Honey Dews, Harry Albrecht, was in the young man's corner, however, and he pushed for Frey to gain a tryout with Nashville of the Southern Association. Frey impressed enough at Nashville that they sent him to Montgomery and then to York in the New York–Penn League, before he finally made his way back to Nashville's Vols.

He became a hot prospect in the Dodger system and had been earmarked to report to Brooklyn in the spring of 1934, after finishing up a final year of seasoning in the minors. Instead, he was pressed into emergency service and reported to the Dodgers in late August, when the Vols received an SOS call from Brooklyn's management.[52]

He reported immediately and it was love at first sight. At least, for a while. Initially, Frey was a huge success for the Bums. He was in his early 20s and was being touted as the "can't miss star shortstop of the future." After hitting .319 in 34 games during the brief 1933 call-up, Frey showed durability and relative consistency the following two years. He hit .284 in his first full season, and though he slipped to .262 in his sophomore campaign, he belted an impressive 11 homers—a surprise power output from a 160-pound shortstop.

His hitting ability, the "can't miss" label, and the way Frey bounced back from a concussion after being hit in the head by a batting practice fastball to turn in an impressive rookie season were all strong indications that he was going to be a keeper for Brooklyn. Prior to the start of the 1936 season, Frey was even named the team captain after Al Lopez was traded to Boston.

It may have been the added pressure of having the squad's captaincy thrust on his still young shoulders or a sore arm that made him rush ground balls and hurry his throws that stalled his progress.[53] Or maybe it was that the great expectations many in the Dodger organization had for him were just a little too great and Frey couldn't possibly live up to them. But no matter what the reason was, by the sixth week in the 1936 season, it was clear that his once bright star had dimmed considerably, due to the plethora of errors he committed. The Dodger captain and once star shortstop even feared he might be traded.[54]

His fears were well founded. The headlines in the Brooklyn and New York papers during the last week of May 1936 told the story: "Dodgers' Captain Unable to Stand Riding from Fans"; "Frey Problem Child: Young Shortstop Can't Seem to Do Anything Right"; "Dodgers' Defeat Breaks Frey's Spirit." Dodger Manager Casey Stengel, who read the papers and heard the derisive remarks of the fans, tried switching him to second base and even the outfield, until ultimately he wound up giving his former star a seat on the bench.[55]

Based on his play in the field, a change certainly was warranted. Up until the time he was benched, Frey had committed 20 errors in 34 games. "A pace like that would have created a new record had Frey stayed in there." His batting average was a paltry .226, which didn't help matters either.[56]

The constant insults directed at Frey from the grandstand at Ebbets Field practically made Stengel's decision for him — it was clear, Frey was finished as the Bums' shortstop. Casey practically admitted as much to writer Edward Murphy.

"Lonnie is sensitive about the way those fans in Brooklyn holler and when they jumped on him, he went to pieces," Stengel said. "I can't play Frey at shortstop in Brooklyn anymore. At least, I don't think so. If he went to that position in our park, those loudmouthed guys in the grandstand might unload on him and he'd never be able to pick up a ball. When some Dodger fans aim a verbal attack on a player they don't miss."[57]

Stengel and the Dodgers were heading out on the road, where Casey said he would experiment using Frey in the outfield. It seemed like a last-ditch effort to save Frey's Dodgers career, giving him a turn to learn the outfield, out of both sight and earshot of his harsh critics on Bedford Avenue. But the marriage between Frey and the outfield wasn't one that would last. The following season, Stengel's confidence in his ability to turn the hometown fans around and reverse his downward slide had evaporated and Frey was dealt to Chicago, where he would play a single season as a utility infielder for the Cubs.

Frey's Star Shines Again

Purchased by the Reds from Chicago the following winter because of his versatility in the infield, Reds manager Bill McKechnie said he "had as good a chance as any man for a regular infield post [on the '38 Reds]"; this despite the fact that he couldn't crack the Cubs starting lineup and appeared infrequently for the Chicago Nine.[58] Originally, McKechnie had Frey slotted in to compete with Alex Kampouris for the everyday second base job. McKechnie wanted to make the switch due to the sore arm Frey had developed back in the minors, where for two years he was unable to throw overhanded and later tended to rush his throws to compensate.[59]

Stengel had reasoned the same thing back when Frey was in Brooklyn and had tried a second base experiment for Frey just as McKechnie was now doing with the Reds. Only in addition to moving Frey from short to second, his new manager did one other thing. He turned Frey from a switch-hitter into a full-time, left-handed batter — thereby enabling the young infielder to worry less about his hitting and focus more on the defensive aspects of his game.[60]

This time, the experiment worked. Lonnie wound up winning the second base battle with Kampouris (later dealt to the Giants) and elevated his game to such a high level that by 1939 he was the starting second baseman for the National League in the All-Star game.[61]

One Brooklyn writer, Arthur Patterson, could hardly believe the turn of events. "Anyone predicting this spring that Linus Frey not only would play a full game at second base in the All-Star game, but also avert a shutout for the National League ... would have been gently led away to the nearest psychopathic ward and barred from the press box for life."[62]

Before arriving in Cincinnati, Lonnie Frey was a "can't miss prospect" in Brooklyn. But things deteriorated so much during his time with the Dodgers that Brooklyn Manager Casey Stengel said near the end of Lonnie's tenure at Ebbets Field, "I can't play Frey at shortstop in Brooklyn anymore ... those loudmouthed guys out in the grandstand might unload on him and he'd never be able to pick up a ball anymore."

But that's exactly what Frey did. In addition to batting .306 for the Reds at the halfway point in the season and leading the league in runs scored (along with teammate Billy Werber), Frey was playing an outstanding second base. As Patterson wrote, "It's Frey's fielding which has everyone talking, particularly those of us who once composed a song about him in Brooklyn, which had one line: 'Makes an error everyday, turning Casey's hair so gray.'"[63]

Frey credited McKechnie's encouraging words and corrections as a reason for his sudden success, claiming that the pat on the back was better than a kick in the pants.

His batting average dipped while he played for the Reds, but his infield play, once he was permanently shifted to second, improved dramatically as did other aspects of his game. In

McKechnie moved Frey from shortstop to second base and turned him from a switch-hitter to a full-time left-handed batter. The result was that Lonnie Frey was the starting second baseman in the 1939 All-Star game.

1940, he batted only .266 but he led the National League in stolen bases, putouts, assists, and double plays and was among the leaders in games played with 150.[64] His increased confidence under McKechnie resulted in three all-star appearances, and for a period of about five years little Lonnie Frey, no longer the can't miss kid in Brooklyn, was the best second baseman in the National League.[65]

Though he was a bust as shortstop for Brooklyn, once Lonnie Frey moved to Cincinnati and was shifted to second, he was according to Bill James, "the best second baseman in the National League for a period of five years."

Billy Myers

Billy Myers, who was half of the double play combination on the 1940 World Champs, had many similarities to his double play partner's playing days in Brooklyn. Like Lonnie Frey in his Dodger days, Billy Myers played shortstop. Also like Frey, he was the captain of his ball club. Finally, he was one of those players the fans rode mercilessly at times. His fellow teammate on the left side of the Jungle Cat infield, Billy Werber, recalled how bad the jitters had got to Myers when Werber took the infield for the first time as a member of the Reds:

> Just before the first game I ever played in a Red uniform at Cincinnati, Billy Myers, our shortstop, said to me behind his glove, "If there's any high pop flies today, you take 'em." Myers didn't feel up to catching pop-ups, and the reason was that he had been ridden right into the jumps and jitters by the critical Cincinnati fans. Billy was a slick fielder, but they had jockeyed him so hard that now, as the 1939 season was about to open, he was temporarily demoralized.... The second Pirate batter that day popped one which flirted with the clouds over shortstop. I left my third base post, with Billy shouting for me to handle it, and chased the ball to within a step of second before making the catch.[66]

Myers got his start with the Reds in 1935 and played his best ball when McKechnie took over the club in 1938. Always a light hitter (his best season was in 1938 when he hit .281 and knocked in 56 runs), his fielding could be erratic — a somewhat deadly combination for an everyday big league shortstop. But McKechnie was adept at transforming the weaknesses exhibited by ballplayers under other managers and turning them into strengths. That happened to be the case in terms of his effect on Myers.

As one writer explained after watching Myers during his first three years in the big leagues and then during McKechnie's inaugural campaign: "Myers isn't the steadiest infielder in the business but he's a clever chap, fast and a play-maker. Incidentally, that's one of Bill McKechnie's achievements that has been overlooked, the effective work he has gotten out of Myers and 'Junior' Frey around second base. These two kids were the most notorious error-makers in the league last year and the year before, but for McKechnie they've dovetailed their play neatly."[67]

He was 24 years old when he saw his first Major League game, which just so happened to be the first game he ever played in — the Cincinnati opener against the Pirates in 1935.[68] Myers was named team captain in his first year, an added dose of pressure for the youngster, when Jim Bottomley left the team. It made Myers the first player to ever captain a big league squad as a rookie.[69]

Homesickness and Other Maladies

Aside from Werber's recollection of the nervousness Myers experienced there were other incidents that showed that Billy Myers seemed to feel pressure more acutely than most. He was a nervous wreck at times due to the taunts of hometown fans, but even prior to that his nervousness almost prevented him from having a big league career at all.

Following high school at West Fairview, Pennsylvania, Myers received an offer to play for a semi-pro team at Lewiston, Pennsylvania, which was 60 miles away from his home. He didn't want to go, but his older brother convinced him to try and offered to drive him there. Myers was nervous the entire ride and said at the time that the trip felt like an eternity and that he thought he'd never get back home.

He played most of the summer there until he joined Waynesboro, a St. Louis Cardinals farm team, in the Blue Ridge League. He performed well in a brief stint with that club and was told to report to the Cardinal Camp at Avon Park, Florida, the following spring.

At the time, the newspapers called it the shortest training trip on record. It took him a reported 36 hours to make the trip from Pennsylvania, and he was placed in a hotel room by himself. With the Cardinals stationed at a hotel miles from the town, loneliness apparently got the best of Myers. He put in a morning's workout the next day, but by noon was headed for home at his own expense. It was said that he had attended a party thrown by his future mother-in-law the night he left and was home the next day to help finish eating the cake.[70]

The Cards didn't give up on him, though. Myers was ordered to report to Danville, Illinois, and he traveled around the Cardinals farm, making stops in Houston, Rochester, back to Danville, Springfield, Rochester (again), Elmira, and Columbus. One season he even caught a souvenir in the form of a stray bat to the head, which sent him home from the Cardinals training camp in 1930.

But his talent persisted and compensated for whatever nervous maladies he suffered from. By August 1934, the Giants had purchased Myers from Columbus for the sum of $30,000, though he never played for them. Cincinnati acquired him in a deal that winter for Mark Koenig and Allyn Stout after the Giants had obtained Dick Bartell to play short.[71]

He seemed to find his place in Cincinnati. With the Reds, Myers made steady progress, especially with his glove, and had his finest seasons under McKechnie's guidance. But by the end of the 1940 campaign, he tested a Reds team that had already suffered through an emotionally wrenching August. Though the Reds had clinched their second consecutive pennant, Myers announced that he had had enough. He was leaving the team and jumped the Reds in late September. Gabe Paul, the public relations director for the club, phoned his boss, Warren Giles, to tell him the news. An incredulous Giles couldn't believe it. "What for?" Giles demanded of his PR director.

"I don't know," Paul replied. "I tried to talk him out of it. McKechnie knows about it too."

Giles tried in vain to reach his talented but distraught shortstop all the next day. When he finally reached him, Giles delivered a threat. "If you don't come back and play in the World Series," he said. "I'll fine you what salary you have coming and see that you aren't cut into the series and you will never play another game."

Myers didn't flinch. "I don't care," he said. "I have personal problems and I don't care if I ever play again. And I don't want any money."

The problems were not disclosed publicly, though some thought it was due to his father's sickness. Giles called Myers persistently, and when he saw he was making progress and wearing his team's captain down, he pressed further. The press had already been told Myers had gone to Columbus on personal business with the club's permission, and that was the story, Giles promised, the team would stick by. When Myers was assured he could come back and act as if nothing had happened, he agreed.[72]

It was a good thing for the Reds that Myers came back, because when Lonnie Frey was injured prior to the World Series, Eddie Joost was in the second base slot and the Reds would have been short-handed had Myers not returned. As Lee Allen wrote, "What would have happened if Billy Myers had stayed in Columbus is not pleasant to think about."[73]

The Thin Man

Eddie Joost was a utility infielder on the Reds pennant winners of 1939–40. He stood 5' 11" tall and weighed 155 pounds. Lanky and quick with the glove, Eddie Joost earned the moniker Thin Man early on due to his frail appearance. Though his ability to withstand the rigors of a full Major League season as an everyday player was often questioned when he first came up (due to his slight build), Joost had staying power and a finesse in the field that made him a player who would be in baseball for the long haul.[74]

He was not an official member of the Jungle Cats, and by his own admission didn't do very well at the plate in the first half of his career. Though he considered his own play subpar at the beginning of what would be 17 years in the Major Leagues, his Reds teams were very successful. Ironically, the Thin Man's best years, and the ones in which he became an All Star, were spent in Philadelphia with the Athletics. Unfortunately for Joost, his Athletics teams were never able to replicate the individual success he had with them in the American League standings.

Before the postwar era, Eddie Joost was branded a utility guy. He spent four years playing for the San Francisco Missions in the Pacific Coast League, earning his chance at the majors, after being sold to the Cincinnati Reds in 1936, for two players and $25,000.[75]

He started his pro career at an early age and was only 16 when he joined the Missions. The young Joost thought he had found paradise. "He was a lean rangy kid, built just about like he is now," his former Missions manager Freddie Hofmann told the *Sporting News* in 1949. He was young and "we'd figured we'd have him around evenings and school holidays and it was with that understanding we signed him."

One day, when the Missions were working out, a stranger approached Hofmann and told him that he was a truant officer and was looking for a boy named Joost who had skipped school. Hofmann said he wasn't there. He told the officer Joost never reported to the team during school hours, but he said he would check the clubhouse just to make sure. As Hofmann told it, he went into the clubhouse and he was surprised to find Joost getting dressed to play. He warned young Eddie of the truant officer and told him to sneak out the side door and to not come back during school hours. Joost took the advice. At least, the first half of it.

"Joost sneaked out but I don't suppose it did any good," Hofmann said. "You couldn't keep that boy away from baseball. Pretty soon I noticed he was around every day."[76]

Baseball was a singular passion for the youngster, which is why he was able to turn professional at such a young age. Though he played solidly in the PCL and Cincinnati paid for the rights to get him, Reds manager Chuck Dressen didn't think much of Joost when he first saw him. That's when he hung the utility tag on him. "Well kid, I don't think you'll ever be a big league ballplayer," Dressen told him at their first meeting. "If we keep you, you'll be a utility player."[77]

Joost appeared in 19 games those first two years (1936–37), spending most of his time (including the entire 1938 season), down on the farm in Syracuse and Kansas City. He was, in the eyes of the big leagues, a potential future sub. Even when he came up for his full season in 1939, it was strictly as a back-up. The Reds thought him valuable because he had the ability to step in and play any position in the infield. A Reds news release touted him as a "fellow whose every move is graceful" and was "one of the easiest and best fielders in baseball. You don't realize it sometimes," the release read, "because he does things so easily."[78]

Though he was a slick fielder and later hit 116 homers in eight years with the A's,[79] his hitting with Cincinnati was anything but easy, as he frequently struggled at the plate batting .252 and .216, in 1939 and 1940, respectively.

"I did not get into the '39 Series," Joost said. "I pleaded with McKechnie to let me play since we were not doing well, but Bill had more faith in Lonnie Frey at second and Billy Myers at short."[80]

Joost's big opportunity came a year later, in the form of an injury to Lonnie Frey, which allowed Joost to play second base in all seven World Series games. His stellar fielding in the series later led McKechnie to make him the starting shortstop after Billy Myers was traded following the 1940 season.[81]

As Joost told it, the injury to Frey was a freak occurrence. One day, toward the end of the 1940 season, "Lonnie Frey and I were sitting at the end of the bench where there was this great big iron water cooler that was full of ice. Frey jumped up for something and the iron lid slipped off the ice and fell on his foot and broke his toe. That's how I became the second baseman for the World Series."[82]

In addition to his hitting, another thing about Joost that wasn't necessarily as easy as his fielding was the way he could rankle a manager. Though most players praised McKechnie effusively as both a manager and a man, Joost saw a different side to the Deacon. He said in a 1999 interview, "McKechnie was a good manager. He knew how to manage his pitchers. But beyond that, we had *good* players. He was a difficult guy personally. He and I didn't see eye-to-eye. He didn't like you to conflict with what he was thinking or saying. Occasionally he was wrong and sometimes I would tell him that. The next thing you know he and I just didn't get along."[83]

After taking up space in McKechnie's doghouse, Joost was jettisoned from the Reds following the 1942 season to baseball Siberia, the Casey Stengel–managed Boston Braves. There he locked horns with another future Hall of Fame manager, with whom he was not impressed.

"Casey was not a good manager," Joost told Stan Gosshandler, long after his playing days had ended. "He certainly was not the guru he was made out to be with the Yankees. He was never on top of the game and was actually a clown. You or I could have won pennants with the players he had with the Yankees."[84]

Joost retold a story that illustrated how strained his relationship had become with Stengel while he was a member of the Braves. As Joost told the story he was batting early in the game with a runner on first and two men out. "I was looking for the signs from third base coach Tony Cuccinello. I was looking for the hit or the hit and run sign but I got the bunt sign. I backed out of the box and said to myself, "What the heck is going on?" I looked again at Tony and he gave me the same sign.

"So," Joost recalled. "I bunted with two outs and Stengel went nuts. After the game I went up to Cuccinello and said, 'What the hell is going on?' He said, 'What do you mean?' I said 'Stengel gave me the bunt sign with two strikes and two outs.' Cuccinello said, 'Casey changed the signs and told me not to tell you.'"[85]

Though he was often at odds with McKechnie, his relationship with the Deacon never got to be as poor as the one he had with Stengel. Although Joost couldn't hit while he was a member of the Reds and never officially made it into the Jungle Club, by the end of the 1940 season, after a stellar fielding performance in the fall classic, Eddie Joost played like he belonged on what was at the time the best fielding infield in Major League history. For one October at least, that was all that really mattered.

5

◆ ◆ ◆ ◆

Armed and Ready

> In my opinion, he lacks guts. He is probably as big a liar as I have ever known. You cannot depend on one word he says. I am not sure just how is the best way to get the most work out of him.[1]

These are the words of Reds general manager Warren Giles in October 1937 discussing Paul Derringer, a man who later became his winning pitcher in Game 7 of the 1940 World Series.

The 1940 team assembled by Giles and his manager, Bill McKechnie, was built on pitching and defense; pitching led by Derringer and Bucky Walters, the co-aces of the Reds staff. But if Giles had not been convinced otherwise, Derringer and Walters might never have had the opportunity to lead the Reds on a run at a world championship.

In the years before Cincinnati moved out of the second division, the burly GM's view of the enigmatic Kentucky right-hander, who became a leader of the Cincy staff, was not that "Duke" Derringer lacked talent, only that it took much effort and prodding to harness it. Giles believed that confronting Derringer was the only way to get the best out of him. In 1937, he seemed tired of all the energy that both he and his predecessors expended on the talented but temperamental hurler. The big rightie with the high leg kick was, in Giles's view, more trouble than he was worth. In a letter to his new manager McKechnie, evaluating Derringer, Giles wrote:

> He was on a bonus contract this year ... and when the pressure was really put on him [he pitched well]; that is when I told him he positively would not get the bonus unless he pitched more effectively, he did good work for a short while after that conversation.... He can pitch better one run behind than with a one run lead.... Personally, I am of the opinion that if we could make a good deal on Derringer, we would probably not regret making it."[2]

The Best Deal

It's the best deal he never made. Giles was right about one thing: Derringer was a hard man to figure. In some regards, he was supremely concerned about how he was viewed, and at other times, he couldn't have cared less. The Duke was one of the best-dressed players in the league, favoring imported shetlands, cashmere, and tweeds, indicating that appearances were important to him; yet in other instances, such as in off-the-field fracases and run-ins with manager Charlie Dressen, he was unflappable, caring little what the public thought as long as he got what he wanted.

One story had it that during the 1936 season, following a game, Derringer and then–Reds manager Dressen got into a fist fight, which ended when the skipper punched Derringer in the face. The next day, an embarrassed and challenged Derringer pitched a shutout. That's one of the reasons that led Giles to believe he was more trouble than he was worth.[3]

How wrong he was. The record shows that Derringer had a manic professional career — extreme highs, followed by extreme lows, that were in turn followed by extreme highs. A former catcher turned pitcher, the good-looking, solidly built Duke won only 11 more games than he lost in his 15-year big league career; he had more losing seasons (eight) than winning ones (six).[4] But for a time, the 6' 4", 205-pound hurler was among the best pitchers in all of baseball.[5]

If his cockiness and arrogance were detriments to his off-the-field personality, they were also significant attributes to his

Warren Giles wrote that Derringer was a liar and told McKechnie, "if we could make a deal for him, we would probably not regret making it."

competitive nature. The unshakable confidence he had in his ability was what led him to the mound in the first place. As Derringer recalled:

> When I played on the Springfield High School team, I was the catcher and had no thoughts of becoming a pitcher until one day some team had licked us about ten-to-nothing and our hurler couldn't get the side out. It was getting late and I wanted to get the game over so I could go on a camping trip ... the way things were going it looked like we'd be there all night, so I volunteered to pitch. I got the game over quick striking out about eight batters. Since then, I've been a pitcher.[6]

It was a conversion that was not without its complications. He was a three-letter athlete at Springfield High School, playing fullback in football and guard in basketball in addition to his prowess on the diamond. Following graduation, determined to make his way in baseball, a young Derringer headed to the coal fields of West Virginia to play semi-pro ball for Coalwood. There he earned his first bonus of sorts. In a 1940 interview, he remembered:

> The mine workers were making big money in those days and bet heavily on the games. I pitched against a team Coalwood hadn't licked in about three years ... and we beat 'em three-to-one. After the game, the miners took up a collection and gave me $301. I didn't know what to do with the money because a lot of it was in change and crumpled dollar bills. Finally, I took off my baseball shirt and rolled the money up in it. I was a pretty happy kid that day.[7]

In 1927, full of confidence and ability, the Duke signed with the St. Louis Cardinals and was so eager to impress the Redbird coaches that during his initial pitching drills, he added even more height to an already lofty leg-kick motion. In doing so, he caught his left shoe in the web of his glove during the windup of his first pitch and promptly fell off the mound; it was an embarrassing first impression, but not a lasting one.[8]

Over the long haul, Derringer's predilection for confounding managers and club executives was surpassed only by his ability to baffle opposing hitters. He combined periods of stellar pitching with some losing seasons and antics on and off the field that led many to believe the end was often near for the frequently unhittable, sometimes temperamental mound ace.

Often, he succeeded in spite of himself. His first spring training in 1927 with the Cardinals was important to his career, not solely because it was his first taste of the big leagues but also because it was his introduction to McKechnie, then a coach on Bob O'Farrell's 1927 Redbirds squad.

He came under both the Deacon's tutelage and that of one of his idols, future Hall of Famer Grover Cleveland Alexander. Ironically, Alexander was the starting pitcher in the first professional game a young Derringer had ever seen. He remembered:

> When I reported to the Cardinals, Alex was there. Despite the fact that he had been a World Series hero the year before, Alex was one of the few who took pains to help me. He drilled one thought home, "If you have something on the ball, control is the main thing."[9]

It's advice Derringer took to heart, and it helped shape his pitching career. In fact, 10 years later, the Duke's control was one of the main reasons McKechnie fought to keep Derringer on the Reds when Giles was ready to jettison him after the 1937 season and a disappointing 10–14 record. McKechnie, partial to pitchers who exhibited control, convinced Giles that Derringer was worth keeping, saying after he assumed the helm of the Reds, "I'll stick with the fellow who can get the ball over the plate. Look at Derringer's record and see who can get the ball over better than he can."

Derringer's control was impressive. For a pitcher who consistently averaged more than 200 innings, and on two occasions threw more than 300 innings, Derringer never issued as many as 70 walks in a single season during his 15-year career. He issued more than 60 bases-on-balls on only two occasions.[10]

Of course in 1927, Derringer was a raw talent, participating in his first spring training and he was sent to Danville, the Triple I league Cardinals affiliate. Danville turned out to be a pennant winner, and the young Derringer posted a 10–8 mark for the minor league club. The following year, he went 15–11, earning a promotion to Rochester, St Louis's top farm team. He was reunited there with McKechnie, after McKechnie (who had taken over for the fired Bob O'Farrell) was himself demoted by Cards owner Sam Breadon for failing to win the 1928 World Series.

During his time in Rochester, Derringer showed he was a quality pitcher. In an impressive two-year stint, 1929–1930, he went 17–12 and 23–11. Those back-to-back performances earned him a trip to the big leagues in 1931.

Not lacking confidence, during spring training of the 1931 season, a prideful Derringer brazenly predicted a 20-win season. Even though he failed to reach that milestone, the Duke opened eyes around the league, going 18–8 for the pennant-winning Cardinals, posting the best winning percentage of all senior circuit hurlers. The performance earned him a Game 1 start in the fall classic as a 24-year-old rookie.[11]

His team fared much better than he did. St. Louis beat the Philadelphia Athletics in a seven-game World Series, but the much-heralded Derringer dropped both of his starts. In Game 1, he opposed Lefty Grove, who coming off his finest season at 31–4, showed the young rookie how much he still had to learn about pitching in big games.

"I was in the game until Al Simmons ruined my dream," Derringer recalled. "He blasted a home run with two men on. That was the end of me."[12]

Though there was no shame in losing his first series start as a rookie to Lefty Grove, Derringer viewed his second series start in Game 6 as a "major disappointment." Up the night before with an abscessed nose, Derringer tried to tough it out and pitch through the pain but saw his mound performance quickly deteriorate. He headed for the showers after four and two-thirds innings' worth of work and four runs scored. An 0–2 World Series record was not the way a deflated Derringer had envisioned his season ending.

The Hangover Strikes

The World Series hangover continued into the following year, and Derringer slid into a sophomore slump that saw him go 11–14 with an ERA of 4.05 — a far different experience than his successful rookie season. By May 1933, the control-oriented Derringer's erratic record had him on the trading block. The Cardinals, seeking middle infield help (Charley Gelbert, their everyday shortstop, suffered an accidental gunshot wound in the leg), trade Big Paul, already 0–2 on the year, to the hapless Cincinnati Reds. Reds general manager Larry MacPhail acquired him along with Sparky Adams and Allyn Stout for Leo Durocher, Frank Henry, and John Ogden.[13]

Derringer went on to lose 27 games that year. It was a season that might have shattered the ego of a less confident hurler, but not Derringer. He posted a respectable 3.30 ERA, and whether it was a matter of ego-boosting or he really believed what he said, Derringer called the 1933 campaign one of his finest in the big leagues. "They licked me time-after-time," Derringer said in 1940. "But I pitched well. I think in about 19 games I was beaten when I allowed an average of three runs per game. The Cincinnati club that year was terrible. I hate to say it, but I think it was about the worst I ever played on."[14] Statistically, it was also his worst season in the big leagues.

Over the course of the next three seasons, Derringer righted the ship.

Though he suffered another losing season the following year in 1934 (going 15–21), he led the Reds in both victories and strikeouts (122). For a squad that sported three different managers and lost more games than the prior year's club, the worst team Derringer had ever played on, it was a significant improvement. The Reds record in 1934 was worse than it had been in 1933 and their standing remained the same — dead last in the National League. In 1935, the Duke regained the brilliance he had shown with the Cardinals in his stellar rookie year, going 22–13 (the third highest win total in the NL), earning a spot on the All-Star team. The Reds, despite escaping the basement, remained mired in the second division, showing little improvement.

The next season, Derringer took a step back. He slipped to a .500 winning percentage, suffered a public suspension by manager Charlie Dressen, and was put on the trading block for failing to slide in an early season loss to the New York Giants. The incident was significant, for it displayed a growing discord between Derringer and Dressen. An accounting of the incident by writer Tom Meany:

> Derringer has been suspended indefinitely without pay for failing to slide home in the fifth inning of yesterday's ball game. Inasmuch as Paul trying to score from second on a single, was waved home by manager Charlie Dressen and thrown out by a length and a half, the chastisement seems ill-placed. It wasn't a smart act on Dressen's part to wave in Derringer and it wasn't a stupid or negligent play on Derringer's part to go without sliding…. The suspension whether merited or not, was more stupid than either his failure to slide or Dressen's sending him to certain extinction against the rifle arm of Moore.[15]

Thomas Swope, a Cincinnati beat writer, emphasized that up until that point Derringer had called Dressen the "greatest manager in the National League," but he cast a skeptical eye as to the reason for the suspension, saying "few persons, if any, believe that Derringer was suspended solely because he didn't slide into the plate, May 3. The general public senses a reason deeper than that." What the reason was, Swope himself claimed to not know, but Dressen and GM MacPhail expected that Derringer's suspension would elicit many trade inquiries. Swope was unsure of whether the Reds would trade him or try to build around him.[16] But despite the difficulties that continued to surround him, his talent won out and Derringer would not be the one who wound up changing his address.

The same could not be said for the two Cincinnati executives. Within two years, Derringer was still wearing Cincinnati Red, but GM MacPhail and manager Dressen were both gone from the Queen City. MacPhail took the GM role in Brooklyn prior to the 1937 season, and Dressen served as a manager "waiting to be fired" by the Reds the following year.

Dressen was eventually fired and for the third time in Derringer's career, Bill McKechnie entered the picture. The Deacon took over the helm of the Reds after being given the job by Cincy's recently appointed GM Warren Giles, a friend from Bill's Rochester days.

"If a pitcher can't win for Bill McKechnie, he can't win for anybody," Derringer said, welcoming the move. True to his word, the Duke promptly won 21 games, nearly pushing the Reds to the pennant in McKechnie's very first season. Though a pennant for the Reds was not to be in 1938, the improvement under McKechnie's guidance was dramatic and Cincy won the NL flag the following year, Derringer's finest season in the majors, a 25–7 MVP-caliber effort.[17]

McKechnie's impact on Derringer was impressive. Ironically, after Giles's assessment of the high leg kicking Kentuckian as an expendable commodity, Derringer flourished under McKechnie's direction. He showed All-Star form, rolling off three 20-plus win seasons, going 21–14, 25–7, and 20–12.

Derringer thought the key to the success of his relationship with McKechnie was that it was built on a fundamental fairness. "McKechnie's been more than fair with me and I try to be fair to him," Derringer said. "It's worked out great for me and I only hope I've played some small part in Bill's success."[18]

In the 1939 campaign, Derringer's 25 victories would have made him an almost certain MVP award winner, but it earned him a spot as merely the second best pitcher on his own team. The Duke finished third in the National League's MVP balloting that season. Instead, the league's highest honor went to his teammate and co-ace, the other half of the best one-two pitching tandem in the National League.

The Workhorse

In 1934, Jimmie Wilson was a player-manager with the Philadelphia Phillies, a team battling the Cincinnati Reds for the cellar in the National League. It's a job that Bill James said was "the equivalent of being a public relations manager for a toxic waste dump."[19] Manager Wilson was not the catalyst needed to reverse Philadelphia's fortunes. The man they called Ace was never able to do much managing the Phils, alternating three seventh-place finishes with two cellar-dwelling eighth-place finishes between 1934 and 1938.

Although he couldn't lead Philadelphia out of the second division in the years he piloted the moribund franchise, Wilson did manage to save a baseball career.

In his first year managing the Phillies, Wilson acquired Boston Red Sox third baseman William J. "Bucky" Walters, who at 23 games into the season was hitting a paltry .216. It was hardly a move designed to change the immediate fortunes of the hapless Phillies. But whatever the merits of the deal may have been and whatever shortcomings Wilson may have had as a manager (or in this case as an evaluator of Major League third base talent), there was no disputing that Jimmie was a quality catcher, solid defensively, and able to successfully guide a pitching staff. He also knew a good pitcher when he saw one. Even, as it turns out, if the pitcher had been playing a different position and had never previously thrown from the mound in a professional game. When it came to Walters though, that was what Wilson saw — a pitcher. He knew his recently acquired third baseman had a strong arm, but the question was, did he have what it took to stay in the big leagues? The answer was, probably not as an everyday player.

The problem facing Wilson was that was all Bucky Walters ever wanted to be. A native of Philadelphia, Walters was an aspiring shortstop in 1929 when the National League's Boston Braves bought his contract from the Piedmont League.[20] Walters tried to make it as an infielder (primarily at third base) with three different teams, including stints with both Boston franchises and the Phillies.[21] He was unsuccessful in all three attempts and could have been earmarked for a career out of baseball. Lucky for Walters, his manager didn't apply a "three strikes and you're out" rule to the struggling third baseman. Instead, Jimmie Wilson saw an opportunity.

Walters was a mediocre everyday player. He had a great arm, was a good fielder, and had the competitiveness managers love.[22] Wilson figured Bucky's arm and spirit should not be wasted, and he sought to harness that talent. He told him, "If you want to make money, be a pitcher."[23]

Initially, Walters wasn't convinced. He wanted to play every day. But Wilson was persistent and, being the man in charge, put the reluctant future hurler in his first pro game during the last week of the 1934 season as an experiment for the playing-out-the-string Phillies. Walters pitched in two games that year, starting one of them. Though he didn't record a decision, he pitched a total of seven innings, posting a 1.29 ERA.[24]

It was hardly a body of work on which to base a pitching career. In fact, one writer's review of Walters's initial effort indicated that there most likely would be no pitching career at all. Wilson's use of Walters on the hill was a "lark," he said and wouldn't have been attempted except that

Wilson couldn't decide which of his three potential third basemen (Johnny Vergez, Mickey Haslin, and Walters) he wanted to play every day the following season.

> Wilson gave Walters a fling on the mound the other day with the hope of relieving the third base congestion, but Bucky did nothing more than to prove he wasn't a pitcher — not yet at least. This does not mean that Walters has been counted out of the running for the three quarters station duties. There are some observers who believe he will gain the job, because at times he flashes such class and batting form that he can hardly be passed up.[25]

Walters didn't get the starting job at third the following year. Instead, Wilson tapped Johnny Vergez,[26] whom the Phillies acquired from the Giants, to be their everyday third baseman. Walters, despite his reticence, was shifted permanently to the mound.

At the outset, the move was half-successful. In 1935, Walters went 9–9, but the following year, he joined Derringer, his future teammate, as a 20-game loser. He endured an 11–21 record for a Phillies team that finished last and lost 100 games.[27]

At that point, things hardly looked more promising for Bucky Walters the pitcher than they had for Bucky Walters the infielder. But Jimmie Wilson knew what he saw, and he consoled Walters. "Don't feel bad because if you weren't a pretty good pitcher you wouldn't have gotten the chance to lose that many."[28]

But losing wasn't what Walters was about. His competitiveness made him study the art of pitching and put into practice the things he learned.[29] In 1937, his third full year as a pitcher, Bucky was still hurling for his hometown Phillies, and though he hated the losing, it had become a way of life. The Phillies finished seventh and dropped over 90 games that year, and Bucky Walters was still an under .500 pitcher, going 14–15.[30] Slowly though, he started to turn things around on the mound. The converted third baseman even represented Philadelphia (as a pitcher) in the 1937 All-Star Game, holding the American League stars, eventual 8–3 victors, scoreless in his one inning of work.[31]

A Historic Day

The next spring, the 1938 campaign looked like it would be another lost cause as Walters started with a less-than-inspiring 3–8 mark for the financially struggling, nearly bankrupt Phils. To help ease the financial crunch, the Phillies began trading off their developing players soon into the season, and Walters was one of those sent packing, traded to the Cincinnati Reds on June 11.[32] It was one of the most storied days in the history of the Reds franchise.

Initially, at least, the significance of the day had nothing to do with Walters. June 11 was the day that Johnny Vander Meer threw the first of his back-to-back no-hit gems against Boston, a feat he matched four days later in Brooklyn.

The city of Cincinnati went wild for the remarkable accomplishments of Vander Meer, a double no-hit southpaw with matinee idol good looks. In the joy that enveloped the Queen City for Vandy's first no-hitter, the acquisition of a bow-legged, former-third-baseman-turned-pitcher with a losing record from Philadelphia hardly attracted notice. But that was about to change.

For the remainder of the 1938 season, Walters went 11–6, pushing his total for the year to 15–14, the first winning season in his pitching career. It was further indication that he was improving as a hurler, but it didn't hint at the greatness yet to come.

The two-headed monster. Bucky Walters and Paul Derringer, the Reds' dynamic duo, led the team to pennants in 1939 and 1940. They are pictured here in spring training in Tampa, Florida.

The following season, a pennant-winning year for the Reds, Walters emerged from almost out of nowhere to become the game's most dominant pitcher. The Reds called it "Baseball's number one believe-it-or-not success story,"[33] and they severely understated the case.

Walters, who had struggled for victories his entire career (and had only one winning record in his years as a pitcher) made his first full-season in a Reds uniform one to remember. The Walters way of pitching, "which ran along orthodox lines, featuring control rather than speed," soon became the talk of the town. His specialty was an inside fastball at the knees mixed with an occasional sinker, and it fooled hitters so frequently in 1939, that he jumped from being a serviceable, workman-like pitcher to the best in league, going 27–11.[34] With his co-ace and fellow 20-game winner Paul Derringer, he led the Reds feared armed forces to the pennant, a turnabout steeped in irony, as both men had previously lost more than 20 games in a season.

Adding to that irony was the fact that although the acquisition of Walters garnered little attention from Reds fans at the time, as historic and incredible as Vander Meer's no-hit performance had been for the Reds, the pitching news on June 11 that provided the greatest impact on the field wound up being the acquisition of Walters. For it was he, not Vander Meer, who was the one to lead the Reds to two pennants and a world championship.

Most Valuable

Casey Stengel called Walters and Derringer "the Number one and two hurlers in our circuit"[35] as the 1939 season was winding down. He was merely stating the obvious.

The Old Professor, who wasn't so old in 1939, wisely didn't say who he thought was number one and who was number two on the Reds staff, and both men posted such stellar seasons that it was hard to select one over the other. The Reds, for their part, called them co-aces. The MVP voters were far more decisive at the end of the season.

So dominant was his year in 1939 that Bucky Walters was named Most Valuable Player of the league, earning 303 of a possible 336 points.[36] The 27-win total topped both leagues, and he led the league in innings pitched (319), complete games (31), and strikeouts (137). It was a special year. Not even Derringer, whose winning percentage was higher (he went 25–7, and finished third in that year's MVP tally) could compare.

Walters was unquestionably the best of the best in 1939. Modest to a

In 1940, Derringer and Walters righted the wrongs of the previous year and won two games each to give the Reds a 4–3 World Series championship over the Detroit Tigers.

fault, he gave much of the credit for his pitching success away — pointing to his former manager and now coach on McKechnie's staff with the Reds, Jimmie Wilson, as the reason for his new-found pitching prowess. His pitching style, a mix of sidearm and overhand deliveries was supplemented by a wicked sinker, the hardest pitch for opposing hitters to hit. He said it was a pitch he discovered when he used to warm up prior to games with Wilson.[37]

So staggering was the improbability of Walters's rise from nearly being tossed on the Major League scrap heap to becoming the most valuable player in the league that the story couldn't be told in the numbers alone.

> Winning the selection as the MVP in the National League for 1939, Bucky Walters steps into a select class, made even more exclusive because only five other pitchers ever won the distinction in all of the polls conducted since they were inaugurated by the leagues themselves in 1922. The others were Dazzy Vance, named by the league

in 1924; Carl Hubbell, picked for the *Sporting News* in 1933 and 1936 and Dizzy Dean, the *Sporting News* Choice in 1934, and two in the American League — Walter Johnson in 1924 ... and Bob Grove, selected by the Baseball Writers' Association in a separate poll in 1931.[38]

Despite his new-found success on the mound, Walters pined to be an everyday player, telling a writer at the 1939 All-Star game, "If I could do what I'd really like to do, I'd be a shortstop."[39] His days as an infielder were gone for good, but his skills as an everyday player were still put to good use. As a Reds press release confirmed during the 1939 campaign:

> It's Bucky's pitching PLUS that makes him stand out with un-par-alleled grandeur in the Red picture. His PLUS is that batting touch which first landed him in the big leagues six years ago. Typical was his 25th victory, September 16, in which he allowed the Giants five hits and socked a double and two singles himself and stole a base.... In his 23rd triumph he came to bat in the 8th with the score tie [*sic*] in Pittsburgh and won his own game with a home run.... Three days before the score was tie [*sic*] in the 10th in St. Louis when Bucky busted a single to center to knock home the winning run.[40]

His ability to hit was an additional bonus, but Walters would have gladly traded his successes at the plate for two more victories in 1939. For though he pitched well in both his outings, Walters lost two games to the Yankees in the World Series that year. It was a disappointing finish, but even the losses on the game's biggest stage couldn't tarnish his outstanding year.

His MVP season was an unqualified success. It also enabled him to earn the most money he ever made as a ballplayer — $22,000.[41] Though the next year didn't see him win as many games, Bucky was a workhorse once again. He won 22, lost 10, and again led the senior circuit in victories, innings pitched (305), and complete games (29). He also came through this time with victories in his two biggest starts, Games 2 and 6 of the 1940 series.

Years later in 1948, when Walters had compiled over 3,140 innings pitched, smacked 23 home runs, and won 198 games, he was signed to manage the Reds. He remained on the active roster because, he said at the time, "I want to make that 200 before I quit as a pitcher." He never got there. But in 1976, a philosophical and retired Walters told Jack Murray, "I won two World Series games. That makes 200."[42]

The Man Who Would Be King

He was born in Prospect Park, New Jersey. And he flashed his brilliance like Halley's Comet. Only his brilliance wasn't separated by 100 years. It was four days. He showed it once in Cincinnati and once in Brooklyn. The fact that he threw back-to-back no-hitters in only the second year of his big league career may have been why Johnny Vander Meer was able to hang around so long. He spent 12 of his 13 years with the Reds—who kept waiting for him to assume his rightful place as the king of the Crosley Field hill. They waited his entire career. When he was through, after 13 years, Johnny Vander Meer wound up finishing with a losing record. The reason the Reds were so patient was because up until 1938 no one in baseball history had ever done what Vander Meer had done. And no one has done it since.

Vander Meer showed the Reds a world of promise and seemed to be preparing for his coronation as the future king of the hill when Cincinnati mayor Russell Wilson presented the Reds rookie hurler with a *Sporting News* award as the minor league's number one player for his accomplishments in 1936. To earn that recognition, Vander Meer struck out 295 batters in 214 innings of work, going 19–6 for the Reds Durham affiliate in the Piedmont League.[43] "He won first five, then 10, then 15 in a row. His stuff was overpowering. In one game, he struck out 20 opponents, and 16- or 17-strikeout games weren't rare.... These kinds of numbers will get you noticed."[44]

He was a wild southpaw, at times unhittable, whose talent the Reds hoped would be harnessed and eventually flourish under McKechnie, who could refine raw pitching talent better than anyone.

There were signs that Vander Meer had the right stuff well before McKechnie's arrival, and he almost cracked the Reds staff even before the Deacon had a chance to work with him. In 1937, Charlie Dressen's final season as manager of the Reds, Vander Meer seemed ready for the big leagues, but his wildness slowed his ascent from minor league standout to Major League ace.[45] He started several games for Dressen but was constantly being lifted from those games due to control problems. In all, he started nine games that season, relieved in others, and finished 3–5, with a 3.84 ERA.[46]

He was returned to the minors, to Syracuse of the International League, where the thinking was that he would be able to start more frequently without the glare of the big league spotlight. At Syracuse, the 23-year-old won 5 and lost 11. He was still as wild as an untamed colt, but the Reds brass was not the least bit discouraged. They saw only a future racehorse.

Johnny Vander Meer marked his place in baseball history with back-to-back no-hitters but was frequently wild and inconsistent in his career with the Reds. A favorite of Warren Giles, he saw limited action in the 1940 season but pitched the pennant-clinching game, earning the ire of some of his teammates.

McKechnie's first spring in Tampa with the Reds was his first time working with the Dutch Master, and he lost little time in going to work on Vander Meer's mechanics. McKechnie and coach Hank Gowdy began observing Vander Meer and made slight adjustments to his delivery.

"What Gowdy and I have tried to do in our long association is to determine the best natural qualifications of any player, particularly pitchers, then show them ways to improve on those qualifications."[47] In the case of Vander Meer, McKechnie noticed the big southpaw was not following through, and so he helped him institute a sort of rocking motion that although it looked awkward, improved Vander Meer's follow-through.[48]

The awkward feel to the motion that McKechnie had instituted wasn't a cure-all. It posed its own set of problems. Gowdy decided to bring in former Red Sox great Lefty Grove, who himself had bouts of wildness until he changed his follow-through, to work with the talented but unpredictable lefty. Under Grove's instruction and McKechnie's watchful eye, the follow-through improved with both the rocking motion and a longer stride. Soon, Vander Meer was hurling darts from the Crosley Field mound.

It was an adventure to be sure. Eddie Joost recalled how the often surprising Vander Meer impacted his friend and team catcher Ernie Lombardi. "I remember Lom sometimes would catch both ends of a doubleheader," Joost said. "If a guy like Vander Meer, who was known for throwing all over the place, was tossing the second game, Lom would be exhausted and couldn't move enough to get his glove to get the ball. He would stick out that big paw of his and catch bare-handed, spit out a wad of tobacco and throw the ball back to Vander Meer."[49]

On April 22, 1938, McKechnie gave Vander Meer a start in Pittsburgh. The Dutch Master was okay, pitching effective ball into the third inning, leading the game 2–1, but then he became unnerved. He walked the first two batters and then retired the next two. He appeared to be out of the inning, but then Gus Suhr singled home the tying run and Vander Meer became unglued. The next batter, Al Todd, tapped the ball back to the mound, and though he had plenty of time, Vander Meer bobbled it. He lost Todd at first but compounded his mistake by throwing the ball wide of the bag, allowing a run to score. The floodgates opened, with the Pirates scoring four runs in the frame. McKechnie, knowing nervousness had got the best of his young leftie, pulled him from the game.[50]

To help quell some of his anxiety, McKechnie used Vander Meer out of the pen in his next two appearances, and Johnny pitched effectively and in control. Everything seemed to have righted itself in terms of his mechanics, and McKechnie was ready to give Vander Meer another start. The Pirates were again the opponent, this time in Cincinnati. The young leftie pitched into the ninth with an 8–2 lead. Those three final outs were the toughest to get, and Vander Meer became anxious when the first hitter in the Pirates ninth reached on an error.

Working hard to maintain his control and not walk anyone, Vander

Meer threw fast and straight. His control was perfect, and the Pirate bats began hitting him as if it were batting practice. After three straight hits, McKechnie pulled him and inserted reliever Joe Beggs to finish what Johnny couldn't. Beggs shut down the Bucs and secured Vander Meer's first victory on the season.[51]

Subsequent starts revealed the schizophrenic nature that marked Vander Meer's entire pitching career. He tangled with future teammate Bucky Walters, still pitching for the Phillies in May 1938, and lost two to nothing. But progress was being made. Vander Meer was able to work through the rough spots and finally finished what he started. His next game against St. Louis was a frustrating affair, as he blew a five-to-one lead in the ninth, due again to his anxiety. He earned a no-decision in what appeared a certain victory.[52]

He showed better form in the Polo Grounds during his next start. Even though he was rocky out of the gate and issued back-to-back walks in the first with one out, Vander Meer settled down, worked his way out of the jam and went on to pitch a five-hit shutout. *The Sporting News* proclaimed that he "had arrived," but they spoke too soon. Vandy was removed from his next start against the Bees due to self-induced anxiety control problems that caused him, in this instance, to again avoid walks at all costs and throw easily hittable pitches across the heart of the plate. After four hits and four runs, Vander Meer was yanked by McKechnie once more.[53]

In his next three starts, things began to turn around. The Dutch Master won all three of those starts and gave up only a single run in each contest. He was setting the stage for baseball history, but not even the most optimistic member of the Reds brass was prepared for what was to come next.

The "Vander Meeracle"

With his record at 5–2, Johnny was off to more than a respectable start in his first season in the big leagues. Then he took the hill against the Bees on June 11 at Crosley Field and shut down Boston without a hit. He walked three but wasn't wild and didn't issue a free pass in any of the last three innings. His next start was on June 15, the first night game at Ebbets Field. His wildness returned, but the Dodgers couldn't hit the Cincinnati southpaw. He walked eight men in that game and put all three men on base via free passes in the ninth, but he was able to hold on for his second consecutive no-hitter, piling one great story on top of another, converting a notable occasion (the first night game in Brooklyn) into "one of the greatest of all sports stories—a 'Vander Meeracle,'" as Colorado Bill Corun called it.[54]

For the last three innings of that contest, the Brooklyn faithful stepped out of character, rooting hard for the Dutch Master to no-hit the hometown Dodgers. As Brooklyn scribe Tommy Holmes wrote, "The applause at the finish couldn't have been excelled had [Vander Meer] been a Dodger pitcher hurling his team to victory in the seventh and deciding game of a World Series—a vague dream all but forgotten in Flatbush."[55]

Holmes went further, stating that from a business standpoint it was lucky for current Brooklyn executive vice president Larry MacPhail, who had inaugurated night ball when he was general manager of the Reds back in 1935, that Vander Meer had pitched a no-hitter four days prior to his equally impressive feat against the Dodgers. As Holmes wrote:

> Everybody could follow the ball. That is, everybody except the Dodgers, but that was entirely due to young Mr. Vander Meer and not any fault of the lighting.... And in one sense L.S. MacPhail ... received a break that few promoters could hope for. The Brooklyn players undoubtedly would have blamed their futility on the lights. They were completely restrained from that alibi by the fact that Vander Meer had proved his ability to pitch no-hitters in the afternoon, only four days before.[56]

The second largest crowd — 38,748 — in the history of the Brooklyn Dodgers sat underneath the lights for the first time on that night in June to see history in the making. Over 1 million watts of electrical lighting units flooded Ebbets Field "to make it the best lighted baseball park in the world."[57] But it took the often wild left arm of Johnny Vander Meer to enable those fans to see the more impressive feat of lightning striking twice.[58]

After Greatness

With his record on the season now at 7–2, Vander Meer's string of scoreless no-hit ball continued for another three and two-thirds innings of his next start, when he finally allowed a hit,[59] bringing his remarkable no-hit streak to a close at 21⅔ innings. With the glare of the spotlight shining ever brighter, offers poured in from advertisers, radio, and others, all of whom wanted a piece of the Dutch Master's greatness.[60] Reds general manager Warren Giles stepped in to act as his pitcher's personal business manager, much to Vander Meer's delight, volunteering his services and promising to separate legitimate offers from the fakes and return to Vander Meer "100 cents of every dollar received" for the young lefty's public appearance and endorsement deals. The agreement was so binding that Vander Meer could talk for publication only with Giles's approval.[61] "Such interviews, of course," Swope quipped, "are given free of charge."[62]

The special arrangement with Giles did not sit well with many of his teammates down the road, and though Vander Meer was likable and a "good friend" to many, there was resentment that Johnny's star may have shined too brightly, too soon.[63] It dimmed for the rest of the 1938 campaign however, as Vander Meer returned to mediocrity for the rest of the season, going 8–8 and finishing the year at 15–10.

Still, it was an extremely promising beginning to a Major League career. It began just as the Reds as a team were beginning their ascent in the senior circuit. They showed more than just a little promise as they contended late into the 1938 season, and many of the prognosticators claimed that a healthy Vander Meer might have pushed the Reds to the top in their run at the NL flag in 1939.

That's because much was made of the fact that an ear infection in July had caused Vandy to be a subpar pitcher after the dual no-hitters and his streak of nine successive victories. The fact that he was "injured" then and was healthy the following year was cause for much optimism. But Vander Meer never regained his pre–ear infection form. He went 5–9 in the Reds pennant-clinching year, hardly what the Reds had hoped; midway through the 1940 season, it was speculated that Vander Meer was the victim of a no-hit jinx, because after the dual no-hitters he quit winning.[64] To his credit, Vander Meer dismissed such talk.

"There's no such thing as a no-hit jinx," he told a reporter. "My no-hit games were good luck. I think that I'll be wining games from now on."[65] He ascribed his recent string of poor pitching performances to a nerve near his spinal column. "I twisted something back there while pitching a year ago," he said. "I'm all right now. For a while, I could throw a fastball but when I went to throw a curve I'd almost faint."[66]

Vander Meer was wrong about how well he would be able to pitch, and Cincinnati sent him to Indianapolis to regain his form. He didn't play with the Reds much in 1940, seeing action in only 10 games. He was recalled late in the year as the Reds were heading for the post-season, which led to an incident that caused tremendous unrest among the team.

As Eddie Joost recalled, "Johnny Vander Meer was brought back at the end of the season after being sent down to Indianapolis and I believe he was ineligible to pitch in the series.[67] A full series share was $5,200,[68] and we voted against Vander Meer receiving a share because he wasn't with the club long enough. But then the commissioner [Judge Kennesaw Landis] came to us and said, 'now, you can't do that. This guy threw back-to-back no-hitters.' So, in the end, we voted him a share and we voted Hershie's [Willard Hershberger's] mother a share as well, which was the right thing to do."[69]

Pitcher Gene "Junior" Thompson remembered that the team didn't vote Vander Meer a share because he didn't figure in the pennant winners all that much in either 1939 or 1940. But he also recalled how Vander Meer was selected to pitch the pennant-clinching game in Philadelphia on Wednesday, September 18, and how unpopular that decision was among the team.

> Well, I think Giles was like an overseer or an agent for Vander Meer. He's the one he wanted to start the game where we were going to clinch the pennant ... a game against the Phillies. Well both Bucky [Walters] and Derringer were okay to pitch that day and they wanted to pitch the clincher. But Giles insisted it be Vander Meer, which we as a team didn't think was fair. I remember McKechnie getting us all around and telling us it wasn't his idea for Vander Meer to pitch what could have been and wound up being the clincher. That was McKechnie's style though, he never made a move that he didn't get us all together to talk about it. Anyway that's why Johnny wasn't voted a share. He wasn't with the club much that year anyway but then the commissioner got involved and Van Der Meer got a full share. Anyway Johnny started the game against the Phils but I don't think he got the win, I think it was Beggs or someone else who came in, in relief.[70]

Beggs did come in to relieve Vander Meer in the 13th inning, but Johnny earned his stripes that day, pitching 12 innings, striking out 10, and earning the pennant-clinching victory for the Reds.

Junior

Gene "Junior" Thompson and Jim "Milkman" Turner rounded out McKechnie's starting rotation in 1940, providing depth beyond the one-two punch of Derringer and Walters and the on-again, off-again reliability of Vander Meer. But Thompson and Turner were more than just a couple of extra arms to throw at the competition in the National League. Gene Thompson was in his sophomore campaign, after going 13–5 in his rookie year, and Turner was in his fourth big league season, his first with the Reds, after having pitched with the NL's Boston Bees for three years.

Pitching on a staff with Walters and Derringer was "quite a thrill," said Thompson, who won 16 games in 1940.

Turner's best season was his 20-win freshman year, which he unceremoniously followed with two losing seasons of 14–18 and 4–11.[71]

For Thompson, who was still a green-eyed Major Leaguer, pitching alongside Walters and Derringer when both were at the apex of their careers, was not only a thrill, but working and living alongside them also had the effect of "rubbing off" as they pushed each other and other members of the staff toward greater levels of achievement.

> It was a blessing to work alongside those guys. They were both outstanding, tough competitors. The four of us who were the bulk of that staff, Bucky, Derringer, Jim Turner and myself had eighty-three complete games that year ... I remember Bucky being outstanding to me when I was a rookie. It was like those two guys had been there forever and they couldn't have been nicer. We really had outstanding camaraderie. You know as teammates in those days, we'd live together and were together on the trains and at the park. We were really together all the time.[72]

Thompson joined the Reds in 1938 making the jump from Class B ball to the majors at the age of 21.[73] It was quite an achievement for a young man who became a pitcher only because as a youngster he had played catcher for church teams in and around his home town of Decatur, Illinois, and was constantly being bloodied as a backstop.

The teams he played on couldn't afford a catcher's mask or chest protector and though Thompson was game and gave it his all behind the dish, he grew tired of all the injuries.[74] After discussing the predicament with his father (Gene Thompson Senior), who himself had played pro ball for a couple of seasons in the Mississippi Valley League; his old man told him to move in front of the plate and taught him how to throw a curve. As the story goes, "Never again did the blonde haired, blue-eyed Thompson offspring come home with a bloody nose and a black eye."[75]

At 17, Thompson attended his first tryout when he made the 178-mile journey from Decatur to Chicago on the last day of the 1934 season. Cubs coach Red Corriden liked what he saw in Thompson's tryout and told Gene to go back to Decatur and the Cubs would call him. They never did.

Instead, Charlie Dressen, who was managing the Reds and also happened to live in Decatur, arranged for Thompson to try out with his club and assigned him to the Reds Jeanette, Pennsylvania, farm team. The franchise was transferred to Monessen prior to the 1935 season, and Gene pitched there for a short time. Later, he pitched for Paducah and went 20–8.[76] At Paducah, he met former Cleveland Indian pitcher Ben Tincup, who managed that club and helped Thompson "a great deal" with his control. He helped refine Thompson's craft the following season as well when Junior followed Tincup to Peoria in the Three-I league. He was with Peoria about half the year in 1937 and then was transferred to Syracuse for the remainder of that season, going 1–2.[77]

He opened the 1938 season in the northwestern New York outpost, but didn't stay long, being shipped to Columbia in the South Atlantic

League.[78] Thompson called the demotion one of the best things that ever happened to him, though he didn't realize it at the time. "I was in the bullpen much of the time at Syracuse and didn't get much chance to pitch," he told *The Sporting News*. "When I got to Columbia ... I got plenty of work there and was soon pitching regularly. The hot weather and hard work did wonders for me," and he went 16–9.

In 1939, the 6' 2" hurler came to Tampa to participate in the Reds spring training workouts. As Thompson remembered:

> I was the most fortunate guy in the world. I went to spring training as a non-roster invitee and some of our starters had gone down with the flu or something, so I got a start against the Dodgers. I combined with another pitcher to throw a no-hitter against them. That caught their eye and earned me another start in the spring. The next game was against the Red Sox. I faced guys like Cronin, Williams and Doerr and pitched against Lefty Grove. Anyway, I won the game 1–0 and managed to stick with the club.[79]

It was clear Thompson had good stuff, especially his curve, which had tremendous movement. Although his call to the majors after one successful season in the South Atlantic League was unexpected, there was little denying that Thompson was ready for the big time, especially when McKechnie said so. As *The Sporting News* said of McKechnie's ability to spot pitchers, he "makes his share of mistakes on infielders and outfielders but when he puts his cheaters on a young pitcher and tabs him as a prospect, Bill is seldom wrong."[80] Thompson concurred. "Bill had some of the best ideas, ideas that guys like [Atlanta Braves pitching coach Leo] Mazzone implement today ... starting guys on different parts of the rubber in spring training ... stuff like that."[81]

In 1939, his rookie season, Thompson pitched on the staff with Derringer and Walters, who were in the midst of their finest seasons, winning 25 and 27 games, respectively — quite imposing for a rookie hurler. At the outset, he was used mostly in relief, getting experience under his belt. Then, in July, McKechnie surprised him by starting him against Brooklyn in a night game. Thompson went eight innings. Shortly thereafter, he pitched his first complete game in the big leagues, going the full 11 to beat the Phillies. By the end of the season, Thompson was 13–5 and had a higher winning percentage (.722) than his teammate, league MVP Bucky Walters.

He started a World Series game in his rookie year, but by his own admission, his performance was forgettable, going only four and two thirds of an inning in the first game at Crosley Field, giving up seven earned runs and four walks against the Yankees. While that Crosley Field start was one he wanted to forget, Thompson had a fondness for the old Cincinnati park. "I enjoyed playing there. All of us did," Thompson said. "We got to know everyone in the ball park and were able to keep the balls from flying out of there. I guess it was sort of a pitcher's park but we had a pretty good staff, too."[82]

His sophomore season was even brighter than his first, and it seemed like he would have joined the 20-win club on the 1940 squad, if it hadn't been for an injury he suffered in a game against the Dodgers. That injury left him on crutches for the better part of two weeks.[83]

It happened during a game in the middle of the summer at Ebbets Field. Lonnie Frey and Pete Coscarart got into a fight. Coscarart lost his temper in the heat of a crucial game and took a punch at Frey. Thompson, who was pitching, headed over to second to support his teammate. Moments later, Reds outfielder Morrie Arnovich pointed to Thompson's ankle and said, "Gene, you're hurt."

Thompson hadn't felt a thing and no one knew how the Reds hurler got spiked. The Dodgers maintained it was one of the umpires who accidentally stepped on Thompson when they ran out to second to break up the fracas. Thompson wasn't sure. He didn't think the injury was serious even after he saw the blood oozing through his sock. It was serious enough that he would be on the shelf for three weeks, and "it took him two weeks more to get his form back again."[84]

He got it back well enough, pitching to a 16–9 record for a successful sophomore year and another trip to the fall classic, though his performance in his second series was little different than the first.

"Sunny" Jim, The Milkman

Like Junior Thompson, Jim Turner also made heads turn when he came up as a rookie pitcher in 1937. But it was for a far different reason.

A career minor leaguer, who had pitched for 15 years in the bush leagues without ever being given a tryout for a Major League club,[85] Jim Turner became a veteran-rookie hurler at the ripe old age of 34. His first season in a big league uniform, as a member of the Boston Bees starting rotation, was the last year of McKechnie's tenure with Boston, and it was a remarkable one for Turner. His persistence and toil in the minors had finally paid off—and he took full advantage of the opportunity, pitching at the top of his form and causing many around the league to scratch their heads and wonder, "Where's that guy been?"

The man who never warranted a tryout in the big leagues promptly won 20 games for the light-hitting Boston franchise, finishing behind only New York Giant hurler Carl Hubbell (22), for the most victories in the National League.[86] He also led the league in complete games (24), shutouts (5) and ERA 2.38.[87]

Though many thought his success remarkable, for such a late start and at such an advanced age, Turner was seemingly unaffected by all the fuss, when he spoke about it in 1938. "Some folks say it was a stunt that I'll never be able to duplicate," he told Paul Shannon of the *Boston Post.* "Yet, I don't know. It may be that life begins at '40,' but I'm sure that a pitcher's life doesn't end at 35."[88]

A rhythmic delivery and pinpoint control helped Turner achieve his success in the minors, success that continued at least initially in his first season in the majors. He had an unworried disposition and possessed a ready

Jim Turner started his Major League career when others his age were ending theirs. He won 20 games for the Boston Bees in his "rookie year" at age 34. McKechnie imported him to round out his pitching staff. He earned the name Milkman because he drove a milk delivery truck in the off season.

grin that seemed to exude a quiet confidence in his own abilities. It's a confidence McKechnie shared, and Turner gave credit to McKechnie for that trust in him even after he had taken a pounding.[89] "McKechnie gave me my chance despite a rather dubious start and an early pounding by the St. Louis Cardinals. He seemed to have acquired a lot of confidence in me and I wanted to show my appreciation. So I bore down from the start and before I realized it myself, I was going along very nicely."

The ability to bear down was a key to his success that first year and as Turner explained, he and his teammate Lou Fette knew the Boston club needed good pitching to keep the Bees competitive. They worked hard every start to provide spot-on pitching, and it was an approach that proved to be effective as they both won 20 games that year.

Though hardly a rookie due to his years of professional experience, Turner sounded a little green when he spoke of continuing his success into the following season. Dispelling any notion that his freshman year was a flash in the pan, Turner was confident his streak would continue.

> I can't conceive of any reason why [it shouldn't continue] … just take into consideration that I had no more stuff in 1937 than I had in the previous seasons. I'll be tossing 'em up to practically the same bunch of hitters … and it goes without saying that I know a little more about those hitters than I did when I made my major-league debut. That's why I think I can at least repeat.[90]

One thing that Turner failed to consider was that the hitters would know him better as well. And it would show. He followed his rookie year with a losing 14–18 season in 1938 and an even more disappointing 4–11 campaign in 1939.

That's when McKechnie, the man for whom he had his finest season, reentered Turner's career. In December following the year they won the pennant, McKechnie and Giles sought to upgrade the Reds in the area the Deacon knew best — pitching. It was already their greatest strength, but McKechnie knew pitchers and knew he could win with pitching and defense. So they traded first baseman Lee Scarsella, who had ability but was excess baggage on a club that had Frank McCormick at first to Boston for Turner.[91]

Though Turner hadn't been much of a success for the Bees in 1939, never regaining his stride after his nose had been smashed by a line drive from Ival Goodman's bat,[92] McKechnie was confident Turner would pitch good baseball for the Reds and be valuable as both a starter and reliever in 1940.

Initially, it was a rocky start for the Milkman, who was viewed as "the biggest disappointment" of the spring. A case in point was a spring game in Tampa, where Turner was leading their eventual World Series opponent, the Detroit Tigers, 8–1, and wound up leaving the game without completing the inning, trailing 9–8. It was generally assumed that the "veteran 'milkman' would be a bigger asset to the club on June 29, than he was on March 29."[93]

McKechnie's confidence in Turner proved to be warranted. He and the other pitching acquisition of that off-season, Joe Beggs, came through with many quality appearances throughout the season to provide more than ample support for the big three of Derringer, Walters, and Thompson.[94] As the Reds pitched their way to another pennant in 1940, Jim Turner was an integral part of the team's pitching success.

Beggs

Long and lanky, the 6' 1", 180-pound Joseph Stanley Beggs,[95] was the great Yankee hurler in waiting. A sinker ball specialist, whose minor league stats were impressive and future Major League success all but assured, Beggs, when he was on his game, was dominant enough to make even the game's greatest hitters shake their heads in disbelief at his ability.

A teammate of Willard Hershberger's, his future batterymate with the Reds, on the 1937 Newark Bears, Beggs had just completed a 22-win season for Norfolk in the Piedmont League, when he became the ace of the Bears staff. In 1937, Newark's championship year, Beggs finished the season for Newark with a mark of 21–4 for the Little World Series Champions. With back-to-back 20-win seasons at the highest levels of the minor leagues in his pocket, Beggs's time to make the leap to the majors was at hand.[96]

The following season, he was invited to the Yankees spring training camp in St. Petersburg, Florida, where no less an authority than Lou Gehrig called Beggs's signature pitch, the sinker, the "iron ball." Gehrig had tried to hit the ball out of the park during batting practice, and when he was unable to do so, he said, "It feels like one of those old-time cannon balls of iron when your bat hits it." Babe Dahlgren supported Gehrig's claim, remembering his tenure with the Bears and having the same experience in batting practice. "It was hard to see and seemed to plop dead when you did get a piece of it."[97]

Beggs's trip to the big leagues with the Yanks in 1938 was an inauspicious start, however, as he went 3–2, with an unimpressive ERA of 5.40.[98] His subpar rookie performance earned him a return ticket to Newark for the 1939 season, where he didn't live up to past accomplishments, failing to duplicate his previous success for the Jersey nine, posting a 12–10 mark in 200 innings of work.[99]

Although the Yankees knew Beggs had talent, they were impatient, and the following season, he was gone. Instead of joining the Yankee staff, in January 1940 Beggs's ticket was punched for the Heartland and he moved to the Queen City, in a trade for Lee Grissom. Most thought the deal was a steal for the Yankees. As *The Sporting News* reported, "Don't be surprised if the systematic way of doing things on the Yankees ... produces a lot of red faces in the National League.... The Yankees certainly put over a sleeper. In any event, they stand to lose little. They had no intention of bringing Beggs back for another trial ... Joe is not fast enough with his limited repertoire."[100]

Some speculated that Grissom may have gone to the Yankees as partial

Fireman to the rescue: Reliever Joe Beggs came to the Reds in a trade with the Yankees following the 1939 season.

payment of the deal that had sent Joe DiMaggio's brother, Vince, from the Yankee-owned Kansas City farm team to the Reds; others believed Yankee GM Ed Barrow was impressed with Grissom's fastball during his brief World Series performance against the Bombers in October.[101]

It was a moot point. New York skipper Joe McCarthy had determined that Beggs was "unlikely to help the [New York] club," though the Yankee leadership, in its arrogance, maintained that Beggs was good enough to pitch regularly for any Major League club except the World Champs.[102] The Reds, for their part, wanted to part ways with Grissom. And so, the deal was made.

McKechnie was delighted. "I've wanted Beggs for a couple of years, since watching him pitch a couple of International League night games in Jersey," McKechnie said, shortly after the deal was consummated. He praised his sharp-breaking curve, ability to keep the ball low, and general control as to the reason Beggs was "a better prospect for the 1940 Reds than Grissom would have been."[103]

McKechnie was right. Though he used Beggs mainly as a reliever, not as a starter as he had originally envisioned,[104] Beggs not only was a better fit for the Reds in 1940 than Grissom would have been, it was also his finest Major League season.

He was the fireman on the 1940 staff and contributed 12 victories against 3 defeats, 7 saves, and a 2.00 ERA. His victory margin and save total were tops in the league for relief pitchers.[105]

The 1940 season was a pleasant reminder of how successful his Newark days had been and was proof that he could perform on the big league level.

6

◆ ◆ ◆ ◆

That Championship Season

The Cincinnati Reds bowed out in four straight games to the Yankees in the 1939 World Series, though the series had been closer than the final tally made it appear. Bill McKechnie believed that a break here or there and the Reds would have been tied with the Yankees at two games apiece and would have had better pitching to take the series. It was partisan thinking to be sure, and a theory to which even most diehard Reds fans probably would not subscribe. But McKechnie fully believed it. He had worked magic in his first two years, first by contending for the NL flag late into the 1938 season and then fulfilling the tease of that year by winning the pennant in 1939. For Reds fans, the Deacon seemed a miracle worker. Who knew? Maybe a tweak here or there would have made Cincinnati the World Champs in 1939.

One thing was certain: The Deacon had made believers of many in the Heartland. Fans had almost forgotten that prior to the Deacon's arrival, the Reds would have been happy just to finish out of the second division. But success bred the expectation for further success, and when the 1939 season ended, Reds fans wanted more than to just make it to the World Series. They believed it was only logical that the team take the next step and make it to the top rung of the ladder.

The Next Step

As early as November, the fans were clamoring for moves that would improve their team and push them over the top. But the Reds didn't make any big deals. Instead, small moves characterized the Cincinnati off-season. Many thought Ernie Lombardi might be placed on the market after his untimely snooze in the final game of the 1939 series. Others thought maybe pitcher Whitey Moore would be packing his bags or that Johnny

Vander Meer was a possibility to move on.[1] But none of those moves materialized.

Instead, smaller deals were made. At first glance the moves were unimpressive, but that didn't mean that they would turn out to be any less important. As writer Lee Allen said of Reds GM Warren Giles, he was always "adroit at making deals that appear to be unimportant but that eventually prove of unsuspected benefit." From the vantage point of the fans that's exactly what Giles appeared to be doing, following the 1939 season, "making unimportant deals."[2]

So, though it was hardly front page news when Giles traded back-up first baseman Lee Scarsella for Braves pitcher Jim Turner (who had won 20 games two years ago but hadn't done much since); the fans collectively yawned when the Reds exchanged relievers with the Yankees, sending Lee Grissom to New York for Joe Beggs; the final story had yet to be written on the field. At the outset, baseball fans in Ohio had little reason to take notice of such minor deals. But as the Reds moved further along into their championship season, the Cincinnati faithful paid closer attention to those "insignificant" preseason moves and noticed the big dividends both hurlers paid, especially in a season where the Reds would win a record-setting number of one-run games.

Despite the relative lack of star power of the Reds postseason moves and the relative ease with which the Yankees had dispatched Cincinnati in the World Series, the loyalty among Reds fans was as fervent as ever. The team sold out their season opener at Crosley Field against the Chicago Cubs by December 13, slightly more than four months before opening day. It was the first sellout for the 1940 season among all the teams in the Major Leagues. "It's not unusual for Cincinnati's club to have an early sellout of Crosley Field for opening day, but this year the sellout came earlier than usual and it also was the largest ever, because since the last opening about 3,000 seats have been added by double decking the right and left field pavilions."[3]

The Business of Baseball

The man behind the insignificant moves and the not-so-insignificant ones that put the Reds on the precipice of a World Championship was general manager Warren Giles.

In conjunction with his hand-picked manager, Bill McKechnie, Giles built (or at the very least put the finishing touches on) what his predecessor, Larry MacPhail, started, bringing pennant-winning baseball back to the Queen City.

Warren Crandall Giles was born in Tiskilwa, Illinois and raised in Moline, where his family moved when he was five years old. He went to Staunton Military Academy in Virginia and was a student for one semester at Washington and Lee University, before his money ran out. He joined the U.S. Army at the age of 21 and served as a lieutenant in the infantry during World War I.

An unlikely baseball executive, Giles had returned home from the battlefields of Europe to join his father's general contracting business. In 1919, he happened to attend a meeting of Moline's community-owned baseball team in the Three-I League and was elected to the unsalaried position of president of that club.

It was quite a career move. Over the next 50 years, Warren Giles devoted himself to a life in baseball, rising to prominence as a shrewd executive, serving as president of the National League during a time of tremendous growth and change, and ultimately earning himself a spot among the immortals of the game in the National Baseball Hall of Fame.[4]

As evidenced by his willingness to serve as general manager of the Moline club without drawing a paycheck, Giles was a man unafraid to take risks. It was a skill that served him well in the rough-and-tumble world of baseball deal-making, though he was more measured and conservative in his approach than many of his peers. His greatest skill was in making the small, subtle moves that in the final analysis became major deals because of the tremendous impact they would later have. This was the case when he was general manager of the Reds, a position he reluctantly accepted at the urging of Branch Rickey, who after Giles's stint in Moline became Giles's boss, mentor, and friend.

Moline

After getting the job at Moline, Giles who admittedly knew little to nothing about running a baseball team said the first thing he did was subscribe to "the baseball bible — *The Sporting News*" and got one of "Louis Heilbroner's Blue Books."[5] That's how he learned the ropes.

By chance, he read in *The Sporting News* that Earle Mack, son of baseball managerial legend Connie, had just been released by Martinsburg in the Blue Ridge League. So Giles arranged a meeting. After meeting with Earle, he signed him to manage his Moline club. As Giles remembered, Connie Mack sent some players his way and before he knew it, the Moline team had moved into the first division. In 1921, Earle Mack won the Three-

I pennant. His first decision had been a smart one and the Moline team's success on the field made Giles a success in the front office.

But even though Giles was carving out a niche as a baseball executive, he still wasn't making any money. His father told him it was time to make a choice to either choose the business of baseball or stick with the contracting business. Being a pragmatist, Giles was ready to give up the game and go back to the contracting business. He wrote Three I-League president Al Tearney to inform him of his decision. Tearney recognized that Giles had talent and a future in baseball and told him about George Belden, who ran a team in Minneapolis and needed help with his farm club. The two met and Belden subsequently offered Giles a *paying* job as secretary of his St. Joseph, Missouri, farm club, a position Giles happily accepted.[6]

Honesty Pays

It wasn't long before the portly, determined baseball executive bought the St. Joe's team from Minneapolis and won a pennant on his own. While at St. Joe's, Giles's baseball fortunes took another positive turn, although it had nothing to do with his winning a title. Instead, it was a player transaction and Giles's honesty in dealing with that situation that cemented his reputation as a good baseball man — at least in the mind of one very influential member of the Major League's GM fraternity, then-Cardinals boss Branch Rickey.

In 1923, St. Louis had a working agreement with the Giles-led St. Joseph's club, and Rickey had optioned an outfielder named Taylor Douthit to St. Joseph's. Douthit was supposed to be recalled by a certain date, and if he wasn't, ownership would revert to St. Joseph's.[7] As it played out, due to an oversight by Rickey, Douthit wasn't recalled by the agreed-on date and he became the property of Giles's club.

Many of the teams in the big leagues, realizing Douthit was a prime prospect, took notice that the outfielder had become the property of St. Joseph's and immediately contacted Giles to try and land the young player's services. Giles was in an enviable position and received several substantial offers for Douthit, including $35,000 from the Pirates.[8] A red-faced Rickey, embarrassed at losing the promising player, yelled and screamed that it was a clerical oversight and said St. Louis still wanted the young outfielder.

With the money dangling in front of him, Giles resisted all overtures for Douthit. He said he couldn't take ownership or the substantial offers on the young outfielder due to what was "a technical oversight."[9]

The Redbirds got to keep Douthit, and he became a star center fielder on their pennant winning teams of 1926–28–30. Rickey was saved from further embarrassment, and though St. Joe's didn't profit from the deal, Rickey and Cards owner Sam Breadon never forgot Giles's integrity in handling the situation. Whether it was simply a shining example of business ethics or a shrewd Machiavellian move designed to make allies of influential Major League executives, there was little doubt that returning Douthit to St. Louis was a smart move by Giles in terms of his future career. As it played out, a few years later, Rickey hired Giles to run the Cards' top farm team in Syracuse.[10]

Fortune smiled on Giles again in Syracuse. And it was there that the future Cincinnati GM believed he really began his start in baseball. "I began to think in bigger terms and tackle near-major problems," he said of his appointment to the western New York city. In short, he started to think like a businessman whose business was baseball. The Syracuse club finished last in Giles's first year, but success was just around the corner. In 1927, Syracuse moved into the first division, finishing second and then, after a franchise shift to Rochester, Giles's team won four pennants in a row and the Junior World Series in 1930 and 1931.[11]

Naturally, the Rochester franchise wanted to ink Giles to a long-term deal after his string of successful seasons, and Giles seemed more than happy to oblige, signing on in 1936 for five more years. After he had signed the deal to remain down on the farm, however, the big leagues came calling.

Larry MacPhail had been ousted as general manager of the Reds and Powel Crosley Jr., needing to fill the void left by MacPhail's departure, came knocking on Giles's door to see if there was any interest for a successful minor league GM to try his hand on the big stage.

The dry-witted and sometimes caustic GM was not quick to jump at the Reds job. Though Rickey had always told Giles he would never stand in his way if he had the chance to better himself,[12] Giles wasn't convinced that taking the job in Cincinnati *was* bettering himself. Though it was a jump to the Major Leagues, Giles knew there were problems in the Queen City. For one thing, the offer was coming from a team that perennially finished in the second division. For another, the Reds were rumored to be about $700,000 in the *red,* which was a substantial figure in 1936. Finally, Giles was a pretty happy man in Rochester. He even joked with Crosley on receiving the offer. "Why, we draw more people in Rochester (350,000) than you do and have more fun by winning," an ever-confident Giles told the Reds president. But despite Giles's protests and doubts, Rickey encouraged him to take the next step and make the move to the big leagues. It would double his $12,500 salary at Rochester and Rickey assured Giles he could have his Rochester job back if he found out that he didn't like Cincinnati.[13]

Farming Success in the Queen City

Once he was in Cincinnati, Giles didn't waver. He knew from the moment he arrived what he wanted to do with the ball club. "When I took over in Cincinnati, I found Chuck Dressen managing the club," Giles said. "Dressen is a fine leader and a fine man. But I felt the situation needed someone with wider experience in handling tough problems."

Giles told Crosley that the man he wanted to manage the Reds was his manager from his Rochester days, Bill McKechnie. McKechnie had done nothing but win in Rochester, and when the Deacon became available in 1938, Giles jumped for him. "I had Bill with me in Rochester and knew exactly what he could do, and how he worked. He was my idea of the greatest manager in baseball."[14] Giles gave all the credit for the Reds turnaround in 1938 to McKechnie, saying that when he assumed the GM reins, the club hadn't improved in his first year and he finished last. The Deacon's first year was different. "McKechnie," Giles said, "had taken that cellar-dwelling club and moved it into the first division, and for a time had some wise baseball men thinking he would win the pennant."

Giles was effusive in praise of the man he put in charge, saying in essence, McKechnie was the secret to his success. "Why there is nothing mysterious in it," Giles explained. "Just a matter of putting a first class man at the helm; keeping players who looked as if they belonged; getting rid of players who looked as if they did not belong; and getting the respect of the opposition ... a good many of the players who are winning for us were not wanted by other clubs. With us, they became set, satisfied and found themselves under competent, sympathetic leadership."[15]

Despite Giles's modesty, it was not all McKechnie's doing. After all, Giles did bring in the Deacon, and then he listened to McKechnie's assessment of his current squad and what was needed to make them better. "We don't have a bad team, Warren," McKechnie told him in his first spring with the Reds. "I think we might fool some people. That big Frank McCormick can play first base. I'm going to put him right in there. And Harry Craft will be all right in center field. I don't know about the pitching. We could use another pitcher."[16]

McKechnie was even brazen enough to predict that he could contend for the pennant with another arm. "If we get one [pitcher] we might have a chance for the pennant," McKechnie told Giles.

"Do you know where there is one?" Giles asked his newly hired skipper.

McKechnie informed him that there were two in Philadelphia that he coveted — Claude Passeau and Bucky Walters. "Of the two, I'd rather have Walters."[17]

Giles went to Crosley for his approval, and that's how the deal for the following season's MVP was made. It was also indicative of how Giles and his manager worked together.

The GM played an integral role in the team's success — even if it was merely exercising patience, showing faith in his farm system, and developing the talent he had already accumulated. As the calendar turned to January 1940, 11 of the 37 players on the big league roster were "purebreeds," having spent their entire professional careers in the Cincinnati organization; nine others had spent at least some time down on the Reds farm.

Established six years earlier in 1934, the Reds' relatively young minor league chain had been home to more than half of the players that Bill McKechnie took to the Major League wars that April.[18] Seven of those players had already drawn full World Series shares for their contributions to the 1939 pennant winner.

The Reds brass may have been confident in their homegrown talent and that they would build off their success in 1938 and 1939, but not everyone, especially outside of the Queen City, had as much faith in McKechnie's team. A 1940 preseason poll of 266 members of the Baseball Writers' Association of America saw it a bit differently, picking the Yankees to repeat in the American League and forecasting the St. Louis Cardinals as the future NL flag winners to set up a 1928 World Series rematch between New York and St. Louis.[19] Of course, players and especially the Reds decision makers paid little attention to what the prognosticators thought.

Thoughts Turn to Spring

As McKechnie's team assembled in Tampa for spring training in 1940, everything seemed to indicate that Cincinnati was improved. Though they were better on paper, that didn't necessarily portend great things on the diamond. Some even expressed more than a little concern when the Reds started sluggishly in the preseason.

The back end of the rotation, most notably newly acquired Jim

Turner, as well as Whitey Moore, Johnny Vander Meer, and Gene Thompson, were clearly in the "need more work" category as the spring season progressed. Yet McKechnie steadfastly believed in his troops and preached patience.[20] The spring schedule included a three-game stopover in Havana, Cuba, to play a group of hand-picked Cuban nationals in a series that drew 100,000 spectators near the end of March; then the Reds played final spring tune-ups back in the United States, before the opener at Crosley Field on April 16 against the Cubs.[21]

Though the infield and pitching were pretty much set in McKechnie's mind, the outfield was something of an unfinished work-in-progress. At the outset, it appeared that Harry Craft, Ival Goodman, and newcomer Mike McCormick, a center fielder who could play left when Harry Craft was in center, would be patrolling the outfield lawn.[22] They were the players who played in the bulk of the games that year, though Craft, who was a promising player and a superior glove man when he took over the center field job in 1938, began producing a series of seasons with diminishing returns. His 1940 season was unspectacular as he hit 6 homers, knocked in 48 runs and hit .244 in 115 games.[23] Goodman was also on the decline. More effective than Craft at the plate, Ival had fallen from his previous All Star status. In 1940, he played in 136 games, hit 12 homers, had 63 RBIs, and compiled a .258 average.[24]

Goodman and Craft

Ival Goodman was the quiet man on the Cincinnati ball club. Known alternately as "Ival the Terrible" and "Goodie,"[25] he wasn't much of a talker, but he did manage to make a lot of noise with his bat, especially in the 1938 season when he shattered the old Cincinnati record of 19 homers in one season by hitting 30 round-trippers, including a record 17 dingers at Crosley Field.[26] The fact that he was able to pound the ball with such ferocity in 1938 may have been part of the reason why his 1940 season was so disappointing. An All Star in 1938 and 1939, Goodman had scored 103 runs (also a Cincinnati record) and knocked in 92 during the 1938 campaign.

Like so many players who played for the Deacon, Goodman had his best years under McKechnie. Originally the property of the Cardinals, Goodman came up thorough St. Louis's minor league system and by 1933–34 was ready for the majors. Though the Cardinals brass knew he was ready for the big leagues, the Redbirds already had a glut of high quality outfielders and no place for Goodman on their squad. In fall 1934 at the minor league meetings in Louisville, the Cardinals traded Goodman (off a good season at Rochester) to the Reds for $20,000.[27]

The Reds were starting to rebuild in 1935, and Goodman saw a fair amount of time in the outfield as a rookie, hitting .269 in 592 at-bats. Jack-rabbit quick on the bases, with a strong throwing arm and good instincts in the field, Ival led the league in triples his freshman season with 18.[28]

His average improved slightly in his sophomore year, but in his third year his production numbers fell off. By 1938, McKechnie had entered the picture and with his guiding hand, Goodman experienced his finest season, helping the Reds stay in the pennant chase until late in the season.

His success wasn't only with the bat. In what many felt was the most difficult right field to play in the majors, Goodman excelled. The way Crosley was constructed, afternoon games had the hot Ohio sun piercing right into the eyes of the right fielder, really making it a "sun field." Goodman, however, was able to make the position his home:

> Goodman seldom loses track of a fly ball in the tough sun field of Cincinnati.... Some other really capable sun fielders lose at least one ball nearly every series they play in Cincinnati. Peering into that blazing sun hasn't dimmed his batting eye either as it has the eyes of some other capable hitters who have played that field. Instead, the more he plays right field, the better hitter he becomes.[29]

Goodman would have success both in the 1939 and 1940 World Series, playing in 11 games and hitting a respectable .295. His regular season production fell off substantially after 1940, and though he was a regular outfielder for the Reds through the 1942 season, he played in fewer and fewer games. After 1942, he was traded to Chicago, where he played the final 2 years of a 10-year big league career. He rebounded for the Cubs in 1943 batting .320 in 225 at-bats, but the next year he was injured late in the season after chasing a fly ball into the outfield wall in St. Louis.[30] He was subsequently released by the Cubs in what was his final Major League season.

From Football to the Majors

Goodman's partner in the Cincinnati outfield, Harry Craft, was born in Mississippi but grew up on a ranch in west Texas. For Harry, like it was for many Texas boys, the game of baseball barely existed. Texas was football country, pure and simple, and it became a young man's game of choice by default. Harry was no exception. A gifted athlete, Craft excelled with the pigskin and received an athletic scholarship in fall 1931 to Mississippi College in Clinton. At the age of 16, he won a spot on the freshman football squad. A star halfback and basketball player at Throckmorton High School, Craft was given the scholarship based primarily on his high school gridiron heroics, though the fact that he was a two-sport athlete didn't hurt. In 1931, he had yet to play a game of baseball.

Even back in the 1930s, it was highly unlikely that a boy with a pedigree like Craft's would have made his way to the Major Leagues. He was riding horses on the ranch and playing football when other boys his age were living and breathing baseball; Craft not only made it to the big leagues but also was a starter on McKechnie's two pennant-winning Cincinnati clubs.

The pride of west Texas, Harry Craft was a football player who began playing baseball in college and wound up a Major League centerfielder.

Craft was quick on the football field — and his coach at Mississippi College recommended that as a freshman, he try out for the track team to stay active in the spring. Young Harry quickly grew bored of track and field. An expert passer on the football field, he soon discovered he could "throw a baseball harder and straighter" than other members on the college squad.[31] His speed proved to be as much of an asset on the diamond as it did on the gridiron, and soon his natural instincts enabled him to adapt to baseball. He developed a batter's eye and learned to go back on a fly and field a grounder better than anyone in the school.

Soon Craft was becoming as renowned for his baseball ability as he was for his football skills, and though he was named an All-Dixie back in 1935 and was captain of the football team, it was baseball that offered him an opportunity to get pay for play.

Milton Stock, a former third baseman for the Cardinals, was scouting and managing for the Reds in the lowest rungs of the minor leagues. He saw Harry play and signed Craft to the Reds Class D affiliate, the team Stock managed in Monessen, Pennsylvania. Stock took away Craft's infielder's glove and told him to concentrate on playing the outfield. With Craft's speed, once he learned the position, Stock reasoned that he would be able to consistently track down fly balls that would elude even more experienced fielders. His instincts were right.

Craft's speed helped him in his first pro season when he hit .317 and stole 39 bases in 103 games. It was a strong enough opening that he was able to move quickly up the Reds farm ladder. In 1936, he climbed one rung to Class C, playing for El Dorado in the Cotton States League. His average fell off there, to .286, but his outfield play attracted notice, and he advanced another rung to Class A in 1937, where he moved his hitting back above the .300 mark. A subsequent promotion to AA saw him again hit over the .300 mark, and by the end of the 1937 season he had made his Major League debut in a Cincinnati Reds uniform, playing the final two weeks of the season and hitting .310.[32]

The following year, 1938, when the Reds began to make their ascent out of the second division, the former football player played every inning of every game for the Reds, who found themselves contending for a pennant. Though he hit only .270, Craft's fielding earned him a place on McKechnie's starting nine because of his excellent defensive ability. He was rumored to be traded along with Lombardi to the Giants for Gus Mancuso and two other players in the spring of 1939; luckily for the Reds, the trade never materialized.[33]

In 1939, Craft was again the starting center fielder for the Reds. It was expected that after seeing a full-season of Major League pitching, Harry would raise his average just as he had in the minors. But two severe cases of tonsillitis and a collision with Lee Gamble in August thwarted any consistency he might have hoped to establish at the plate.

"I had hit in sixteen straight games just before that collision," Craft said, "and felt I was coming along nicely. I was meeting the ball well. A player knows when he has the right feel at bat, when he is timing his swing correctly. After I was out several weeks, it was hard to get it back. My neck and shoulder remained stiff and sore.... I believe the injury prevented me from hitting as well as I did last year or a little better."[34]

He played in 139 games in 1939 due to the injuries and batted .257. Like Goodman, his average dipped again in 1940 to .244, though he was still a strong fielder. By 1942, after a six-year big league career and a world championship with the Reds, the former footballer-turned-center fielder's big league career, all of it with the Reds, was over.

Though both Goodman and Craft peaked a little too early and had their best seasons as the Reds were rising in the standings prior to 1940, they still had enough gas in the tank to provide reliable, solid defense in the Reds championship season.

As unspectacular as Goodman and Craft's statistics were in 1940, they were as much of a sure thing as McKechnie had in the outfield. In the spring of that year, left field was another matter entirely and proved to be the most difficult spot to fill. Johnny Rizzo, a former Pirate, played there briefly, until he was dealt away 31 games into the year after he got into an altercation with a fan that annoyed McKechnie. He was followed by Morris Arnovich, a former Phillie, who took over for a short time after that.[35] But rookie Mike McCormick, who impressed in the spring, wound up being slotted in the outfield more frequently to play both left and center field for the National League pennant winners. For McKechnie, the second Mr. McCormick on his team was something of a find.

Gold in the Crosley Field Lawn?

Born at Angel's Camp, California, where the discovery of gold led to the rush of 1849, Mike McCormick (no relation to first baseman Frank) joined the Reds as a rookie in the 1940 outfield. McKechnie was hoping he had found California gold, and the local scribes said McCormick looked like "pay dirt as a left fielder,"[36] after he earned the job in the spring when several members of the Reds outfielding corps suffered preseason injuries.

The original plan was for McCormick to split time in left with Vince DiMaggio, but with the various ailments afflicting the Reds outfielders, McCormick saw significant playing time in March, and he performed at such a high level that it became his job to lose. Standing an even six feet and weighing 193 pounds, the native Californian came to the Reds when they purchased his rights in a working agreement they had with Indianapolis.

McCormick had found his way to Indy after being the property of the Cleveland Indians and had somehow been playing under "a gentleman's agreement" with the Buffalo Bisons, through a bit of sleight of hand on the part of the business head of the Bisons, Leo Miller. Technically, though, he still belonged to Cleveland. At least, that's what the Indians thought.

The Indians were quite adept at using "a bit of magic" to attract prime prospects like McCormick. As the story goes, McCormick was playing high school baseball for the Stockton team, when Carl Zamloch, a former pitcher for the Chicago Cubs who was working as a scout for Cleveland, spotted him. Zamloch was a master of the sleight of hand, an actual magician who could eat glass, swallow fire, and perform a host of magic tricks. He performed these tricks to large groups of up-and-coming young players out on the West Coast, which served as an ice-breaker to a more in-depth conversation about the player's future. That is how it transpired with McCormick. In 1934, when Mike turned 17 and was playing semi-pro ball, he magically signed with Zamloch as a Cleveland optionee.

From that point, the Indians optioned McCormick, first to Monessen then to Butler in 1935 and finally to New Orleans in 1936, which used up his three option years. In 1937, he became a Buffalo Bison, under the gentleman's agreement worked out by Leo Miller. The next year, Baseball Commissioner Judge Kenesaw Landis, investigated that gentlemen's agreement deal and felt something wasn't right about it and declared Mike McCormick a free agent. As a free agent, Landis originally had a stipulation in the ruling that prevented McCormick from signing with Indianapolis. The Indians (the nickname for the Indy franchise) was one of the teams included on the list of ineligibles. They were prohibited from signing him, primarily because Miller had left Buffalo to run Indianapolis's business operations.

But Miller was persuasive in arguing that Indianapolis shouldn't be penalized for something he had done with the Bisons. Landis acquiesced, and Miller had McCormick in the fold once again, this time as an Indy outfielder.

Though he injured himself by sliding into second halfway through that first year in Indianapolis, McCormick rebounded in

A rookie on the 1940 squad, Mike McCormick saw ample playing time in the Reds outfield after his stellar play in spring training.

1939 when he hit .318 for the Hoosier City, earning himself a look from the Reds, who ultimately purchased his contract in 1940.

He impressed them enough in the early spring to earn the spot as a rookie over the veteran talent that McKechnie had assumed would land the job. After leaving Florida, the Reds tangled with the Red Sox nine times in various minor league cities as a final preseason tune-up, and McCormick further cemented his spot among the starting nine, when he hit .382 over the nine games with Boston.[37]

An outfield of McCormick, Goodman, and Craft wasn't an outfield that was going to hit a lot of homers or knock in a lot of runs, especially after Goodman's production had started to slide. But McKechnie believed in their quickness and their defensive ability. As the season wore on, defense would not be enough, and the Reds, in an effort to get more production from the outfield, made a key acquisition that proved to be integral to their run at the world championship.

Out of the Gate

Because the pitching struggled early in the spring, and the Cincinnati offense seemed to sputter in Florida rather than start, there were some who believed that the club would go the route of previous National League pennant winners and fail to repeat (or even contend).[38] The ever-patient Deacon knew that games in March and April (especially when they didn't count), were hardly the ones to get excited about, and he calmly waited for his team to gel and play the kind of ball he knew they were capable of playing.

"Teams slaughtered by the Yankees never are the same again," went the preseason naysayers. "Watch the Reds crumble."[39] But the Reds weren't about to crumble.

When they took five of eight games against the Red Sox in their final spring tune-ups, it appeared as if those who harbored any doubts about McKechnie's troops could put those worries to rest. For those who believed the spring was still the spring and wanted to wait until the regular season began before believing the Reds had dusted all the cobwebs out, the first month of the season allayed any fears they may have had regarding a pennant-inducing hangover in Cincinnati.

The Reds won the first two games of the season by one run, besting the Cubs by identical 2–1 scores, foreshadowing the nip-and-tuck style of games they would play through much of the season.[40] Although the opening day win was good news for Reds fans, it wasn't even the premiere baseball story in Ohio.

On that April 16 opening day, Ohio's Junior Circuit franchise, the Cleveland Indians, bested the White Sox at old Comiskey Park in Chicago behind the no-hit pitching of 21-year-old phenom Bob Feller. Strangely, Feller was pitching on two days' rest (having been shelled in a Saturday exhibition game in Cleveland) and recorded the only opening day no-hitter in baseball history. Even more impressive was that he performed the feat in frigid, 35-degree temperatures.[41] He went on to post a 27–11 record for the Tribe that year, and along with Bucky Walters and Paul Derringer, gave Buckeye State fans some of the highest-quality pitching in big league history.

Like Feller, the Reds were also off to a torrid start. By May 13, just about one month into the season Cincinnati had the highest winning percentage of any club in the majors,[42] having won 15 of their first 19 games.[43] As Swope wrote, "They are showing the rest of the league no mercy as they attempt to pile up such a lead for the flag that they cannot possibly lose out through a slump in the closing weeks of the campaign."[44]

As of mid–May, the Reds had won 4 in a row, 9 of their last 10, and were 5 games ahead of their pennant-winning pace from the prior year. They had just won three straight from the Cardinals, whom many predicted would overtake them for the NL crown, demolishing the Redbirds in their own park by scores of 12–5, 7–1, and 13–4.[45]

Though the Reds had shot out to an amazing start, equally impressive was the start of the Brooklyn Dodgers, who on May 13 held the second best winning percentage in all of baseball. At the close of play on that date, Brooklyn was one-half game behind the NL-leading Reds.[46]

The Reds may have been playing well, but they were hardly on Easy Street. They only had to glance over their shoulder to see that their could be no let-up in their approach. If they so much as lost a step, the Dodgers were ready and waiting to pounce and take the top spot.

In fact, the battle with Brooklyn went back and forth for much of the first half of the season. The Reds had to overtake the Bums on seven different occasions to move into the National League lead, and though Cincinnati posted winning records in each of the season's first three months, going 6–3 in April, 19–7 in May, and 16–11 in June, the Dodgers hung right in there with them.

The Reds were pacing the National League and winning at a steady clip, and by the end of June, St. Louis (despite getting the preseason nod from the experts) wasn't a threat to Cincinnati's aspirations to repeat as NL champs. The Redbirds weren't even playing .500 ball and were a full 15 games behind the Reds, barely visible in Cincinnati's rearview mirror.

The Dodgers were a different story. They just wouldn't go away, shadowing the Reds throughout the first three months of the season. They appeared to have staying power, as well, matching the Reds victory for victory. They went 9–0 in April, 12–10 in May, and 17–11 in June. But it wouldn't last. Though the Dodgers kept pace in those first three months, they couldn't keep up. Cincinnati's superior pitching and defense eventually outpaced the Bums, as Brooklyn wore down through the heat of the summer and on into September.

A Break for the All Stars

The Reds placed two fewer players on the National League's 1940 All-Star squad then they had in 1939. Only four players represented the Queen City franchise at Sportsman's Park in St. Louis for the 1940 midsummer classic. Bill McKechnie managed the NL squad, and Frank McCormick, Bucky Walters, Paul Derringer, and Ernie Lombardi joined him as representatives of the Reds. Two players who had represented Cincinnati in the previous year as All-Star starters, Ival Goodman and Lonnie Frey, were not selected.

In part, the fewer number of selections was due to the fact that the Reds as a team were far less successful from the plate than they had been in 1939. That didn't mean the 1940 Reds were inferior to the 1939 squad, just different — especially in the way they went about winning ball games. The 1940 club was stronger defensively and won through defense, pitching, and "a well-timed but light attack." After 63 games, the point where they broke for the All-Star Game, the 1940 Reds were 41–21–1 with a batting average of .261. The 1939 version had gone 40–23 and hit for a .275 average over the same number of games. Every man on the team, with the exception of Harry Craft and Eddie Joost, hit considerably higher in 1939 than they had in 1940.[47]

Fortunately for the Reds, their outstanding pitching and defense were able to compensate for a multitude of sins at the plate. While as a team they were successful at the unofficial halfway point of the season, entering the All-Star break playing .666 baseball with a half-game lead over the second-place Dodgers, there were concerns.

First baseman Frank McCormick, who had been an All Star the previous two seasons and was in the midst of an MVP campaign, was almost going to be a no-show in St. Louis due to an impacted wisdom tooth. The tooth was bothering him so much that he had played with difficulty and had been slumping. For whatever reason, the pain had subsided in the days leading up to the game, and McCormick changed his mind about using the three-day break to have the dental surgery and recover. He opted instead to have the procedure at the end of the season.[48]

McCormick's pain wasn't the only issue McKechnie and company needed to address. Bucky Walters, who had won the MVP in 1939, had started off like a house on fire in 1940, but then he got stuck on victory number 9 — going six full starts before landing victory number 10 in the first game of a June 30 twin bill killing against the Cubs.[49] Walters, who lost four of those six starts, blamed only himself but saw no reason for panic. "I'm not blaming anyone … for those losses," Walters said. "I lost them because my control and batting eye strayed. I quit helping myself with my bat and I pitched too many balls where I didn't want to pitch them and they were hit for damaging blows."[50]

In addition to righting Walters, the Reds also sought to bolster their chances of a more successful pennant push by sending Johnny Vander Meer down to Indianapolis to work on his control. Vander Meer's wildness, which had plagued him since (and in fact during the second game of) his double no-hit performance in 1938, was too much of a liability to be used frequently in such a close race for the pennant. He had been spending a lot of time on the bench and was unable to gain the pitching time he needed to regain his control.

The Reds sent him to Indianapolis a week before the All-Star Game, and the hope was that Vander Meer would find the answer to the control question and be a force for the Reds as they moved toward the NL flag in the latter part of the summer. The experiment started off well as Vander Meer fanned 10 in his first start down in Indy on the last day of June.[51]

Critical Games?

After the All-Star break, the Reds began to distance themselves from the Dodgers. Immediately following the midsummer classic, the Reds faced Brooklyn at Crosley Field and took two of three from the Bums, behind Walters and Derringer. As they prepared for a three-game series at Ebbets Field at the end of the month, the Reds held a not insignificant five-game lead over Brooklyn, having gone 6–2 since the break. Brooklyn was 6–8 during the same period, tiring after playing doubleheaders on three successive days in the middle of the month, even though they recorded a split in the six twin bills against the Reds and Pirates.[52]

With over two months left to go in the season, it was still too early to deem a series on July 23 critical, yet the Dodgers wanted to keep Cincinnati in their sights and show the Reds they would be in a dogfight 'til the

Vander Meer was sent to Indianapolis halfway through the 1940 campaign to work on his control problems so he could be a force in the push for the pennant.

end. Trailing by five games, they didn't want to lose more ground, so the Dodgers and their loyal contingent of 40,583 who packed Ebbets Field were ready to duke it out with McKechnie's boys. As it turned out, that's exactly what happened.

In the eighth inning of the first game, tempers flared when the Brooklyn fans' former punching bag, Lonnie Frey, attempted to break up a double play on a ball hit by Frank McCormick. McCormick had grounded to shortstop Pee Wee Reese, who threw the ball to Pete Coscarart, covering the bag at second. Frey came in with spikes high, in an effort to break up the double play. He cut Coscarart on the knee, and Coscarart threw weakly to first, unable to complete the double play. Coscarart began pummeling Frey for the spiking, and a riot ensued on the field.

Dan Daniel reported that the riot was a "long-delayed reaction" from a 1939 game in which Frey had injured Dodger pitcher Whit Wyatt's leg so badly that the pitcher's career had seemed over. It wasn't, because Wyatt was on the hill for the Dodgers in the very same game and in the melee he "kept walloping the prostrate Frey over the head with his glove." It was so bad that Frey's face was said to have looked like it had been "massaged by a tank."[53] Reds pitcher Junior Thompson also got hurt in the fracas when he was spiked on the ankle and wound up missing a few starts.

Though the Dodgers delivered quite a few blows in the eighth, they weren't the kind of blows that won ball games. The Reds wound up winning the first game in extra innings 4–3 and won the second game by a walloping 9–2 score. It was their 10th doubleheader victory of the season, against no losses and four splits. When the Reds completed the sweep of the series the following day, they led the Dodgers by eight games in the standings—and a series that wasn't crucial at the outset proved critical now as the Dodgers fell far behind the pace.

The Ripple Effect

Brooklyn was hardly in the business of helping a division rival, especially one whom they trailed in the standings, had developed a special kind of hatred for, and was the only team separating them from the National League pennant. But in the latter part of August 1940 that is exactly what the Dodgers did. On the morning of August 22, Brooklyn trailed the Reds by six and a half games. As Warren Giles went through his mail that day, one of the letters contained the list on whom National League teams had asked waivers. One of the names caught his eye, and he circled it and brought the list to Crosley Field to show Bill McKechnie so he could ask the Deacon what he thought.

The name he circled was that of Jimmy Ripple, a journeyman outfielder who had spent the bulk of his professional career in the International League with Montreal, though he did make his way to the majors, playing four seasons with the New York Giants.

McKechnie looked at the name and told his general manager, "Well, he's over thirty. But he's a money ballplayer. He might be just the man we need in the World Series. Yes sir, Warren, if he's in shape let's get him."[54]

McKechnie's statement later proved prophetic as the former house-painter, wallpaper hanger, and "money ball player" turned into a World Series hero for the Reds. Giles followed his hunch and plunked down $7,500 to land Ripple from Brooklyn's minor league affiliate north of the border. Though Giles was quick to react in claiming Ripple, the waiver transaction proved to be anything but smooth sailing, and it took a lucky break in the form of a decision from Commissioner Landis to ensure Ripple would be the property of the Reds.

It was not the first time Jimmy's ballplaying future would be altered by a quick turn of events. Jimmy Ripple's career was one that was filled with swift, unexpected breaks. The first break was when he decided to give professional ball a try, signing with Jeanette of the Mid-Atlantic League in 1929.[55] While there, he hit an impressive .336 and was sold to Montreal, where he again impressed, attracting the eyes of Major League scouts in 1932. The White Sox were interested and were about to acquire the outfielder when one of those quick breaks almost derailed his big league aspirations, when he broke his collarbone attempting to make a diving catch against Jersey City. After the injury, the White Sox nixed the deal, and Ripple remained trapped in the minors, playing in Montreal for three more seasons before being sold to the Giants prior to the 1936 season for the sum of $35,000.

Though Ripple didn't make an immediate impact as a rookie, once he got the chance, he played a key role on the Giants' back-to-back pennant winners.

> Ripple didn't create any excitement in the Giants ranks until well after the 1936 season opened. The club was in a slump and Bill Terry re-juggled his outfield, putting in the rookie Ripple. Immediately, the Giants started to click and went on to the pennant. Jimmy hit .305 in 96 games and then in the World Series that fall, he batted .333 against the Yankees.[56]

The following season, on August 23, the Giants were being beaten by the league-leading Cubs going into the bottom of the ninth, 7–2. The

Giants pushed two runs across and then got another two men on. With one out, Ripple came to bat and homered to tie the score, igniting the Giants' play. As it turned out, the Giants swept the doubleheader from the Cubs and went on to best Chicago for the NL pennant by three games,[57] though they fell to the Yankees in the World Series.

As successful as he had been in the Giants' pennant push, Ripple's play fell off by 1938, and his average dropped to its lowest point in his professional career, .262. Giants manager Bill Terry was ready to move him, and Ripple knew it was coming. Terry traded him to Brooklyn in a deal for veteran catcher Roy Hayworth.[58] Jimmy played with the Dodgers through the end of that season, but by spring 1940, his future in Brooklyn didn't look so bright. He was past 30 on a Dodger team with a glut of outfielders that was trying to get younger. He wasn't going to last long in Brooklyn, so Larry MacPhail gave the outfielder permission to make his own deal. He garnered only lukewarm interest, and a proposed trade the Reds made, offering Lee Gamble to the Dodgers in an exchange of outfielders, was turned down.

Dejected but not defeated, a determined Ripple returned to the minors and Montreal. He told *The Sporting News*, "I knew I was better than a lot of outfielders in the National League and I made up my mind that I'd start all over again and get back up there. I kept punching and it finally paid dividends."[59]

It paid dividends for the Reds as well, when Giles paid the $7,500 to pluck him out of Montreal. The Dodger affiliate, no doubt at the behest of the parent club, tried to prevent the deal from going through for 10 days, due to a clause they said existed in their contract with Ripple. That clause would have prevented Jimmy from joining the Reds for 10 days and by league rules would have made him ineligible for the postseason. But as it turned out, Landis ruled in favor of the Reds, and Ripple reported to Cincinnati on August 29, two days before the eligibility deadline expired.

"I found out about the Reds claiming me from Clyde Sukforth, Montreal manager, but it was a shock that I might not get to join them until it was too late for the World Series," Ripple said. "It was one of the happiest moments of my life when Commissioner Landis wired me to report to the Reds."

He provided a much-needed tonic for the club when he arrived. For prior to Ripple joining the club, a member of the Reds sent an unwelcome chill through the summer heat of that baseball season — a chill that would continue to be felt by some members of the Reds more than 60 years after it happened.

7

♦ ♦ ♦ ♦

"Hurting More Than We Knew"

As it is with every baseball August, the turning of the calendar from the last day of July to the first day of the cruelest baseball month signifies the beginning of what players and fans call the dog days. The stultifying heat of late summer weakens the strong arms of spring, causing fastballs to float slower through the strike zone and breaking balls to hang just a split second longer. The bat speed slows in the late summer, as does the step of those on the base paths and the concentration of those in the field. Pretenders are eliminated from contenders when August is done. Even for those who are going well, August is a month a player endures more than enjoys. For the Reds, August 1940 was no exception.

Dog Days

The dog days actually began a week early for Cincinnati in 1940. On the night of July 26, Ernie Lombardi twisted his ankle after stepping awkwardly on the first base bag in a game against the Dodgers in Brooklyn, a game the Reds later won. The "Big Slug" (for slugger) was diagnosed with a sprain and the "Little Slug" (as Willard Hershberger was called due to his smaller stature and role as Lombardi's understudy) was pressed into service.[1]

The Reds had distanced themselves from Brooklyn and developed what was now a commanding lead in the division, putting eight and a half games between themselves and the second-place Dodgers. But as the Reds ran into a string of extremely hot weather in the East, they began a swoon that had everything to do with the oppressive heat, their comfortable lead in the standings and the complacency that often comes from playing games from a position of power (at that point in the season, the Reds had won 7 in a row, 18 of 20 and 24 of 29).[2] The slump was bound to happen, and most agreed it had little to do with Lombardi being injured and out of the lineup.

Even the team's harshest critics, its beat writers, saw the timing of Lombardi's injury and the slumping of the team as a coincidence. The reality was that the Reds had won so often, they were due to lose a little. But the perennial backup from Lemon Cove, who was thrust into a starting role, saw things differently.

Sportswriter Thomas Swope wrote, "Hershberger had filled in for Lombardi with eminently successful results. In fact, he was hitting better than anyone on the team. This time, however, the hot weather in which the Reds played during Lombardi's absence sapped Hershberger of much of his stamina. His playing declined as did that of the Reds as a whole."[3]

Hershberger's play began slipping as soon as he assumed the bulk of the backstop duties. Earlier in the season, he had hit well and called a good game when he spelled Lombardi on the back end of doubleheaders or when the Big Slug was given the odd day off. Even during the game in which Lombardi injured his ankle, Hershberger played the understudy's role perfectly as his sole hit drove in the first two Cincinnati runs, in an eventual 9–5 victory over the Dodgers. At the time, his average was .368. The Reds were winners of seven in a row.[4] But things were about to change.

Over the course of the next eight games on that East Coast swing, Hershberger caught six of them. The Reds posted a 1–5 mark in those games, and Hershberger went hitless in all five losses.[5] His average plummeted sharply to .309, and as his performance waned, the seeds of his own destruction began to show.[6] A young man who became distant and withdrawn to his high school friends after his father's suicide, Hershberger was now brooding more openly than he had before. But those who thought the deterioration of his mental health and his poor self-worth were tied solely the team's poor performance couldn't have been more wrong.[7]

In the one game of the six that the Reds won, Hershberger went three for four, but it offered little solace to the troubled catcher. Something wasn't right. Even in victory, he blamed himself for handling the pitchers poorly and constantly referred to himself as the reason for the defeats that had cut into the Reds first-place lead.[8]

The stifling heat took a physical toll on him, causing him to lose 15 pounds and display symptoms of dehydration and exhaustion. Terrible bouts of insomnia coupled with his teammates' merciless taunting for being the team hypochondriac all began to contribute to Hershberger's downward spiral.[9] As Gene Junior Thompson recalled, "Hershie spent an inordinate amount of time with team trainer Doc Rhode, complaining

As a back-up to Lombardi, Hershberger excelled, but when he was thrust into a starting role, his play fell off, and he blamed himself for the team's losing streak.

constantly of feeling ill … asking him to check the whites of his eyes." As Hershberger would leave the trainer's quarters, Thompson remembered teammates calling out, "'You look a little peaked Hershie, are you all right?' He would get upset by it," Thompson said. "Of course, at the time, we got a big kick out of it, laughing thinking it was all funny. I remember bottles of pills would wind up in Hershie's locker, as part of the practical jokes, that kind of thing."[10]

"He was a different person, kind of a recluse," teammate Eddie Joost, remembered nearly 60 years later. "We kidded him all the time, but he was hurting more than we knew. I felt badly for many years for the way I treated him."[11]

Bottom of the Ninth

On July 31, taking on the Giants in New York's Polo Grounds, the Reds behind pitcher Bucky Walters were ahead four-to-one. With two out and the bases empty in the bottom of the ninth, the Reds had all but

marked the game down as a win. Walters was one strike away from winning the game on four different occasions. He failed on all four.

Walters was the most reliable pitcher on the Reds staff, and he was cruising along in the ninth when he ran the count to 3–2 on Bob Seeds, who eventually walked. He reached the same count on the next batter, Burgess Whitehead, before serving up a homer, just inside the right field foul pole, which cut the Cincinnati lead to 4–3. Hoping to get the victory without going to his relievers, McKechnie decided to leave Walters on the hill to face the imposing Mel Ott.[12]

Ott, the most feared hitter in the New York lineup, battled the Cincinnati ace and drew the count to 3–2. Again, Walters failed to convert, and he put Ott on with the second

More than 60 years after Hershberger's suicide, Gene Thompson still feels the effects. "Since then, I haven't made fun of anybody."

walk of the inning. With no move from the manager, Harry "the Horse" Danning, who in a 10-year career of nearly 3,000 big league at-bats hit a total of 57 homers, stepped into the batter's box. Walters got ahead in the count with two quick strikes and then inexplicably threw a ball that hung over the plate, which Danning promptly deposited into the upper left field balcony, giving the Giants a 5–4 victory. As Danning circled the bases, a disgusted Walters left the mound for the Reds clubhouse.

Hershberger was too stunned to move. He stayed behind the plate, standing in disbelief, as his teammates left the field. Hershberger had called for a fastball, trying to put the victory in the books, when he probably should have

Eddie Joost said of Hershberger, "He was hurting more than we knew. I felt badly for many years for the way I treated him."

wasted a pitch. Walters had shaken Hershberger off the first time he called for the heater, but Hershberger insisted, calling again for the hard stuff. Walters threw the pitch Hershberger called for — a pitch that didn't fool Danning and enabled the Giants to steal a victory.[13]

The box score for that game is shown[14]:

Cincinnati Reds vs. New York Giants
July 31, 1940, at Polo Grounds, NY

Cincinnati Reds — Player, Pos.	AB	R	H	RBI
Bill Werber, 3b	4	1	2	1
Mike McCormick, cf	3	0	1	0
Lonnie Frey, 26	4	1	0	0
Frank McCormick, 1b	4	2	1	2
Willard Hershberger, c	3	0	0	0
Ival Goodman, rf	3	0	1	0
Morrie Arnovich, lf	4	0	0	0
Billy Myers, ss	4	0	1	0
Bucky Walters, p	4	0	0	0
Totals	33	4	6	4

New York Giants — Player, Pos.	AB	R	H	RBI
Bob Seeds, lf	4	1	1	1
Burgess Whitehead, 2b	5	1	2	2
Mel Ott, rf	4	1	1	0
Harry Danning, c	5	1	2	2
Babe Young, 1b	2	0	1	0
Frank Demaree, cf	4	0	1	0
Tony Cuccinello, 3b	3	1	0	0
Mickey Witek, ss	4	0	1	0
Bill Lohman, p	2	0	0	0
Johnny Rucker, ph (a)	1	0	1	0
Jo-Jo Moore, ph (b)	1	0	0	0

(a) Singled for Bill Lohman in the seventh inning.
(b) Batted for Paul Dean in the ninth inning.

Cincinnati	2	0	0	0	1	1	0	0	0	4
New York	0	0	0	0	1	0	0	0	4	6

Cincinnati Reds

Pitcher	IP	H	R	ER	SO	BB
Walters (L)	8.2	10	5	5	5	5

New York Giants

Pitcher	IP	H	R	ER	SO	BB
Lohman	7.0	6	4	4	3	1
Dean (W)	2.0	0	0	0	1	0

E — Whitehead, Witek. 2B — Werber, Witek. HR — F. McCormick, Werber, Whitehead, Danning. DP — Cincinnati-1. LOB — Cincinnati-3, New York 8.

It was a devastating loss. Even from their secure position at the top of the National League standings, the Reds in the middle of a slump could not afford to give away games they should have won.

There was plenty of blame to go around for the loss: Walters, for giving up the runs, especially the 0–2 homer (Walters had two strikes on each of the four batters he faced after the first two outs in the inning), and McKechnie for going too long with an obviously fatigued pitcher. But Hershberger took the loss the hardest, blaming himself for calling the wrong pitch to Danning and for calling the wrong pitches throughout the ninth. He went beyond the Giants game, blaming himself for every one of the team's losses in Lombardi's absence, telling third baseman Billy Werber, "If Ernie had been catching, we wouldn't have lost those ball games. We'd have never lost that game tonight."[15]

Werber told his teammate that he was talking nonsense, but Hershberger was not convinced. As Werber remembered:

> The next day was an off day and I went to a movie with Hershberger. I shall never forget that picture. It was "Maryland." It was a good one, too, but Bill got up several times during the most interesting parts, to take a turn around the lobby. He was jittery, upset; kept blaming himself for the loss of that ball game the day before, which he had felt had taken money right out of the pocket of every man on that Red team. I tried to console him but he had it figured out this way ... "Bill," he said "Walters is a great pitcher he won twenty-seven games last year.... What happened yesterday couldn't have been his fault ... that sort of thing doesn't happen when Lombardi is catching...." He blamed himself for everything, always did. Carried the team on his shoulders or tried to.[16]

Following the loss to the Giants, the Reds boarded a train and traveled from New York to Boston for a series of three consecutive double-headers against Casey Stengel's hapless, last-place Boston Bees. The Bees had finished in the second division four times since 1935, finishing above .500 only once in five years, thanks in large part to the miraculous work of McKechnie (who as Boston's previous manager even won a manager of the year award for the perennially woeful Boston club). The trip to Boston was cause for optimism on a disheartened Reds team. If anything could cure a National League losing streak in 1940, a trip to Boston for a series against the Bees seemed as likely an antidote as any.

Boston

Things in Boston started off miserably for the Reds. They dropped both ends of the first twin bill, and while they were sitting atop the NL with a six-game lead, it felt anything but secure. With the double-dip loss, the team believed it had hit the low point of the season. But the worst was still to come.

In the second game of the doubleheader, a 12-inning affair, Hershberger went hitless in five trips to the plate. It marked the first time the Reds lost two games on the same day, 10–3 in the first game and 4–3 in the nightcap. Hershie, who had come up five times with men on and five times failed to deliver in the clutch, was more distraught than ever. In addition to failing at the plate, he was failing behind it as well. His play was so listless that he didn't field Max West's slow topper, forcing pitcher Whitey Moore to make a play on a ball that should have been handled by the catcher.

After the Reds set down the side, McKechnie approached Hershberger to tell him of his error. From the dugout, the manager pointed to the spot on the field, where the ball landed. "That's your play," McKechnie told a disinterested Hershberger. "Is there something wrong with you? Are you sick?"

"There's plenty wrong with me," Hershberger responded. "I'll tell you about it after the game."[17]

Hershberger's despondency became consuming. McKechnie noticed something wasn't right, and after the game the genial manager, whose reputation as a kind and compassionate man was never put to greater test, sought out his 29-year-old catcher to try and console him. He kept Hershberger behind after the other players left the stadium and sat with him in the grandstand of the Bee Hive, talking, trying to ease the mind of the troubled catcher. Knowing he would need back-up, McKechnie enlisted the help of Coach Hank Gowdy to help bring Hershberger out of his depression. They talked with him, and eventually the three men returned to the Copley Plaza Hotel. For the next several hours, McKechnie sat with his young receiver in his hotel room suite, telling him that his slump would pass, as would his troubles, and that he was confident Hershberger would begin his timely hitting once again and that the Reds would soon be back to their winning ways.[18]

During the meeting, Hershberger revealed to his manager that he had planned to kill himself. He told McKechnie he was going to do it that very day but lost his nerve. There were a number of ways to end his life, he confided in the 54-year-old skipper; swallowing iodine was first on the list, but he decided that wasn't appropriate. He also thought of using a razor, but because he strictly used electric razors and did not own a straight razor, he had given up on that method.

He cried repeatedly in front of McKechnie, both in his office following the game and on through the evening. The discussion was wide-ranging and exhausting, with Hershberger telling McKechnie during one exchange, "My father did it and I'm going to do the same." McKechnie counseled and consoled Hershberger over the course of several hours until gradually the young man's mood lifted and his despondency passed. The two men went to dinner. After finishing their meal, McKechnie, believing he had saved his player's life, went back to his room and fell asleep.[19]

After joking with his teammates in the lobby, Hershberger appeared to be in a better frame of mind. But later that night, when Hershberger's roommate, Bill Baker, returned to the room, he found his teammate sitting in the dark, smoking a cigarette, the antenna of his radio uncoiled on the floor with Hershberger staring at the wire.[20]

Hershberger told Manager McKechnie, "My father killed himself and I am going to do it too." He fulfilled that promise, slitting his throat with his roommate's safety razor.

The next morning, Hershberger told Baker he wasn't feeling well but went downstairs with the other members of the team. He had breakfast with *Cincinnati Enquirer* beat writer Lou Smith, who tried to joke with him, but Hershberger was unresponsive.[21] The Reds players milled around the Copley lobby waiting to leave for that Saturday's doubleheader against the Bees. Around noon, Hershberger was in the lobby, surrounded by his teammates. He responded to several requests from players, who encouraged him "to come along," that he would be out right away. Paul Derringer, Cincy's number two pitcher in the midst of his third consecutive 20-win season, was the last of the Reds to leave the hotel. Hershberger told him, "I'm going to come out soon, catch one game and get four for four."[22]

A Sick Man Among Us

Hershberger never left the hotel. When he did not arrive at the park by 1:10 that afternoon, road secretary Gabe Paul, at the behest of McKechnie, called Hershberger's room. The catcher promised Paul he would come right out to the game. "I'm sick and can't catch," Hershberger told Paul. "But I'll come right out and watch the games."[23] The Reds won game one, but there was no sign of Hershberger at the park. McKechnie grew worried. Between games, he asked Dan Cohen, a Cincinnati shoe store owner and friend of Hershberger's who was visiting Boston during the series, to check on the catcher. Cohen had used Hershberger as a spokesman for some of his store's advertising and had a dinner engagement scheduled with him for later that night.[24] McKechnie told Cohen, "Tell him we won the first game and that he won't even have to get into his uniform but to come right out."[25]

As Cohen left for the hotel, McKechnie addressed his players prior to the start of game two. "We have an unusually sick man among us," the manager said "who must be treated differently than we are in the habit of treating one another. We must cease playing jokes on him and above all else we must stop asking him how he feels. He is so sick mentally that we must overlook anything he does and try to raise his spirits back to normal."[26]

Cohen arrived at the hotel and went directly to Hershberger and Baker's room. He found the door locked and no answer to his repeated knocks. He searched out a maid, who unlocked the door for him. On entering, Cohen found the room still and empty. He made his way toward the bathroom and noticed towels spread neatly along the floor. As he neared the bathroom he saw his friend's lifeless body, lying slumped over the bathtub, his shirt and coat removed, his jugular vein sliced open.[27]

Hershberger had told his manager the night before that he did not own a straight razor and that was the reason he had not killed himself. His roommate did use a safety razor however, and Hershberger found it and in the same manner of his father, retired to the bathroom to violently end his life. Boston medical examiner Timothy Leary was immediately summoned to the scene. He confirmed that Hershberger had been dead an hour or so.[28]

Cohen left the hotel and returned to the stadium, where he informed McKechnie of Hershberger's suicide in the fourth inning of the second game. "When I saw Dan Cohen come running down to the bench," said back-up third baseman Lew Riggs, who shared an apartment in Cincinnati with Hershberger, "I knew something terrible had happened to Hershie."[29]

McKechnie received Cohen's news and told coach Hank Gowdy what had happened. The manager left the dugout and told Gowdy the team was in his hands. He instructed his coach not to tell the players about Hershberger until after the game was over. McKechnie left for the hotel with trainer Doc Rhode and Cohen and cried inconsolably on arriving back at the Copley. The Reds players knew something was amiss when the three men left the ball park without a word, and they turned in a listless performance, dropping the second half of the twin bill, 5–2.

At the end of the game, Coach Gowdy called the players together and asked for quiet. It was their second meeting that day about Hershberger. "I want to tell you something," the coach said quietly. "Willard Hershberger has just destroyed himself." The team, much the way they do after a

On hearing the news of Hershberger's death, McKechnie left the park in the middle of a game against Boston. After the game, Coach Hank Gowdy called for quiet in the locker room and told the team, "Willard Hershberger has just destroyed himself."

painful defeat, dressed in silence and left the stadium quickly. That night they gathered in McKechnie's hotel suite, where the manager had composed himself and told his players of the previous night's meeting with Hershberger. Hershberger left no suicide note, and many on the squad were left searching for answers. McKechnie answered what he could. He told them how Hershberger's father had killed himself and how Willard said he knew that he would do the same one day. McKechnie also said Hershberger had revealed some personal problems to him in confidence, which he would not discuss, only that it had nothing to do with anyone on the team.[30]

Since Then, I've Never Made Fun of Anybody

Eddie Joost recalled, "McKechnie never told us what any of that was about. He just said it was personal and private. It was something though

... and it's probably the wrong word but it took some kind of courage and a strange mix of desperation for a guy to slit his own throat ... we discussed it years later we'd sit down you know and wonder what the hell did he do."[31]

As to the reason Hershberger used a straight razor to end his life and not a gun, McKechnie had his own theory.

> Ever since he was a youngster Hershberger had a love for firearms. There was something about a gun which seemed to fascinate him. The beauty of design perhaps. His collection of revolvers was notable ... he knew many collectors and spent much time in their company. When his mind collapsed, why didn't he use a gun? My thought is that guns had been his hobby for so many years, that he developed such a close association with that — well to use one to end his life would be a form of desecration.[32]

Gene Thompson continued to feel the effects of Hershberger's suicide even 61 years later. "My first thought was did we have something to do with it? I've thought about it so many times. I don't think we had any idea how this was hurting that young guy. Since then, I've never made fun of anybody. That will stay with me for the rest of my life. Perhaps, it would have happened anyway, but I don't think we helped it."[33]

Riding Hershberger seemed to be on the minds of many of the players following his suicide. Undoubtedly many felt guilty or troubled by the way they treated the young catcher, wondering if a joke here or there tipped him over the edge. An article by Thomas Swope, written shortly after Hershberger's death, even referred to him as "highly good-humored and highly popular with fellow players. He could take kidding better than any of them," Swope wrote, exonerating players who were not being accused of anything. In the period of self-examination that followed the tragedy, Dan Daniel, in his column "Daniel's Dope," wrote of the relationship between writer and player:

> There are men in the major leagues who are built for the buffetings of defeat and the responsibilities of victory. But there are many others in the player ranks whom nature constructed just a little too fine. These are the brooders. They worry if they lose. They worry if they win. They keep wondering what their manager thinks of them, they read every line written about them.[34]

Then, in explaining the writer's relationship with players who are made of less than the strongest stuff, he wrote:

> The writers feel that if a man makes a profession of baseball he must expect the occasional harsh line. But the Hershbergers make the

writers stop and think—and sometimes just stop. Sometime back, Bill Terry was quoted in a magazine article as having said that baseball writers' severe criticism had driven a member of the Giants to the point of suicide. We haven't the faintest idea of who that player could have been. But we do know that as soon as the writers spot a man for a brooder they "lay off" him.[35]

McKechnie concluded the meeting with the players in his suite the night of August 3 by calling on his players to pull together: "We must now win the pennant and give Hershie's mother a full share of the World Series money and I know you fellas will win it."[36]

It took the manager over a week to recover from the suicide. "Hershberger was a moody type, a growing mental case, and how I failed to miss the symptoms, I just can't tell you," he told Joe Williams in 1940.

"I didn't recognize the condition he was in until the day he ended his life. He missed a play on the field and when I talked with him about it, there was a strange, fierce gleam in his eyes, a look I had never seen before in a normal man.... We talked for a couple of hours. If he had any real pressing troubles, I couldn't get them out of him. When he left me he seemed thoroughly composed. I was still disturbed about him, remembering that look he had in his eyes at the game, but somehow, I figured he'd snap out of it."[37]

Billy Werber remembered that Hershberger's suicide shook Bucky Walters worst of all. "We usually roomed together, Bucky and I, but on that particular trip we had been given separate rooms," Werber recalled. "He came to me and said, 'Bill you've got bunk with me tonight. I can't bear being alone after this.'"

Werber tried to tell Walters he'd be all right. He told the pitcher that he was already unpacked in his room and didn't want to switch rooms and repack. "When I came up from dinner there wasn't a thing left in my room," Werber said. "Walters had packed everything in my bags and taken them to a larger room he'd hired, and unpacked everything again. That night I saw what Walters was going through. The pressure was on all of us, heavier after that, but particularly on him."[38]

It was the end of the Hershberger episode. Thirteen years later, after the 1940 season had long passed into history, another catcher from that Reds team tried to follow in his footsteps and took a safety razor to his throat.

8

♦ ♦ ♦ ♦

The Hall of Famer

The car wheels rolled along the California road, the big man they affectionately called the Schnozz and his wife, Bernice, drove east through the beginnings of the Golden State's spring bloom. It was early April 1953, a time for another baseball season, so many of which Ernie Lombardi had spent in the California sunshine. At 45, the two-time National League batting champion was now a liquor store operator, five years removed from his final baseball season, one spent with the Sacramento Solons. The Lombardis were on their way to see relatives in San Leandro, California, but this trip was not undertaken for the purpose of visiting with Lombardi's sister and brother-in-law, Mr. and Mrs. Arthur Van Ness.

The visit with relatives was merely a quick pit stop on the way to an appointment at a sanitarium in Livermore to treat the former catcher's growing depression — a depression that had intensified in recent weeks. At some point, during the day-long visit with his sister, Ernie Lombardi complained of not feeling well and excused himself to the bedroom. When her husband didn't return after several minutes, Bernice went into the bedroom to check on him. And in circumstances eerily similar to those of his Reds understudy Willard Hershberger, some 13 years earlier, she found her husband, the solid 6' 3" foundation of a man on whom the Cincinnati pennant winners of 1939 and 1940 relied, lying on the bed with his throat slit from ear to ear, a self-inflicted wound from a safety razor the big man had found in the bathroom.[1]

Still alive, Lombardi was rushed to nearby Fairmont Hospital, strongly fighting the attempts to save him. He screamed, "Let me die!" over and over again until he was gradually brought under control by health care workers. The wound was so severe, the attending doctors decided to transfer him to Oakland and a hospital where he stood a better chance of recovery. Even there, he was given little chance for survival.[2]

But as the hours passed into days, it became apparent that Lombardi

Lombardi at bat. Pictured in profile with two of the things he was most famous for — his large nose and his mighty bat. Ernie "Schnozz" Lombardi was a two-time batting champ and National League MVP who was posthumously elected to the Hall of Fame.

was not going to die. Just as in his baseball career, Lom proved resilient and staged a comeback. Eventually he was removed from the critical list and avoided joining his fellow backstop from the 1940 World Champions as a baseball suicide.

How had the quiet, unassuming giant of a man, former Most Valuable Player and two-time batting champion, come to this? Like Hershberger before him, there was no easy answer.

Hershberger had a family legacy of suicide and suffered from a mental illness that caused him to view destroying himself as the only option. Lombardi took a longer but equally painful road; though the reasons for Lombardi's desperation were not as obvious as Hershberger's, clearly the absence of baseball at that point in his life played an integral part.

From the time he was a young boy, the only life Lombardi knew or cared about was one that had baseball at the center. It was a life that included 17 years as a Major Leaguer, the pinnacle of a lifelong love affair with the game that began even before Lombardi played semi-pro ball for Ravioli's Meat Market at the ripe old age of 12.

How passionate was he about the game? Family members often recalled the story of a preteen Lombardi leaving for a game one morning and never showing for a family wedding that night. Even as a youngster, Lombardi was most

An out-of-baseball Lombardi, in a manner similar to his back-up, Willard Hershberger, tried to commit suicide by taking a razor to his throat. He survived the suicide attempt, but his life after the game was marked by bitterness and difficult times.

comfortable on the diamond. A permanent fixture on the sandlots of Oakland, he would have been a star on any high school team, yet he did not take to traditional schooling. On finishing grammar school, his chance to letter in the sport he loved was lost when he skipped high school to work in his father's grocery store. Though he eschewed classwork, Lombardi continued his education on the diamond, playing baseball at the semi-pro level into his late teens.[3]

An Oak Grows in Brooklyn

Initially, at least, Lombardi and his shotgun arm patrolled the outfield. It was an uneasy marriage, though, as his canon of an arm was attached to a plodding body that was slow to react to balls hit to the outfield. His manager, Al Clark, took notice of the hulking teen's powerful release and soon-to-be legendary lack of speed and realized that Lombardi, an unnatural fit in the outfield, had the potential tools to become a solid backstop. From that moment on, with Clark's guiding hand, the Schnozz's rapid-fire release came from behind the plate — a manager's instinct that later helped a quality slugger earn his keep in the big leagues.

As Lombardi learned the ropes behind the plate, scouts for the Pacific Coast League scoured semi-pro games throughout the Bay Area and his play, especially his bat, began to raise eyebrows. Initially, a contract offer came from the Oakland Oaks, but Lombardi was fearful that Oakland might try to send him to a farm team away from his home for some seasoning (he was not yet a quality receiver). So he rebuffed the offer. He was young and still attached to his hometown. But after a trip his father took away from home left Ernie in charge of the family store, the teenager knew that a life running a grocery was not for him. At 19, he took matters into his own hands and placed a call to the Oaks to see if they were still interested. Fortunately, they were — and Lombardi signed his first professional contract for the remainder of the 1926 season, a deal consummated before he reached his twentieth birthday.

Lombardi's initial reticence at signing with the Oaks later proved to be more than just teenage jitters when in his second professional season the converted catcher discovered that his defense was not quite up to Pacific Coast League standards (at least as far as the Oaks decision makers were concerned). He was demoted to the Oaks farm club in Ogden, Utah, a place literally up in the hills. Ogden was a long way from California, and the man who later earned fame in part because of his famous schnozz, was in the initial stages of his career suffering because of it. As a member of the Utah nine, Lombardi experienced severe nosebleeds due to the altitude, became sick, and began to lose weight.

In spite of these hardships and what the Oaks considered questionable defensive skills, not on par with other backstops in the Coast League, there was nothing questionable about Lombardi's bat. He hit .398 over 50 games in Ogden and soon found himself and his no-longer-bloody nose back in Oakland, where for the next three seasons his lumber crackled off seasons of .377, .366, and .370.

"I don't know whether they [the Oaks] brought me back to save my life or because I was hitting so good," Lombardi said. "But I'm sure glad they did." His three successive seasons hitting above the .350 mark convinced the Major Leagues the time was right to take a chance on the big man with the big nose and in 1930, the Brooklyn Dodgers bought themselves an Oak for the sum of $50,000.[4]

Brooklyn proved to be a far from an idyllic experience. In 1931, his rookie year, Lombardi rode the bench behind veteran Al Lopez, who batted a light .260 but played in part because he was seasoned and a favorite of manager Wilbert Robinson. As an understudy to Lopez, Lombardi managed to get into 37 games for the Bums and post a healthy .297 average. His rookie year was marked by a brief flirtation with pitching (again, another baseball man trying to harness Lom's powerful arm) but never got beyond the tryout stage. His rookie year also marked the first and only time Lombardi was pinch-hit for in his entire career, when Robinson sent Ike Boone, a reserve outfielder, up to bat for the gentle giant.[5]

Although Dodger skipper Robinson toyed with the idea of putting Lombardi on the hill for the Dodgers as late as September 1931, come April of the following year, the big man had traded Dodger blue for Cincinnati red and a permanent pair of shin guards.[6]

Catching Fire in Cincinnati

The move to Cincinnati was perfect for Lombardi, and he caught on famously in the Queen City, moving immediately into a starting role. His bat sent balls bouncing off the Crosley Field wall, as he hit an impressive .303 for a woeful Reds team. His fielding also improved, and despite the insults hurled his way for being oafish and lumbering, he was agile behind the plate, covering pop fouls well and throwing out runners who dared to run against his strong arm.[7]

"My only weakness was my lack of speed," Lombardi used to say. "I couldn't move as fast as Rollie Hemsley or Mickey Cochrane."

There were plenty of stories about his slowness. One of the most often repeated tales was of the time he stole second base against the Dodgers, one of eight stolen bases in his 17-year career. After singling off Dodger hurler Kirby Higbie, Lombardi took off for second, and catcher Mickey Owen reared his arm back to throw, but neither stunned shortstop Pee Wee Reese nor disbelieving second baseman Billy Herman moved to cover the bag. "They couldn't move when I stole," Lombardi jokingly recounted. "I was just too fast for them."[8] Teammate Eddie Joost recalled that Lombardi would try to steal one base a year and was usually successful. "It was usually in September," Joost remembered. "And the other team would be so stunned, when they saw him coming they wouldn't know what to do."

A good-natured sort, Lombardi didn't appear to mind the constant needling, whether it was about his nose or his speed, even taking part in it himself. "In Cincinnati once, I hit the left field wall and they threw me out at first base," he said to a reporter, laughing about the incident.[9]

His slowness was a trait he was kidded for almost as much as his huge nose and was one that bothered him as he got on in years. Many speculated that the perception of Lombardi as a lumbering oaf (one that was reinforced and unfairly magnified by his swoon against the New York Yankees in the 1939 World Series) was part of the reason he was underrated for so many years.

In 1974, an out-of-baseball and bitter Lombardi told a reporter, "All anybody wants to remember about me was that I couldn't run. They still make jokes. Let them make jokes. I had a couple of bum years but not many and my lifetime batting average is .306."[10]

Later, the story he once laughingly told about being thrown out at first after hitting the left field wall met with a decidedly different response. "I've heard all those stories. About nine-tenths of them are trash.... They make fun of me. I went six for six one afternoon. All of them line drives off the wall. I once had four doubles off four different pitchers in four consecutive innings. Hey, I was a hitter."[11]

If Lombardi believed his hitting should do his talking, there was little denying it spoke well of him. Though he never slugged more than 20 dingers in a season and in fact reached the 20-homer mark only once, he smoked the ball when he hit it, developing a unique interlocking golf grip in the minors after a blister on his finger prevented him from holding the bat properly. The grip allowed him to hit in spite of the blister and the ensuing success he had in Oakland ensured that the grip stuck around long after the blister disappeared.[12]

The hits coming from that unique grip was one of the few things Cincinnati fans had to cheer about in the beginning of Lom's Reds career, as his personal prowess at the plate directly contrasted his team's performance. The early 1930s were lean times for Cincinnati as they occupied a permanent position in the second division. From 1932 to 1937, the Reds employed four different managers and finished last four times. In spite of the team's lackluster play, Lombardi shined — batting over .300 in each of those seasons, except for a .283 mark in 1934. In the years 1935–37, the Schnozz's bat spoke loudest as he went on a tear compiling impressive marks of .343, .333, and .334.

A Very Good Year

At the end of the 1937 season, the fortunes of the Reds and Lombardi himself were about to change, as the Charlie Dressen era ended and Bill McKechnie, winner of pennants with Pittsburgh and St. Louis, was given the reigns of the Cincinnati ball club. McKechnie overhauled the starting lineup, replacing five of the starting nine on the last-place 1937 team, and brought in Bucky Walters to shore up the Cincinnati pitching staff. The improvement in the Reds was dramatic. They moved into the first division in McKechnie's first year at the helm, finishing the season 6 games off the pace of the league-leading Chicago Cubs, a 34-game difference from the prior year. Lombardi flourished under the Deacon as well, posting a .342 mark, winning both an MVP Award and the first of two batting titles.[13]

Yet there were other reasons for Lombardi to celebrate. The 1938 season marked the only time in Major League history that a pitcher threw consecutive no-hitters and Lombardi was on the receiving end of both of Johnny Vander Meer's gems. On June 11, the often wild Vander Meer took his 5–2 mark to the hill against McKechnie's former team, the Boston Bees, who were managed by Casey Stengel. With Lombardi behind the plate, the 23-year-old southpaw pitched a gem of a game in rendering the stingless Bees hitless. Four days later, with Vander Meer's next start as the first ever night game at Brooklyn's Ebbets Field, Lombardi was again behind the plate, trying valiantly to steer the wild leftie through the Brooklyn lineup. Among the 38,000 in attendance that night, 700 were family and friends of Vander Meer's, some of whom presented him with gifts in a pregame ceremony that was also attended by Johnny's boyhood idol, Babe Ruth.

Vander Meer kept the fans and Lombardi on their toes as he continued throwing no-hit stuff throughout the night, but went to one 3–2 count after another, walking a total of eight in the game. The Reds carried a 6–0 lead into the ninth, but with one out, Vander Meer walked the bases loaded, putting his no-hitter and shutout in jeopardy. With the bases full of

Dodgers, Vander Meer induced a grounder to third from Ernie Koy, forcing pinch runner Goodwin Rosen at the plate. The only thing standing between him and baseball history was Brooklyn's next batter, player-manager Leo Durocher. As Durocher later recalled, "I hit it as hard as I could hit it. Harry Craft, their fine centerfielder caught it right off his shoe-tops."[14]

"Vandy was real hard to catch because he was so wild," Lombardi said later. "You never knew where the ball was going to end up when he was pitching. When you caught Vandy for nine innings you knew you were in a game. All you'd want to do after that was go home to bed." For his part, Lombardi maintained the secret to the second no-hitter and preserving the shutout was calling fastball after fastball. "I had more of a chance to catch the fastball than the curve … he could bounce the curve."[15]

Although 1938 was a magical one for Lombardi, winning the batting title, the MVP Award, and catching Vander Meer's consecutive no-hitters, the seeds for the end of his career with the Reds were already being sown. At the Reds' year-end banquet in 1938, Lombardi got "kind of loaded." When a radio announcer stuck a microphone in front of the big man and asked if he had anything to say, a more than half-drunk Lombardi offered a poorly timed swipe at Reds General Manager Warren Giles saying, "Giles is no good, he's an old goat."

"And then," Lombardi recounted, "I passed out." The radio interview got back to Giles and although it would have been imprudent to trade Lombardi off of an MVP year, Giles filed the remark away — making a note to get rid of him as soon as his play faltered.

Lombardi struggled with club owners to get a raise for the following year, but gradually managed to persuade the Reds to move his annual $13,000 salary in 1938 to $17,000 for the next season. That $17,000 proved to be the highest salary he earned in his big league career. Years later, he recognized the comments he made in a moment of drunken liberation hurt him with the Reds front office. "As soon as I had a bad year [.264 in 1941] I was gone." It would also hurt him later on, after his playing career ended, when Giles, a stalwart of the Hall of Fame Veterans Committee, consistently blocked Lombardi's election to Cooperstown.[16]

King Kong Keller and the Play That Won't Go Away

The season following Lom's 1938 MVP campaign, the Reds returned the pennant to Cincinnati for the first time since the tainted 1919 championship thrown by the Chicago Black Sox. Lombardi was key to the 1939 effort, and although his average dropped significantly to under .300 for the second time in his career (.287), the drop was partially offset by his career high in homers (20) and his steadying influence with the Reds quality staff. It also marked Ernie's first appearance in the World Series and, ironically, the low point of his professional career.

The collision at the plate in Game 4 against the New York Yankees, where Charlie "King Kong" Keller crashed into him as the ball arrived, that seemed to forever tarnish the glitter Lombardi earned from being MVP just one year earlier. The pundits said the "Schnozz slept," called him "Sleeping Beauty," and maintained that he allowed DiMaggio to round the bases while the ball remained only a few feet from his huge, motionless body (Lombardi was knocked woozy from the force of the collision). Even though he was injured, the run actually scored due to the failure of Reds pitcher Bucky Walters to back up the play. In the final tally, DiMaggio's run didn't impact the series or the game, but the event made Lombardi, in the words of baseball historian Bob Broeg, "look ungamely."

The fans howled as Lombardi lied prostrate on the field, but more than the physical pain from the collision, the taunting crowd wounded the proud man emotionally. To be derided for his big nose or legendary slowness may have hurt Lombardi inside, but on the outside he went along with it well enough. Lombardi was agreeable, even self-effacing about it — whether or not he truly saw the humor in it. However, making a caricature of him as if he was a cartoonish figure when he was hurt seemed to question his desire and showed a lack of respect, not only for his ability but also for his humanity. The fans jeering at him while he lied sprawled on the ground undoubtedly hurt Lombardi — but the real pain came from the way the play followed him throughout his life. That DiMaggio rounded the bases was hardly his fault. In one of the more unjust characterizations in baseball history, Lombardi was branded a goat as if he single-handedly lost the series to the Yankees.

As home plate umpire Babe Pinelli recalled, Keller unintentionally kicked the big backstop in the groin on the play. It was one of those collision plays at the plate where the runner gives it everything he's got and the catcher takes the hit. Unfortunately for the Reds, in the crash, Lombardi took the worst of it, and while Lom tried to stay on his feet, the pain to his groin was just too intense.[17]

"Blaming Lom for that mess was so unfair," Eddie Joost recalled.

> If you go back today and get a film of that play called "Lombardi's snooze," Keller slid into him and Lom was knocked out. He was unfairly criticized for years for allowing DiMaggio to round the bases and come in and score. But if you look at it from strictly a base-

ball point of view, it was Bucky's fault because he didn't back up the play. Nobody ever mentions that.[18]

Almost a year after the World Series loss to the Yankees, Manager Bill McKechnie seemed intent on setting the record straight regarding what happened to Lombardi during the Keller collision. Lombardi had remained silent about what occurred, but the play followed him everywhere. McKechnie told Joe Williams, a writer profiling the Cincinnati skipper for the *Saturday Evening Post*, "If you can work something into your piece about what [Umpire Babe] Pinelli told me (about Lombardi being kicked in the groin), I'd appreciate it. You can't imagine what a going-over Lombardi has taken and without a protest. A dead-game stand-up fellow he is."[19]

Injuries and a World Championship

In 1940, Lombardi had little opportunity to erase the final image of the 1939 season, even though he was playing for a pennant winner and eventual World Series champion. He again raised his average above the .300 mark, hitting .319 in 109 games; however, it was not his hitting but the two injuries he suffered that served as strange catalysts for the Reds championship season.

The first happened in Philadelphia on July 26, when Lom injured himself by twisting an ankle, forcing Hershberger into a regular starting role. Hershberger, who had excelled in Lombardi's shadow as a quality backup, suffered mightily as a starter, and the Reds begin losing. During the next 10 days, Hershberger's internal demons surfaced. His deterioration and eventual suicide shocked the team as they were driving toward their second consecutive pennant in early August.

In the wake of Hershberger's death, Lombardi returned to his backstop duties but suffered a second injury to the ankle in Brooklyn on September 15, virtually ending his season. He made spot appearances in the World Series that year, but the second injury, in an ironic twist, served as the impetus for another Reds catcher to shine in series play. Forty-year-old coach Jimmie Wilson came off the bench to have an excellent World Series, hit .353, and put a positive exclamation point on an 18-year Major League Career. Later, the irony of the positive impression made by a single World Series performance was not lost on Lombardi as he doggedly tried to escape the ghosts of his own World Series past.

"I did manage to make a hero of Jimmie Wilson in the '40 series, when I tripped on first base and sprained my ankle," Lombardi later said.

"Wilson was a coach and he hadn't caught in four or five years. They taped him up like a mummy and he had a great series."[20]

As writer Will Grimsley succinctly summarized the catcher's legacy both as a World Series performer and everyday player, "The shame is Lombardi is remembered more for the awkwardness of his 6' 3", 230-pound frame and that bizarre World Series incident than for his natural skills."[21]

It should have been a glorious afterglow, the year following the championship season, but the Reds did not duplicate their pennant-winning form in 1941, dropping to third with an 88–66 mark. Lombardi suffered at the plate, as well, his average dropping to .264, his lowest ever to that point. His already testy relationship with GM Warren Giles did not improve, and Lom asked to be dealt to the New York Giants but was sent instead to the lowly Boston Braves following the 1941 season. Adding insult to injury, Lombardi was forced to take a $6,000 cut in salary.[22]

As Giles and McKechnie tinkered with the lineup following the 1941 campaign, moving Lombardi proved to be an easy decision for Giles. Although it was true Lombardi was a successful and likable player, Giles sensed the time couldn't be better to move him. And he was right.

There was hardly an uproar in Cincinnati over the deal. The Reds were, after all, one year removed from a championship, and even diehard fans would spend less time focusing on baseball and the fortunes of a single player, turning their attention instead to the war their country had just entered in Europe and the Pacific.

A Second Batting Title

As the 1942 season began, many of the game's more stellar players were in a different kind of uniform, trading their baseball flannels for army fatigues; yet the games went on. President Franklin D. Roosevelt gave the green light order calling for baseball (even if the talent was watered down) to be played during wartime for the good of the nation. Lombardi, now playing in Beantown, took the chance to play ball to heart. He revived his powerful stroke, returning to his old form in hitting .330 for the Braves. He won his second batting title and earned the distinction of being the only catcher in the game to twice lead his league in hitting. Whether it was revenge at Giles, the man who traded him, or the fact that he was simply able to again find his swing and show the baseball world just what he was capable of, Lombardi relished the personal renaissance, even receiving the best possible compliment a traded player can hope for, from the man who replaced him, Cincinnati catcher Ray Lamanno.[23]

During a Reds–Braves game that year, Lamanno gave Lombardi the news every traded player longs to hear when Lom stepped to the plate. "You're driving McKechnie crazy with the way you're hitting," Lamanno told the big man. "He's pulling his hair out."

After a single year with the Braves, where he led the league in batting for the second time, Lombardi finally got that trade to the Giants. At 35, he still had the desire and the skills to make his presence felt. In four years with New York, Lombardi posted seasons of .305, .255, .307, and .290. He even managed to find himself a roommate (Giant pitcher Bill Voiselle) for the team's road trips, something that was a rarity for the big man during his years in the big leagues.

Rena Lenhardt, Lombardi's sister, explained that "when Ernie snored, it sounded like he was about to die." It was so bad that Don Brennan, Lombardi's last roommate on the Reds, told team officials he'd pay his own expense before rooming with Lombardi again. Writer Jay Mariotti retold the tale of "one roommate, Chick Hafey, who tried to slip a clothespin over Lombardi's nose but had to remove it when Lom's face started turning purple."[24]

"Nobody would ever room with me," Lombardi explained. "They said I snored too much." When asked how he managed to handle Lombardi's incessant snoring, Voiselle offered, "I've got bad ears. I can't hear him."[25]

Hard Times

After his Major League career ended with the Giants, Lombardi played in the minors for Sacramento in 1948 and then fell on hard times. For years after his playing career had ended, Lombardi hoped for a job in baseball somewhere. In 1949, an opportunity seemed to present itself when former teammate Bucky Walters wanted him on his Reds staff. "But Gabe Paul said no," Lombardi recalled. "A lot of people said no after that."

After he recovered from his suicide attempt in 1953, there were rumors that he was broke and his three sisters had to support him. He worked for a time as a steward in the press box of the San Francisco Giants until an insult from a sportswriter caused him to quit. For his part, Lombardi maintained that the press box job was just to be close to the game. Others thought it was out of necessity. He worked in an Oakland gas station for a time and also tried to land any kind of work with the Oakland A's. He was refused and at that point turned his back on baseball.

For years, he regularly participated in old timers games, but after the A's turned him down for a job and then invited him to participate in an old timers celebration honoring Casey Stengel, Lombardi "just put a check on the form that I wouldn't be there."[26]

Of all the unkind things he had to endure, perhaps the greatest insult he received was the yearly snub by the Hall of Fame. For the first 15 years of eligibility, he was ignored by the writers and then for the next 18 by the Veterans Committee. It was true that he led the National League in passed balls for 10 seasons (a reason often given for his exclusion from Cooperstown), but there was no denying his prowess at the plate in the form of two batting titles and an MVP season in 1938. Lombardi was bitter about not being elected to the Hall, so much so that toward the end of his life he told writer Wells Twombly:

> If they elected me I wouldn't show up for the ceremony. That sounds terrible. But every year I see my chances getting smaller and smaller ... who wouldn't be bitter? The great Yogi Berra was one of the great catchers of modern times. He's in the Hall and you know what his average was? It was .285 and he only played in about 300 [actually 267] more games than I did. I'm not putting him down, but he wasn't that much faster than I was.... They've waited too long and they've ignored me too long. I was the National League batting champion twice.[27]

Despite the Hall's failure to elect him, there were moments of recognition. In 1971, Lombardi was honored when a former classmate of Willard Hershberger's, then President Richard Nixon, voted him on to his all-time team in the 1925–45 category. Even that honor had its downside, when sportswriter Red Smith challenged Nixon's list saying the president took Lombardi for sentiment over a more deserving Jimmie Wilson (whom Lombardi "made a star" by being injured in the 1940 series).[28]

Recognition

Every so often, in the years preceding his death, Lombardi was the subject of a "Where Are They Now?" article with a headline invariably calling him "bitter" or a "recluse," but it was more accurate to see a man who was longing for respect from the game that since his playing days ended rejected him at every turn.[29]

Why was he kept out of the Hall when other players of lesser stature are elected? At least when the vote was in the hands of the Veterans Committee, his former general manager Warren Giles, an influential Hall of Fame member, successfully lobbied against it. There were those who pointed to the fact that he led the league in passed balls for 10 seasons or that he resembled Cyrano De Bergerac and was more often an object of satire than of greatness as reasons for his exclusion.[30]

Yet despite his detractors, Lombardi put up solid numbers. Near the end of his life, his bitterness increased each year as he once more was excluded from the Hall of Fame. One could almost hear Lombardi pleading for recognition in the interviews he gave in the years before his death. Although he said he would never appear at the Hall of Fame if elected, there was hardly anything that mattered more to him. He was a prideful man, who although good-natured about the sometimes hurtful comments directed his way, was concerned about how he was perceived both as a man and as a ballplayer. As one oft reported story went, one day after a game at Crosley Field a kid handed him a piece of paper to sign. Lombardi shook his head no, walking past the youngster. Further on up the road, there was another boy asking for an autograph. When Lombardi again refused, the first kid yelled to the second, "Don't pay any attention, he can't write." From then on, the story went, the prideful Lombardi never refused to give his signature to a fan.[31]

On September 26, 1977, Ernie Lombardi died in Santa Cruz, California. He was never given the option to turn down the Hall of Fame's induction invitation because the Veterans Committee did not elect him. Two years later, his former GM Warren Giles died. Finally, in 1986, Rena Lenhardt, the older of Lombardi's two older living sisters, got the opportunity to speak for her deceased brother at his induction ceremony in Cooperstown.

9

◆ ◆ ◆ ◆

Champions of the World

Perhaps the most encouraging sign awaiting the Reds as they entered October and their second consecutive appearance in the fall classic was not that they had put such distance between themselves and the second-place Dodgers in the wake of Hershberger's suicide (the Reds went on to win a total of 100 games and finished 12 games ahead of the second-place Bums) but that their opponent would not be the New York Yankees.

The Detroit Tigers were the 1940 American League champions, and they arrived at the fall classic after squeaking by the Cleveland Indians by a single game and besting the World Champs from New York by a mere two games to take the AL flag. With a .584 winning percentage, the Tigers were not a great team, but they sported a powerful offensive lineup led by left fielder Hank Greenberg's monster season (.341, 41 homers, 150 RBI), aging second baseman Charlie Gehringer (.313 batting average), and first baseman Rudy York (33 homers and 134 RBI). They also benefited from a career year from veteran righthander BoBo Newsom, whose 21 wins and 2.83 ERA are second only to Bob Feller (27 wins and 2.61 ERA) in the junior circuit.[1]

Was it a blessing or a curse that the Reds did not have to take on the Yankees? Most would have agreed that the Reds were better off taking the train to the Motor City than the Big Apple, primarily because the Yankees were a better all-around team than the Tigers, whose sole advantage was its heavy hitting lineup. Yet despite this general consensus, not everyone saw it as a less pressurized series for McKechnie's troops. J. Roy Stockton, a writer for the *St. Louis Post Dispatch*, took the opposite tack. He believed the Reds, by not facing the Yankees, were carrying an "unusually heavy load of responsibility" entering the 1940 series.

> The responsibility is greater this year for the Reds because they no longer will have the excuse of meeting a super team. In recent World

Series the Yankees have been overwhelming favorites ... the American League champions dominated their circuit as well as world title competition. This year it's different. The great Yankee machine cracked and sputtered down the stretch ... the Tigers are only one of five evenly matched American League teams ... [a Reds loss] would be taken as a sign of [American] league superiority. That is the extra load the Reds will carry.[2]

The first day of October, the day before the series began, newspapers from around the country focused on events in an increasingly unsettled world. Albert Einstein was sworn in as a citizen of the United States, and Adolf Hitler and Benito Mussolini scheduled to meet again at the Brenner Pass, as the Luftwaffe bombs dropped over Britain.[3] Yet in the midst of all of the global uncertainty, in Cincinnati, where games one and two were scheduled to be played, the focus of the city seemed to be solely on the world of baseball.

The big questions in the Queen City, at least for the first two weeks of October, were: Will it be Derringer or Walters in Game 1? Will injuries to Lombardi and second baseman Lonnie Frey keep them out a game or two or for the entire series?

As Cincinnatians prepared for their second World Series in as many years, the American League champion Tigers—cocky, confident, and healthy—were installed as five to six favorites.[4] Due to the uncertainty of Lombardi and Fry's status, the Tigers' considerable prowess at the plate and their faith in the strong arm of ace Newsom, Detroit had reason to feel confident. They swaggered into Crosley Field, fresh off a tight AL pennant race, believing that the string of American League World Series successes will continue with a championship for the Detroit nine.

There were flaws, to be sure. After Newsom, the Tiger pitching staff was extremely suspect; and age and slowness in the infield had many prognosticators more than a little concerned. Yet the Tigers exuded confidence, partly because the National League had not won a World Series game since Game 4 of the 1937 contest when the Giants beat the Yankees, 7–2. Also contributing to the Tigers' sense of aplomb was that the senior circuit had not won a fall classic series since the Cardinals beat the Tigers four games to three in 1934. Of course, it was the Yankees and not the Tigers who were the reason for the American League's recent superiority. But by beating the Yankees for the 1940 pennant, the Motor City squad acquired a healthy dose of self-esteem. To a man, they believed they were more than ready to do battle with the light-hitting though pitching-rich Reds.[5]

Perhaps sensing that this World Series would be closer than the last (and might be the last one for a while, should America be drawn into the war), hotel rooms throughout Cincinnati were sold out. Lobbies over-flowed with "baseball people" and fans, many of whom were turned away at city hotels and found themselves referred to the Chamber of Commerce for hotel lodgings in the Cincinnati suburbs. As the *New York Times* recounted:

> It seemed impossible to take a step without encountering a baseball figure, either in hotel lobbies or on adjoining streets. Practically every club president, secretary and manager and every major league executive from Commissioner Landis on down the line, was to be seen. Scouts, minor league managers and major league stars of the past are here in profusion too.[6]

The overflow business of lodging the out-of-town visitors extended beyond the city's limits. As the *Cincinnati Enquirer* noted on the eve of Game 1:

> Offering a good front room for $10 a night, a Rose Lawn housewife threw in the use of a parking lot 200 feet from the ball park as an added inducement. Another woman said she had "two good rooms for only $35 a night," and that she would give two tickets to the games as her bonus. The average price for rooms within ordinary distance of the center of the city was $2 a night. A Bellevue woman said she had four rooms for fifty cents a night, adding, "they are nice, comfortable clean rooms."[7]

In addition to the new-found hoteliers, scalpers did a brisk business at the outset as tickets with a face value of $5.95 per game or $16.95 for the series sold for $25 a strip and $50 a pair.[8] For a sport that was just over 20 years removed from the betting scandal and fixing of games that nearly destroyed it, newspaper accounts still reported on wagering — explaining that there was light betting at the opening (due mainly to the gimpiness of Lombardi's slow-healing sprained ankle).[9] UPI staff in London, in the midst of their twenty-sixth night of the German blitzkrieg, sent the following message to their New York headquarters: "Beleagured exiles would greatly appreciate daily World Series scores and batteries," a message that reemphasized how ingrained the game was in America's conscience — even in the midst of shells falling in what was at the time a foreign war.

Without Lombardi, and with Hershberger's suicide in early August, the Reds seemed to be undermanned behind the plate. Much was made of the fact that 40-year-old coach Jimmie Wilson would be called into service in the event that Lombardi couldn't go; an event that seemed more likely as game time approached.[10]

On game day, 31,793 fans packed the ball park in Cincinnati. Many of those without a ticket watched from nearby loft building windows, roof-tops,[11] and even, as the *New York Times* reported, a scaffolding thrown up on a truck parked where it would offer a distant view of the game from the back of center field. Red, white, and blue bunting stretched along the upper and middle decks of the park on a warm, sunny October afternoon that seemed more like summer than early fall. Righthander Paul Derringer, who was winless but pitched well in the 1939 series against the Yankees, got the Game 1 nod from McKechnie.

The Deacon also announced that Lombardi and Frey would sit out the opener and be replaced by Jimmie Wilson and utility infielder Eddie Joost, respectively. Lombardi, who was batting .319, was one of only two power hitters in the Cincinnati attack. With his injury, an unprotected Frank McCormick, whose 127 RBI signified a real threat, was the only slugger likely to give an opposing pitcher pause from the Reds mostly singles hitting lineup.[12]

"Old-man Wilson," who in the 16 games he had played since returning to the active list, hit an unimpressive .243, was not expected to do much with the bat; neither for that matter, was the slick-fielding Joost, whose paltry .216 was even weaker than Frey's hardly robust .267. But their hitting was not really what brought them to the series in the first place. The Reds were here because of pitching and defense, and at least as one Pittsburgh scribe saw it, the systematic smarts of Reds manager Bill McKechnie. How else could one account for McKechnie's one-punch lineup (the punch belonging to first baseman Frank McCormick) coming this far? As *Pittsburgh Sun-Telegraph* writer Charles Doyle explained, though his city's Pirates, guided by Frankie Frisch, scored 100 more runs than the Reds, McKechnie's team outsmarted the seven other National League clubs en route to their second consecutive pennant. Doyle wrote that if one took McCormick out of the lineup it revealed an offense absent any hint of power. "Analyze the rest of the Cincy cast and you will look at some weazened batting averages almost devoid of the old wallop," he wrote. "They don't even compare favorably with the marks made by clubs of 30 years ago, in the days when there was no thought of a lively ball."

The reference to a lineup that wasn't even up to "dead-ball" era standards aside, Doyle praised the Reds for outsmarting their opponents and their uncanny ability to leave the rest of the league "groggy and ready to be counted out." Much of that ability had to do with the Reds muchvaunted pitching staff and McKechnie, "who probably knows more about pitchers than any of his contemporary pilots."[13]

Forty-year-old Jimmie Wilson came out of the coaching ranks to put the shin guards on one final time for the 1940 World Series. Lombardi said of Wilson, "They taped him up like a mummy but he had a Great Series." Wilson hit over .350 in the fall classic and even stole a base.

As Game 1 was about to begin, the Reds arms were ready to take on the Tigers bats, in a series that most agreed was a virtual toss-up.

Game 1, October 2, 1940

Paul Derringer, the big right-handed Kentuckian whom many considered the best pitcher in the game (though he had lost all of his previous three World Series starts), took the hill for Cincinnati on an unusually mild October day in the Heartland. As Derringer dug at the dirt in front of the pitching rubber, about to launch into his trademark high leg kick, the 31,000 plus who filled the stadium on Western Avenue and Findlay Street were nearly bursting from anticipation.

In the first inning, the Cincinnati faithful had reason to be hopeful. Derringer seemed to have his best stuff, and he retired the first three Tiger batters to face him. Big and loud, BoBo Newsom, the Tiger hurler in Game 1, didn't seem to be Derringer's equal in the bottom half of the first.[14] Though Newsom substituted a dizzying wind-up for Derringer's high leg kick, the 210-pound Southerner appeared a bit unsettled in Detroit's first visit to the fall classic since 1935.[15] In the first, he gave up a double to Mike McCormick and faced the Reds only real power hitter in the lineup, Frank McCormick. McCormick stepped into the batter's box with two outs, and Newsom mistakenly threw a high fastball that the big first baseman launched deep into center field. The ball looked like it might clear the wall, and the fans rose to their feet in anticipation, but Detroit center fielder Barney McCosky backed up against the green fence and made a one-handed stab, catching the ball and thwarting the Cincinnati threat in the first.[16]

As the Reds took the field for the second inning, Derringer's flawless opening quickly faded with the first hitter he faced. Detroit slugger Hank Greenberg singled to left to start the inning. Greenberg thought about stretching the single into a double, but about halfway between first and second he changed his mind and raced back to the first base bag. An alert play by Cincinnati shortstop Billy Myers, who took the relay throw, might have caught Greenberg at first, but Myers's back was to the first base side when he took the throw. None of his teammates called for him to throw over to first baseman Frank McCormick, a minor but uncharacteristic miscue for the usually stellar Cincinnati defensive corps and a mental lapse that proved costly.[17]

Tiger first baseman Rudy York, the next batter to face Derringer, singled over second, and again Greenberg made a base-running blunder. The big Tiger touched second, rounded the bag, and again overextended himself. Halfway to third, Greenberg changed his mind for the second time in as many plays, stopped dead in his tracks and headed back to second. Myers took the throw from center field but didn't look back to second, where a good throw would have gotten Greenberg. It was the second time the Reds failed to make Detroit pay for a base-running mistake, another atypical mental lapse for what appeared to be a jittery Reds defense.[18] There were two on and no one out, and although not credited with an error, the Reds infield seemed to be feeling the acute pressure of the big game.

The sixth man in the Detroit lineup, right fielder Bruce Campbell, sacrificed down to the usually sure-handed Billy Werber, the National League leader in fielding percentage, at third. Werber fielded the ball cleanly, but his throw to lanky, 24-year-old Eddie Joost, who was covering the bag for McCormick after the first baseman charged the bunt, pulled Joost off the first base bag. Werber was charged with a throwing error, and the bases were full of Tigers with nobody out. Derringer set from the stretch and dug again at the front of the rubber as he prepared to face the bottom of the Detroit order. To that point, all three Tiger batters to face him in the second reached base, and Detroit looked as if they were poised for a big inning.

Third baseman Frank (Pinky) Higgins lined a single to center, and the first two runs of the 1940 series scored, giving Detroit a 2–0 lead. With runners on first and second, two runs in, and still nobody out, the usually steady Derringer became unglued. He walked the number eight hitter, catcher Billy Sullivan, again loading the bases, to face opposing pitcher BoBo Newsom. Newsom grounded the ball to first, and Frank McCormick fielded it cleanly and threw home to get the force on Campbell.[19]

With one out, the top of the order came up. Shortstop Dick Bartell slipped a single to center, scoring Higgins and Sullivan; center fielder Barney McCosky added another single to score Newsom, sending Derringer to the showers, with one out in the second inning. McKechnie was hardly able to get reliever Whitey Moore warm, but Moore came in and did an admirable job to squelch the flames, setting down the Tigers without any more runs scoring in the inning.

It was only the middle of the second, and the Tigers held a commanding 5–0 lead. Derringer, a stellar regular season performer, had again failed on the big postseason stage.

After only an inning and a third worth of work, a despondent Duke headed to the showers. In the empty clubhouse behind the left field stands, Derringer, whose biggest goal since he was a kid was to win a World Series game, watched it slip away for the fourth time in as many tries.[20]

He stood in the dimly lit clubhouse, looking for a fresh shirt, as sportswriter Henry McLemore waited to hear in the Duke's own words what exactly happened out there. Derringer took the jersey with the big number 30 off his back and uttered an audible sigh.

"That's baseball for you," Derringer offered to McLemore. "You get all ready. You have all your stuff and then they tee off on you. I'm telling you, I had anything I ever had. I was putting the ball right where I wanted it. Still, they kept hitting anything I threw up there."

"You'll get another whack at 'em," McLemore said. "Next time, it'll be different."

"It's gotta be," the Reds ace said. "You know how much I wanted to win. For myself, I mean. But believe me the real reason I wanted to win was for McKechnie. He's tops and I feel pretty bad about letting him down."

Derringer finished dressing and though he heard a roar from the crowd as reliever Whitey Moore set down the side, he knew not only he but also the Reds were done for the day.[21]

Cincinnati added a harmless single run in the fourth, which was followed by a Detroit fifth where Rudy York tripled and Campbell homered him home. In the eighth, the Reds scored a solo run, but that was the end of the scoring as BoBo Newsom settled into a groove and the Tiger bats belted the Reds around for a 7–2 thrashing.

The Game 1 loss, the fifth straight World Series defeat for the Reds and the tenth straight World Series conquest for the American League, tied a series record held by the 1927–28 Yankees and 1929 Philadelphia Athletics. The *Enquirer* reported that after the Detroit onslaught in the second, the game was about as interesting to watch "as a circus parade is to an elephant rider."[22]

In the clubhouse following Game 1, there was little celebration from the Detroit manager and as expected no sign of quit in the Reds. Tiger skipper Del Baker explained that Newsom had not pitched up to his standards but had enough to win. "BoBo didn't have his usual stuff, but he had control. They just couldn't hit him. Derringer had a lot of stuff but we were just hitting. Tomorrow I'll pitch [Schoolboy] Rowe. I'm not predicting the outcome, we'll just be in there doing our best as we were today."

Newsom took a different approach. Like a carnival barker under the big top, BoBo took center stage and had plenty to say. He was known for being a talker, and although the Tigers to a man were quiet and respectful following the Game 1 victory, Newsom was brash, boldly predicting, "If we hit as we did … we may win it in four straight. I don't think we'll be back in this ball park after we get through with the Reds in Detroit."

In the Tiger dressing room following a Game 1 performance that saw the Reds scatter eight hits and score two measly runs, BoBo received many congratulatory backslaps and "nice goings," from his teammates.

"It was the first one I ever pitched," he told reporter Bob Bohne of the series victory. "My dad was there, too," he added proudly. "It was only the second time he has seen me pitch. I didn't think he'd get here. Been sick in South Carolina, but he made it."[23]

The Reds dressed quietly in the home clubhouse, dejected but not defeated. McKechnie was matter-of-fact about the Game 1 defeat and not at all bothered that it was his fifth consecutive series defeat. "Derringer had plenty of stuff but they just hit everything he threw up there," he said. "They just hit Derringer and we couldn't hit Newsom." Lombardi or Frey wouldn't be coming to save the day in Game 2, though. "I'll pitch Bucky Walters tomorrow. Wilson will catch and Joost will be at second. I expect Lombardi and Frey to get in before the series is over, but I can't say when. I don't want to take any chances with the big fellow until he is ready to play." For those who may have doubted the two-time NL champs' resolve, the agreeable McKechnie offered, "We were beaten without being disgraced. We're not down. Tomorrow is another day."

But not everyone agreed. "Really, it looked like our boys were a trifle stage frightened in the early stages of the game … they did not play heads up baseball like they did in the opening game of the Series at Yankee Stadium last year," wrote the *Enquirer*'s Bob Saxton.[24] Another writer added that the only consolation of the Game 1 massacre was that there would be cash refunds for Game 6 tickets and it will be "just like finding money."[25]

Game 2, October 3, 1940

Henry Quillan Buffkin Newsom was not a well man. He suffered from a chronic heart condition that restricted much of his movement even in and around the Hartsville, South Carolina, town where he lived. Yet despite his ailments, the 68-year-old former farmer and father of Tigers pitching ace boarded the train in South Carolina for a trip to Cincinnati so he could watch his son pitch Game 1 of the World Series against the Reds. He had only been in the stands once before when Buck had pitched, but this was the World Series, after all, and the elder Newsom was determined to watch his son on the sport's greatest stage.[26]

His father made it to the park and was in the Crosley Field stands as Buck Newsom beat the Reds, getting the double thrill of winning a World Series game while his father proudly watched from the seats. In the early morning hours before Game 2, still in the afterglow of his son's victory, Henry Newsom suffered a heart attack at his room in the Hotel Netherland Plaza. Buck rushed to his father's bedside, and although the son told his father he would get well and watch him pitch again, the elder Newsom shook his head no and told him he had seen everything he had wanted to see. He died shortly thereafter.[27]

The doctor who attended to Henry Newsom did not attribute the death to excitement over the game, saying it probably would have occurred had he stayed at home. Buck told reporters his father had told friends back home that he would not be back. He said that his father died simply because he had lived long enough to see his son pitch a World Series game. If he had not pitched yesterday, he was sure his father would have lived long enough to see him do it another day. He also told the reporters he would pitch again in the series. "I'm going to pitch again and win for Dad. He would hate me if I didn't do it."[28]

As Newsom stayed with his father's body at the funeral home, his teammates got ready for a Game 2 showdown with the Reds. Lynwood "Schoolboy" Rowe, the Tigers' number two starter, brought a 16–3 mark to the hill against the bowlegged second ace of the Reds staff, converted third baseman Bucky Walters.

The truth is, Walters was probably the number one ace of the staff at the time. In 1940, Bucky led the senior circuit in virtually every important pitching category (22 wins, 27 complete games, 2.48 ERA) and held the opposition to a .220 average that also led the league. He was the best (if not the last) hope for the Reds to break what was now a five-game World Series losing streak.

How important was the Game 2 start for Walters? Dropping the first two games at home with their best pitchers on the hill was not the way the Reds envisioned going into Detroit, and it would have virtually assured them of losing any probable chance of winning the series. In essence, winning Game 2 took on tremendous importance, not only for the team's collective psyche and to make believers of their increasingly frustrated fans but also to give them any realistic chance of winning the World Championship.

The crowd topped the 30,000 mark once again, but although they were just as boisterous as the throng that attended Game 1, about 1,000 fewer fans showed than the prior day. The bandwagon jumpers probably thought they had seen enough after the Tigers had whipped the Reds pitching in Game 1.[29] With Frey and Lombardi out again, the less than faithful figured they would cut their losses instead of waiting for the losses they were certain would come. The city's scalpers fared poorly after the Game

1 loss, as the *Enquirer* reported that many tickets were sold for the regular price or less and that it appeared likely that a number of registered scalpers would have no profits to report when they filed their returns on November 10.

Those who stayed away must have believed they made the right decision when Walters's shaky start put the Reds behind early. He walked the number one and two men, Dick Bartell and Barney McCosky, in the Tigers lineup and appeared unnerved as he tried to find his rhythm in front of a quickly quieting crowd, who watched the game under a brilliant, cloudless sky. McKechnie, not wanting the game to get away, sent Gene Thompson to warm up in the Cincinnati bullpen before Walters had even recorded an out.[30]

The uneasiness in the crowd grew when Detroit's number three hitter, Charlie Gehringer, attempted to advance the runners with a sacrifice but failed to lay down the bunt. Tiger skipper Del Baker changed his signals and with Gehringer free to hit away, he singled to right, scoring Bartell and advancing McCosky to third, putting the Tigers ahead, 1–0. With runners on first and third and nobody out, the mighty Hank Greenberg stepped to the plate; Walters and the Reds were in a world of trouble. But Walters got Greenberg to ground the ball to third baseman Billy Werber, who threw to second baseman Eddie Joost, who in turn tossed to Frank McCormick for the double play. The Reds conceded a run, as McCosky crossed the plate, but the double play seemed to settle Walters and energize the crowd. Walters fanned the next batter, Rudy York, on four pitches and although the Reds took their turn in the bottom of the first, down 2–0, they entered their dugout realizing it could have been much worse.[31]

The problem, of course, was that the Reds offense had been so ineffective that spotting the Tigers any sort of lead put Cincinnati at a distinct disadvantage. It forced their pitching and defense to be nearly perfect, as the offense tried to make up the runs. Tiger starter Schoolboy Rowe did little to give the Cincinnati faithful confidence as he retired the Reds in order in the home half of the first. Walters settled down, regained the confidence and poise he exhibited throughout the season, and pitched a scoreless second, giving the heart of the Reds order a chance to even their early deficit.[32]

The first batter in the bottom half of the second, NL MVP candidate Frank McCormick dug in and lanced Rowe's first pitch to left for a single. Jimmy Ripple followed with a harmless pop into short left field that was grabbed by Dick Bartell for an easy out. With one on and one out, Lombardi's understudy and the oldest player on either roster, Jimmie Wilson, took his turn in the batter's box. He singled to right, advancing McCormick to second as the Reds went station to station. Light-hitting Eddie Joost followed Wilson with a single to center, scoring McCormick. With runners at first and second, the number seven man in the Reds lineup, Billy Myers, readied himself for his turn against Rowe and hit the first pitch into left, scoring Wilson with the tying run and moving Joost into scoring position.[33]

With four consecutive hits by the Reds, the Crosley Field fans were ecstatic at suddenly seeing a new game. An errant pick-off throw to second by Tiger catcher Birdie Tebbetts allowed Joost to go on to third and Myers to advance to second. Rowe got Walters to fly out to short center, preventing Joost from tagging with the go-ahead run. With the top of the order up, Rowe walked Billy Werber on a 3–2 pitch to load the bases. The Reds were seemingly on the verge of a big inning when Rowe got Mike McCormick to swing at his first pitch, which he popped to short to end the inning. The game moved to the third, with the score tied at two.

It was a brand-new game now that the Reds had fought back. After the blip in the opening frame, Walters was near the top of his form, pitching like a true ace. The Tigers were set down in order in the third, and Cincy took the lead for good in the bottom of the inning, when outfielder Jimmy Ripple smacked a two-run homer into the bleachers that proved to be the lift the Reds and their fans had been waiting for. He gave the home team the lead for the first time in the series.

Walters again retired the Tigers without a hit in the top of the fourth and then aided his own cause in the bottom of the inning, when he showed that although he threw like a front-line starter, he hadn't forgotten how to hit as an everyday third baseman. He doubled past third with one out. The current third baseman, Billy Werber, then followed Walters's lead with a double of his own. That chased Schoolboy Rowe from the game and gave the Reds a five-to-two lead.

In the Detroit sixth, Hammerin' Hank Greenberg doubled home Charlie Gehringer, who was on first after the Reds erased lead-off hitter Barney McCosky on Gehringer's fielder's choice. The score narrowed to five to three. Rudy York came to the plate and drove the ball deep into center field, where Ival Goodman made the grab but couldn't prevent Greenberg from advancing to third. Walters then induced Bruce Campbell to ground to Eddie Joost at second, to end the Tiger threat.[34]

Detroit reliever Johnny Gorsica entered the game when Rowe left for the showers and traded zeroes with Bucky Walters in the seventh and eighth innings. In the top of the ninth, with the Reds first World Series victory in 21 years within their grasp, the Crosley faithful held their collective breath as Tiger sluggers Hank Greenberg and Rudy York prepared to take their licks.

Greenberg batted first in the inning and believed he had Walters's timing down. As Walters whipped the ball toward the plate, Greenberg waited on the delivery and smacked it deep to left toward the Crosley Field scoreboard, where it was corralled by Ripple for the first out. Walters then fanned Rudy York for the second time in the game. When shortstop Billy Myers squeezed Bruce Campbell's pop-up in the webbing of his glove for the twenty-seventh and final out, Cincinnati had its first series victory in 21 years.

For the fans, it was as if a cork had been popped from a bottle of champagne. As the *Enquirer* told it, it wasn't just the fans in the Crosley Field stands who celebrated. "In downtown Cincinnati — where mighty little work was done between 1:30 and 3:30 o'clock there were whoops of joy and the biggest shower of ticker tape and torn-up phone books since Armistice Day. Fourth Street between Walnut and Vine Streets was ankle deep in bits of paper."[35] Forty-five minutes after the final out, paper was still dropping to sidewalks on Fourth and Walnut. All of this and the Reds had only won a single game.

Game 3, October 4, 1940

As the Reds and Tigers boarded the train from Cincinnati after Game 2, Manager Del Baker remained confident. He gave the Reds compliments for having "plenty of heart and fight-back," but he said, echoing the sentiments of BoBo Newsom expressed just a day earlier,

> We've got three games coming up at Briggs Stadium and I don't think we'll need to return here for a sixth series game. We've seen the best pitching the Reds have got and we ran Derringer out of the box and came within a hit of having Walters out of there. My boys have a lot of respect for Walters, particularly in view of the fact that he made himself a pitcher after failing as an infielder, but they want one more crack at him.

Game 3 at Briggs Stadium was not a sell-out, though with the stadium being bigger than the Reds park, the third game, the first one in Detroit, attracted nearly 53,000 fans. The game was a battle of 34-year-old Tennesseans, as Jim "Milkman" Turner squared off against Tommy Bridges, a slender, right-handed curveballer who was pitching on 10 days' rest.[36]

The Reds were feeling confident off their Game 2 victory and, in a surprise move by manager Bill McKechnie, welcomed back a gimpy Ernie

Lombardi to the lineup. Lombardi's presence gave the Tiger hurlers an extra thumper to face, though prior to game time it was uncertain how effective the big backstop would be with a swollen ankle. Inspired by their win in Game 2, the Reds picked up where they left off in Cincinnati, as lead-off man Billy Werber lanced Bridges's first pitch down the left field line for a double. Mike McCormick struck out, enabling the Motor City faithful to settle in; but when the third man in the Cincy lineup, Ival Goodman, singled to center to score Werber, the crowd went silent once again. Bridges held the Reds in check for the rest of the inning, as Frank McCormick lined out to right and Jimmy Ripple struck out to end the first. The Tigers came to bat trailing, 1–0.[37]

Milkman Turner, who was 14–9 on the season, strode to the hill for the Reds and had his curveball breaking, fooling the Tiger batters as he set them down in order in the bottom half of the first. In the Reds second, Ernie Lombardi doubled, but three outs were recorded by Bridges in quick succession, leaving the wounded backstop stranded at second. The teams traded zeroes until the Tigers came to bat in the bottom of the fourth.

In the fourth, McCosky took Turner to center for a lead-off single, the first hit off the Cincinnati hurler. Gehringer followed with a low line drive that shot past Frank McCormick at first and allowed McCosky to take third. With runners on the corners and nobody out, the ever-dangerous Hank Greenberg stepped into the box. Turner induced the big man to hit a double-play ball to Bill Werber at third that allowed McCosky to tie the score. Bruce Campbell then bounced to first to end the inning.

With the score tied at one, the Tennessee hurlers kept the hitters at bay as both Cincinnati and Detroit failed to score in the fifth and sixth frames. Cincinnati put another zero on the board in the top half of the seventh, and then the wheels came off the Milkman's delivery truck. Turner went to three-and-two on Hank Greenberg to open the bottom half of the seventh, and with the count full, Greenberg lined Turner's next offering over the second base bag for a single.

With Greenberg taking a slight lead at first and Turner pitching from the stretch, a hanging curveball was delivered to Rudy York, who smacked the ball high into the air. Left fielder Jimmy Ripple went back to the very edge of the outfield wall and appeared to settle under it, but the ball carried just over the screen for a two-run homer.[38]

York circled the bases behind Greenberg to a "deafening roar of applause" as the Tigers went ahead, three-to-one. Rattled by the home run, Turner gave up a hit to the next batter in the Tiger lineup, Bruce Campbell, and then Pinky Higgins sent Turner to the showers with "a mighty swat high into the upper deck of the left field stands 390 feet from home plate."[39]

McKechnie went to the bullpen and replaced Turner with Whitey Moore. Moore came in, and after he retired the first two Tigers to face him, he spent some tense moments as he allowed the next two runners to get on. He managed to squirm his way out of the inning without further damage as Charlie Gehringer fouled out with runners on second and third. The Tigers led five to one as the game moved to the eighth.[40]

Though they started the inning four runs in the hole, the Reds didn't quit. They strung together three singles in the top of the inning to narrow the score to 5–2. But the Tigers bats came alive again in the bottom half of the eighth, determined not to let the Reds back into the game. The National League's number one fireman, Joe Beggs, took the mound in the eighth. Hank Greenberg promptly welcomed him with a 415-foot line triple to right center field. Bruce Campbell singled Greenberg home and later scored on a looping double by Pinky Higgins to put the game out of reach. The Reds added two more runs in the top of the ninth, but it was too little too late, as Bridges went the distance for a 7–4 victory.[41]

In the moments following the game, McKechnie closed the clubhouse door to reporters for five minutes. He was terse with his postgame analysis in the mostly sullen locker room. "You guys saw what happened out there today. That's the way it is in baseball. When they start to go — they go fast — slip right out from under you." The only positive McKechnie took from Game 3 was that Lombardi actually got to play, though he was removed once the game got out of hand. Even though the big man managed to double in his first at-bat, his future role in the series remained in doubt. "I was glad Lombardi was able to get in there, but I don't know whether we'll be able to use him again except for pinch-hitting. His right ankle is swollen and sore right now."[42]

In contrast to their National League counterparts, the Tiger players were confident, and they celebrated, knowing the burden had shifted back to Cincinnati. Amid the back-slapping and bear hugs being administered to York, Higgins, and winning pitcher Tommy Bridges in the victorious clubhouse, Del Baker sounded off on his National League opponents, "Say these fellows are nothing but nubbers. I never did see so many hoppers for hits. That's all they do, they just nub the ball along. I don't want that trip back to Cincinnati. We can beat those fellows, and we will, unless they have good enough pitching to stop our hitters."[43]

In Game 4, the nubbers enacted their revenge.

Game 4, October 5, 1940

After Game 3, Paul Derringer and Bucky Walters entered the team's jammed hotel lobby together and Derringer, who was yet to record a World

Series victory, was mobbed by autograph seekers. Walters, the man who pitched the three-hitter that gave Cincinnati their first series victory since 1918, stood alongside him, unrecognized, waiting patiently for 15 minutes as Derringer signed his name. Maybe the fans hadn't recognized the unassuming Walters, or maybe they knew Derringer's luck was about to change.

Derringer wasn't scheduled to start Game 4, and McKechnie frequently dangled sophomore Junior Thompson as his projected starter to keep the Tigers guessing.[44] At the eleventh hour, however, McKechnie decided on the Duke. His reasoning was sound. Rather than have a youngster face the prospect of having the Reds go down three games to one, with one more game to be played in Detroit, McKechnie instead turned to a veteran who had pitched in four World Series games. The logic was sound, except for one small detail. On the game's biggest stage, Derringer had come out on the short side every time.

It was a pivotal game for the Reds. Down two-to-one in a visiting park, McKechnie was pinning his hopes on Derringer and the belief that he would regain his form and pitch like the 20-game winner he was and not the pitcher who got shelled in the second inning of Game 1. Although confident in the Kentucky rifleman as a legitimate ace, McKechnie knew Derringer had been snake-bitten when it came to the fall classic.[45]

The Duke's rather inglorious history in series play went back to 1931 when hurling for the Cardinals. He blew up twice in that year's World Series against the Philadelphia Athletics. In 1939, he lost two tough decisions to the Yankees; in Game 1, a mere few days ago, he imploded in yet another attempt at a World Series victory. Should he lose Game 4, he might take the hopes of his teammates along with him.[46]

Perhaps counting on Derringer to defeat himself or figuring the law of averages said a pitcher of Derringer's capability had to win some time, Detroit manager Del Baker surprisingly countered with a right-handed rookie, husky Dizzy Trout, who along with Fred Hutchinson had posted the worst mark of any Tiger hurler during the regular season at 3–7. It was a curious move, because Detroit could really grab control of the series. But instead of looking to deliver a knockout blow by throwing BoBo Newsom and making the Reds beat their best, Baker opted for Trout and gave Cincy a chance to breathe again.[47]

Admittedly, Baker didn't have many options. Newsom, Rowe, and Bridges were the best his team had and they had each already pitched. There was precious little depth beyond those three. Baker's boys were a team that relied on hitting and Newsom and Rowe. Baker was saving Newsom, who was still smarting over the death of his father, for Game 5. He would just have to live with whatever effort his fourth starter could muster.

A 54,000-plus crowd filled Briggs Stadium, hoping to watch the Tigers pounce on the Reds and chase Derringer from the hill once again. An early morning drizzle turned into a downpour as the fans, many of whom dressed for a damp fall day, gathered in hope that a game would be played and their Tigers would be victorious. Their faith was rewarded (at least partly) as the clouds dispersed, giving way to sunshine and warmer temperatures by game time.

The Reds knew they had little room for error and broke from the gate quickly. In the first, Billy Werber walked to start the game but was erased at second on Mike McCormick's fielder's choice. The game's third batter, Ival Goodman, liked what he saw from Trout as soon as he stepped into the batter's box and slammed the first pitch into the left field corner for a double, scoring McCormick all the way from first. Clean-up hitter Frank McCormick followed with a bouncer to third baseman Pinky Higgins that advanced Goodman to third. Higgins's error on the next play, a Jimmy Ripple smash, scored Goodman and enabled the Reds to spot Derringer a two-run lead before he took the mound.[48]

With the help of a double play, the Duke set down the Tigers in the first, and the teams went scoreless in the second. In the top of the third, Goodman again connected with a Trout offering and singled to center. McKechnie, looking for his nubbers to put some distance between the singles-hitting Reds and the Detroit lumber company, called for a hit-and-run that was perfectly executed by Frank McCormick, leaving runners at the corners with nobody out. Jimmy Ripple slammed Trout's next pitch into left for a double, scoring Goodman and moving McCormick over to third.

After Ripple, the Tiger skipper had seen enough of his fourth starter and pulled Trout in favor of Clay Smith. With runners on second and third and nobody out, Smith dug in to face Lombardi's replacement, catcher Jimmie Wilson. Wilson bounced one weakly to third, forcing the runners to hold their position. Eddie Joost followed with a pop-out to second, and Myers was intentionally walked, loading the bases for Derringer. The big Kentuckian failed to help his own cause as he grounded into a fielder's choice, third to second, to end the inning. The Reds threat came to an end, though they led the Tigers 3–0 going into the bottom of the third.[49]

The Tiger bats, asleep until this point, began to nub away themselves in the bottom half of the inning. Dick Bartell led off with a bouncer back to Derringer for the first out. Barney McCosky walked for the second time, and Derringer ran the count to 3-and-2 on Gehringer. The Tiger second-sacker grounded out to short but advanced McCosky. The next batter,

Hank Greenberg, smashed a double down the left field line that scored McCosky. With a walk to Rudy York, the Cincinnati dugout began to get nervous, sensing Derringer might implode. But he didn't. Instead, Big Paul recovered in time to strike out Campbell, leaving the tying runs aboard as the Reds head to the fourth, ahead 3–1.[50]

The Reds answered Detroit's run with one of their own in the top half of the fourth, once again providing themselves a three-run cushion. Billy Werber began the inning with a walk on four pitches. The next batter, Mike McCormick, doubled — hitting a pitch that sent chalk flying on the right field line as Werber advanced to third. With second and third and none out, the Reds were poised for a big inning. Ival Goodman, who was swinging a hot bat, was next up for the Reds, and he sent a deep fly to left center that Hank Greenberg corralled. Werber scored, making it 4–1, and Mike McCormick advanced to third on the sacrifice. Frank McCormick, always a threat, proceeded to pop out to Gehringer. Jimmy Ripple received an intentional pass, and with two on, Jimmie Wilson struck out swinging to end the inning and the Cincinnati threat.

Both teams failed to score in the fifth, and the Reds went quietly in the sixth, continuing to hold their three-run lead, keeping the Detroit faithful silent for much of the afternoon. In the bottom of the sixth, Derringer retired Greenberg and York and appeared to be setting the Tigers down in order when Campbell lined a single to right for Detroit's fourth hit of the day. Pinky Higgins then smashed a Derringer fastball off the right field wall for a triple, scoring Campbell and narrowing the Reds' lead to two, bringing the roar of the Tiger crowd back into the game.

Tiger catcher Billy Sullivan, the next batter to face Derringer, was intentionally walked to a resounding chorus of boos. Del Baker sent Earl Averill in to bat for reliever Clay Smith, and he flied out to Goodman in right, leaving the tying runs stranded and the National League champs, still in the lead, 4–2. The Tigers and Reds both put up zeroes in the seventh. In the top of the eighth, a Mike McCormick single drove Billy Werber home for the final run of the game and a 5–2 Cincinnati victory that knotted the series at two games a piece and ensured a return to Crosley Field.

A chorus of "Great going Duke," and a host of congratulatory back slaps greeted Derringer as he returned to the victorious visitors' locker room with his first-ever series victory. The win brought a smile not only to Derringer's face but also to a clubhouse where a mere 24 hours ago not a single grin could be found. "That sure was a long time coming," Derringer offered. "It's great to have it at last." McKechnie was all smiles, too. "We had to win this one today; that's why I pitched Derringer. If we lost today that might have been our finish. When you're in a spot like that you must give everything you have, and the best I had was Derringer ... he proved that out there."

A more caustic review came from Del Baker, who saw his opportunity to take command of the series fade away. "They beat us with a fast ball pitcher," Baker grumbled, "that's what. We had many opportunities to knock in a run with men on base but we just didn't hit. Maybe Derringer was too good or maybe my hitters were too weak. Derringer deserves praise for his game. He was fast and had a lot of stuff and got better as the game went along. But make no mistake about it, we'll get 'em."[51]

Game 5, October 6, 1940

The fifth game and the final one in Detroit promised to be an emotional affair, as BoBo Newsom took the hill, only three days after his father's death. Del Baker knew his ace could have gone one of two ways. Either the big righty would be so distracted over the loss of his father that the Reds would get to him early and drive him from the game or he would "pitch a game for Dad" and be at his best. In Game 4, Baker had gambled and lost on his hunch that the Detroit bats would pound Derringer and give Dizzy Trout enough of a cushion to patch together a workman-like effort. Now with the series tied at two, Baker knew Newsom would have to be at the top of his game — especially if McKechnie were to pitch Walters in Game 5. With the series heading back to Cincinnati, this was one gamble the Detroit skipper couldn't afford to lose.

In the pregame interviews, McKechnie told the writers that it would either be Junior Thompson or Walters as his starter for Game 5. The scribes took their notes, but were none too pleased with the fact that McKechnie had misled them about his Game 4 starter (pitching Derringer instead of Thompson). Perhaps angered by the Deacon's gamesmanship, a rumor rose among the press corps that McKechnie was planning on leaving Cincinnati after the series to take the newly vacant Cleveland Indians managerial job and replace the recently departed Oscar Vitt. It was a distraction the Reds hardly needed, and it forced McKechnie into issuing a pregame denial, saying he hadn't been approached by any Cleveland officials. "I'm perfectly happy at Cincinnati," the Deacon said. "I have no intention of making a change."[52] As for his Game 5 starter, McKechnie opted for sophomore Junior Thompson, a reliable hurler who had posted a 16–9 mark during the 1940 campaign.

As game time approached, it was clear it would be a perfect day for baseball. A cloudless sky and a game time temperature in Detroit that rose into the 80s truly breathed the life of summer into the Motor City's final ball game for the year. Thompson and Newsom matched zeroes for the first two innings, but it was clear from the outset that Newsom was about to pitch a game nearly as perfect as the weather.

Thompson, on the other hand, was suspect from the very start — barely escaping the first two innings without allowing a run — after surrendering four singles and a walk. In fact, so shaky was the performance of his Game 5 starter that McKechnie had relievers warming as early as the first inning. But the skipper held his breath and postponed a decision to go to the bullpen, as Thompson uneasily squirmed out of the first two frames.[53]

The Tigers were not so kind to the sophomore in their half of the third. Barney McCosky and Charlie Gehringer hit back-to-back singles, and then Hank Greenberg, who had already singled in the game, launched a moonshot off of Thompson that "sailed through one of the portals in the upper deck of the left field stands, three-hundred and fifty feet from home plate and some sixty feet above the ground." The blast sent the Briggs Stadium crowd into delirium, and forged the Tigers into a commanding three-to-nothing lead. Greenberg rounded the bases to deafening cheers. And though Thompson escaped the inning without further damage, with the way Newsom was throwing, Detroit did not need another run.[54]

The Tigers added more however, scoring four runs in the fourth and one in the eighth, as they piled on the hits. Cincinnati pitching contributed to the rout as well, allowing 10 walks and 13 hits, as the Detroit carousel circled around the bases to the delight of their adoring fans, thumping the Reds, 8–0. In truth, the only bright moment for the Reds came in the fifth, when the partisan Detroit crowd cheered wildly for past glories, when Johnny Vander Meer was announced as a reliever. "They'll never forget those two no-hitters," the *Enquirer* recounted in its editions the following day.

Despite the relentless assault from the Detroit batters, Game 5 truly belonged to Newsom. As writer Judson Bailey wrote, the luster of Newsom's hill performance dimmed the bombardment of the Tiger bats so thoroughly that after the game "scores of the 55,189 fans who packed the big steel and concrete arena came down onto the diamond just to admire with proper awe the deep holes that Newsom ground into the dirt next to the pitching slab."[55]

Newsom had promised his father he would win his next start, and he delivered the finest performance of his 20-year career, cruising through a Cincinnati lineup that offered meager resistance. Uncharacteristically quiet prior to the game, the usually verbose Newsom let his pitching speak more brazenly than even he ever could, posting a final tally that left little doubt as to the game's brightest star. His final line was a pitcher's dream—a complete game shutout, three harmless singles, eight strikeouts, and only two walks. It was a triumph, pure and simple.

Out of respect for Newsom's father, there was no whooping or hollering in the Tiger clubhouse—only a quiet satisfaction from a team that had played the most complete game of the series to date. "It was the hardest game I ever wanted to win," said a still-grieving Newsom, in the victorious locker room. "I felt great, no kidding. Naturally, I didn't feel as good as I should have. I pitched this game for my dad and I hope he knows what I accomplished. I knew in my heart he wanted me to win. This was the one I wanted to win most."[56]

Game 6, October 7, 1940

As his team boarded the train for home, Bill McKechnie knew there was little mystery left to the task at hand. His team was going back to Crosley Field trailing in the series, three games to two. Having been beaten badly by the Tigers the day before, McKechnie knew there wasn't any room left for a poor performance by his squad, especially from his front-line starters. Still, the wily manager liked his chances. He had two aces up his sleeve in the form of Game 6 starter Bucky Walters and what he hoped would be Game 7 hurler Paul Derringer. Plus, he had the added advantage of playing in his home park. Although Detroit would likely throw their number two and number one pitchers again, the short rest Newsom would have in the event of a Game 7 winner-take-all finale seemed to favor the Reds. But Game 7 was just a possibility. The Reds had to get there first.

The Deacon was quietly confident as game time approached. A steady morning rain fell in Cincinnati, and it appeared unlikely that Game 6 would go on as scheduled. A postponement of Game 6 would no doubt benefit the Tigers—because it would give BoBo Newsom another day of rest and virtually assure his taking the hill for the Motor City in Game 7.

But as it had been throughout the series, by game time the rain had stopped. Though an overcast sky remained, at 1:30 in the afternoon, the soggy field was deemed ready for a game, the prospect of rain finished for the day.[57]

Perhaps due to the less than ideal weather conditions, or maybe due to a creeping sense of pessimism among the Cincinnati less than faithful, the crowd assembled slowly for Game 6. For the first time since the series began, it was game time before the bleachers filled. As the *Enquirer* reported, scalpers took a terrific beating on Game 6 tickets. They were offered freely around hotel lobbies, and many were trying to unload them by the handful outside the park. Some of the tickets in the grandstand sold for as little as a dollar. "There is something in the air," Joe Garretson wrote, "that gave the impression that the fans thought the series would end in six games."[58]

The Reds sought to put an end to that sense of uncertainty in the minds of their fans and quite possibly any lingering doubts they may have harbored themselves. To do it, they turned to their sinker balling co-ace, the lean and lanky Bucky Walters.

In the first inning, Walters quieted the Tiger bats that roared so loudly in Game 5, setting Detroit down without a hit, mercifully enabling anxious Cincinnati fans to find some comfort as they settled in for the do-or-die contest. The Reds, needing to show Schoolboy Rowe they meant business, wasted no time in getting to work in their half of first.

Billy Werber, batting in the lead-off spot, smacked a double off the left field wall to the delight of the adoring crowd. McKechnie, who played for the first run early, had his number two hitter Mike McCormick lay down a sacrifice, that moved Werber over to third. The next batter, Ival Goodman, bounced to the right side of the infield. First baseman Rudy York fielded the ball cleanly, but a mental lapse by Schoolboy Rowe, who failed to cover the first base bag on the play, allowed Goodman to reach first safely and Werber to score. The 30,000+ crowd went wild as Cincinnati scored the first run of the game.[59]

The Reds weren't through. Clean-up man Frank McCormick smashed a rope just inside the third base bag that looked like a sure double. But the ball bounced into foul ground and hit the jury box in left field, giving the Tigers a break with a favorable ricochet that prevented it from being a double and forced Goodman to stop at second. It was a short-lived reprieve.

Jimmy Ripple stepped into the batter's box and singled between first and second, for the fourth Reds hit of the inning. Goodman scored, putting the Reds up by two, and McCormick advanced to third, planting the seeds for a big inning.

With only one out and runners on first and third, Del Baker had seen enough. He pulled Rowe in favor of reliever Johnny Gorsica. Gorsica rose to the challenge. He struck out Jimmie Wilson swinging and then induced Eddie Joost into a fielder's choice, to end the Cincinnati threat. After one inning, two Reds had crossed the plate on four hits. The Reds may have had a two-to-nothing lead, but the Tigers also knew it could have been much worse. With their heavy hitting lineup of Greenberg, York, and Campbell waiting to unload, Baker's boys knew the Reds lead was hardly insurmountable.

But as the game moved through the middle innings, it was clear Walters was pitching with command in front of a superb Cincinnati defense. It began to feel as if the two first inning runs would stand. The pessimism that permeated through the crowd prior to the game had all but disappeared, and as the teams traded zeroes in innings two through five, Cincinnatians began to believe their team would live to see a Game 7.

In the sixth, outfielder Jimmy Ripple started the Reds off with a single to center. Catcher Jimmie Wilson followed by bouncing a chopper over first baseman Rudy York that advanced Ripple to third. With runners on first and third and no one out, Eddie Joost walked, loading the bases to give the Tigers a force at any base.[60]

The Reds, with an opportunity to put the game away, stumbled. Billy Myers bounced a high chopper back to the mound that Gorsica promptly fielded and threw to Birdie Tebbetts, retiring Ripple for the first out. With the bases still full of Reds and one out, pitcher Bucky Walters dug into the box to try and help his own cause. As a converted third baseman, he was a better hitter than most pitchers, but he too bounced a Gorsica offering. This time, however, he bounced it high enough down the third base line that Pinky Higgins's throw home was too late to retire Wilson, and the Reds tacked on another run, going ahead three-to-nothing. Billy Werber, who was the Reds' hottest batter, was the next man up, but he hit into a double play to end the inning.

The Tigers and the Reds went scoreless in the seventh, and Detroit failed to score again in the top of the eighth. In the bottom of the inning, Fred Hutchinson replaced Johnny Gorsica, who had pitched into trouble several times but each time had managed to survive, allowing only a single run in a workman-like relief stint of seven and two-thirds innings.

In the eighth, Hutchinson struck out Billy Myers to open the inning. But then, as if to show the Tigers who was in command of the game, Bucky Walters smacked Hutchinson's first offering deep over the left field wall, just inside the foul pole, for the Reds' second homer of the series and a four-to-nothing Cincinnati lead.[61]

The 31-year-old Walters set down the Tigers again in the ninth, without allowing a run to complete a virtuoso performance that the *Enquirer* called "one of the greatest games of his short, but brilliant pitching career."[62] Much of the credit went to Walters for the Game 6 victory as he shut out the Tigers on five-hit pitching, but the Cincinnati defense was just as stellar behind him.

While Walters's buddies were beating him into a swayback, he was surely mindful of what they did for him to tie the series.... Billy Werber timed grounders at least three times so perfectly that he looked like a robot going on to complete double plays. Eddie Joost checked one potential hit at such an angle that he had to throw in a loop to McCormick at first.[63]

In the victorious clubhouse, the blond ace with the crooked smile grinned from ear to ear. He accepted the hearty congratulations of his teammates and told the reporters, "My control was better today than in the second game." He was a hero for all Cincinnati to love. As Sue Goodwin wrote in her action-away-from-the-action column, "Skirting the Field," "There was one word you couldn't escape last night, on the street corners, in the hotel lobbies, in the office buildings, everywhere the key word was 'Bucky.'"[64]

The city of Cincinnati was jubilant. But there was still one more game to be played.

Game 7, October 8, 1940

As the seventh and final game approached, the one thing that both Bill McKechnie and Del Baker believed in was the maxim that said to save the best for last. Each man selected his Game 1 hurler to start the seventh and final game of the 1940 fall classic. A smiling McKechnie revealed as much in the winning clubhouse after Bucky Walters's Game 6 victory. He knew immediately that Derringer would take the hill for the Reds, although he was pitching on a scant two days' rest.

"It will be Big Paul," he told reporter Lou Smith. "And I won't have to sleep on the decision. It will be Big Paul today, tomorrow or any day the final game is played."[65]

For his part, Baker was more coy. Newsom, far and away his best pitcher, would have had to go on a single day's rest if he were the starter. Conventional wisdom had Baker leading toward throwing Tommy Bridges and keeping him on a short leash, inserting Newsom from the pen, the moment Bridges got into trouble.

There was good reason to believe that was how Baker would approach his mound choice. After Game 5, BoBo was complaining of "miseries in his powerful ham-like right hand." He said he was tired, and it hurt when he gripped the ball.[66]

But despite his maladies, Newsom was a strong man who thrived on work. He had on several occasions during the 1940 season appeared in

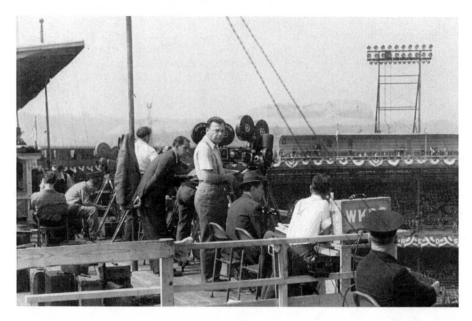

Bringing the news to a waiting world. The press records the 1940 World Series at Crosley Field.

both ends of a doubleheader and toward the end of the season was the pitcher of record for both ends of a twin bill against the White Sox.

Baker said he wouldn't make up his mind until after he watched his pitchers warm up prior to the game. But after the warm-ups were done, Baker decided to go with his ace on only one day's rest.

The weather for Game 7 was nearly perfect; a cloudless sky and a high of 67 degrees. It provided an ideal baseball climate once again, but it didn't guarantee a sell-out. As one reporter wrote, there were far more than a few empty seats. It was strange that this deciding World Series game did not attract close to a capacity crowd (in fact, it was the lowest attendance of all seven games), especially since Reds fans had been waiting for more than 20 years to be on the brink of a World Championship. But as the *Enquirer* duly noted, "Though there were plenty of empty seats ... the windows of the factories on the other side of York Street were more than well-filled."

For the 26,000+ who did watch Game 7 from inside Crosley Field, Newsom and Derringer did not disappoint. The two aces, both of whom had posted three consecutive seasons of 20 wins or better, locked into a classic pitcher's duel, pitching like they were supposed to—like their baseball lives were on the line.

A crowded Crosley Field plays host to the world.

If either veteran hurler felt the jitters of a Game 7 start, it didn't show. Derringer set the Tigers down in order in the top half of the first, and Newsom mirrored that performance in the bottom half of the inning. In the second frame, each team recorded their first hit. Though both teams advanced a man to second, the Reds through Jimmie Wilson's unexpected steal, the game remained scoreless.

The Tigers began chipping away in the third. Billy Sullivan led off and hit the ball past first. Frank McCormick knocked it down, but Sullivan beat Derringer to the first base bag. BoBo Newsom sacrificed Sullivan to second, and when Dick Bartell popped to second baseman Eddie Joost, the Tigers had a man on second with two out. The next batter Barney McCosky walked, putting runners on first and second. Tiger second baseman Charlie Gehringer was next in line, and he smashed one to third, where the usually sure-handed Billy Werber stabbed the ball but made a low throw that skipped by Frank McCormick, allowing Sullivan to score from second with the game's first run.

For a long while, it looked like that might be the game's lone run. Both Newsom and Derringer blanked their opponents into the seventh. For Newsom it was 16 consecutive innings that he had held the Reds scoreless. Against the Tigers top pitcher at least, the Reds were — as many of the reporters had taken to calling them — the hitless wonders.[67]

That is, until their bats came alive in the bottom of the seventh. That's when Frank McCormick punched Newsom's first offering into the left field corner to bring the Crosley Field crowd to its feet. The Reds redhead, Jimmy Ripple, rescued by McKechnie from the minor league scrap heap, smacked Newsom's second pitch of the inning to the opposite corner of the park. It bounded off the right field bleacher screen, missing a home run by a couple of feet, sending the crowd into hysterics.

Tigers right fielder Bruce Campbell played the ball off the screen and whipped it back into the infield, but the deafening roar of the crowd prevented cut-off man Dick Bartell from hearing a pleading Pinky Higgins, who called for a relay throw to the plate. As McCormick crossed home to end Newsom's shutout streak and his air of invincibility over the Reds, Ripple took second base. Suddenly, the Reds, who only an inning ago seemed as if they might go home as bridesmaids once again and suffer a second shutout against Newsom in three days, were in position to take the lead.[68]

Catcher Jimmie Wilson, batting .353 for the series, followed the Deacon's direction and laid down a sacrifice to bring Ripple over to third. With weak-hitting Eddie Joost scheduled to bat, McKechnie went to his bench and sent the most powerful man he had on his roster — Ernie Lombardi — up to pinch-hit. As quick as Lombardi left the pine Del Baker was off his bench as well, instructing Newsom to walk the Schnozz. McKechnie countered by sending Lonnie Frey in to pinch-run for Lombardi.

That set the stage for Billy Myers, who was hitting a light .130 for the series. Branded a goat in the prior year's pasting at the hands of the Yankees, Myers stepped in to face Newsom with runners on first and third. He ran the count to three and one. On the fifth pitch of the at-bat, Myers atoned for his sins against the Yankees a year earlier as he connected off Newsom, lifting a tremendous fly deep to center, backing Barney McCosky up against the fence, 385 feet away. McCosky caught the ball, and Ripple tagged at third to score easily, breaking the tension in the most nerve-wracking game of the series, putting the Reds ahead two to one.[69]

As the Reds and Derringer took the field in the eighth, they were ready to face the top of the Tiger lineup — Gehringer, Greenberg, and York. With the crowd still buzzing from the Reds two-run seventh, Gehringer started off the Detroit eighth with a single to right, putting the tying run on first. But before the Tigers could mount a rally, Derringer snuffed any potential threat as Greenberg lined out to Billy Myers. Derringer then got fly outs from York and Campbell to leave the Reds three outs away from their first world championship in 21 years.

In their half of the eighth, the Reds got a runner to first when Mike McCormick beat out a bunt to Pinky Higgins. But the Reds never advanced him to scoring position and went quickly in their half of the eighth. A one run lead. Three outs to go.

The Tigers had sent their most ferocious batters up in the eighth, but Derringer still had to get the three hardest outs of his career to send the city of Cincinnati into a world championship frenzy. Though his faith in Derringer had been rewarded up to this point, McKechnie wasn't taking any chances, and he warmed both Bucky Walters and Joe Beggs in the bullpen, just in case.

He didn't need them. Derringer made it look easy, retiring the first two batters to face him without the ball ever leaving the infield.

As the crowd neared baseball nirvana, Earl Averill was sent to pinch-hit for Newsom. He grounded the ball to Lonnie Frey, who threw on to McCormick for the final out. And then bedlam ensued.

Cushions given to fans at the start of the game were hurled onto the playing field from the upper deck as the championship celebration began. Gene Thompson's wife fainted from the tension and excitement leading to the game's final out and was being revived by fans in between the whoops and hollers of the delirious patrons around her. Jubilation spread like wildfire, beginning on the Crosley Field diamond, gathering strength in its stands and ultimately moving beyond the ballpark, into the far reaches of the city and suburbs.

"Cincinnati," the *Enquirer* reported, "had become a city without reason."

> The civic madness started at Crosley Field a split second after the final out and, spreading like chicken pox in a playground, swept the entire city, from suburb to suburb and city limit to city limit…. Automobile horns, thousands of them, played their sweet symphonies; Factory whistles screamed … thousands of persons just walked around yelling, singing whistling and clapping hands … the traffic was so congested that before a gal could cross the street, her dress was in danger of going out of style.[70]

A paper blizzard fell in the city's financial district, and the celebration extended far into the night as the city's streetcars and automobiles were rerouted out of the Main Street area to give the thousands of fans celebrating in the downtown district "an opportunity to express their exuberance without traffic hazards."[71] By all accounts, it was some party.

The biggest celebration, however, occurred among the Reds themselves. Gene Thompson was first into the dugout, followed by his grinning manager and then a "whooping singing bunch of ballplayers" whose hands ferociously, joyously slapped one another's backs. They hugged,

Ode to Joy. A Game 7 victory celebration on the field that soon spread throughout the city of Cincinnati.

some kissed, and they lofted the Duke and the Deacon up onto their shoulders and paraded them around the locker room — the conquering heroes of the 1940 baseball world. The two men rode in triumph, as a throng of well wishers numbering over 200 crammed into the small quarters to be part of the mayhem.

Detroit Manager Del Baker came into the locker room to congratulate McKechnie. "The best club won, I guess," Baker told the Reds skipper. "If we had to lose, I'm glad we lost to you, Bill; you're a great guy."

McKechnie returned the compliment, saying the hard-fought series was "the best I ever saw in all my experience in baseball. You've got a great team."[72]

Jimmie Wilson kidded about being a helluva base-runner, with his 40-year-old legs copping the only stolen base of the series. Even the injured

Derringer is hoisted on the shoulders of his teammates after the win in Game 7.

Lombardi, who was used sparingly, joked that with enough spring training under his belt Wilson would be quite a catcher.

The clubhouse attendants cleared a path through the sea of well wishers so that Commissioner Landis could congratulate McKechnie, general manager Warren Giles, and team owner Powel Crosley Jr. on the World Championship. Ford Frick, president of the National League, beamed proudly as his league finally snapped the AL's World Series winning streak, capturing the senior circuit's first title in six years.[73]

McKechnie's squad had finally won its championship, just as it had won so many games that championship season with pitching and defense. And like 41 of its 100 victories that year, they had won the championship by a single run.

The reporters left the locker room and wrote through the early evening, analyzing how this team of light-hitting nubbers had managed to become World Champions. In the next day's newspapers, people throughout the Heartland who hadn't been part of it knew exactly how it had been done.

(Left to right), Landis, McKechnie, and Giles after the World Championship.

But for now, as the confetti fell from the downtown buildings and the joyous screams of children and adults filled the streets and yards, it hardly seemed to matter how they managed to do it. They had done it. McKechnie's boys, the Cincinnati Reds, were finally the champions of the world.

10

♦ ♦ ♦ ♦

And Then...

In the moments following the Reds' World Series victory in Game 7, an elevator boy at the *Cincinnati Enquirer,* in classic understatement, said, "My old man's gonna be awful happy about the Reds winning the series."

"So's everyone else," said one of the passengers. "So what?"

"So, my old man's a rag picker," the boy replied. "And all this paper they've thrown into the streets is gonna be like money from home."[1]

In the midst of a city gone wild, the Crosley Field crowd lingered, trying to savor the glow of a World Championship for as long as possible. The sportswriters wrote their articles for the next day's papers to put the games in their proper context one final time for all those who had seen, listened to, or followed the series. Yet despite all the ink and platitudes detailing the exploits of the Reds and Tigers, the young elevator boy's comment proved most prescient. The old order was about to change, both in the world of baseball and the world as a whole. Practicality would soon rule the day as the war in Europe and a new one in the Pacific was about to be brought home.

Baseball would have one more glorious season, marked by two stunning individual achievements, before the bombing at Pearl Harbor plunged America into war. In the summer of 1941, Joe DiMaggio hit safely in 56 consecutive games, collecting a hit in each game he played from May 15 to July 16, replacing Wee Willie Keeler's mark of 44 straight games set in 1897. Similarly, in Boston, Ted Williams set a record of his own. Williams established the standard for hitting excellence in modern baseball, when he hit .400 over the course of an entire season.

Williams's average rose over .400 for the first time on May 25, and he continued on that pace to the All-Star break. On September 27, the next-to-last day of the baseball year, he was hitting .401 and his manager, Joe Cronin, suggested that he sit out the last two games so he could preserve his .400 average. Williams declined. He went one-for-four, dropping his average under the .400 mark to .3995. On the season's final day, Williams went six for eight, raising his average to .406.[2]

The hitting achievements of the Yankee Clipper and Splendid Splinter enthralled baseball fans for much of the summer, but as the Yankees disposed of the Dodgers in the 1941 Series, the world of both America and baseball would never be the same again.

The economy shifted into wartime mode and the United States underwent an industrial revolution that condensed what would more naturally have occurred over a period of months and years into days. America's gross national product increased from $100 billion to over $200 billion, and wages and salaries rose from $50 billion to $120 billion.[3]

President Franklin Roosevelt saw to it that America's game would continue to be played during wartime with his famous Green Light Letter, but baseball, like all sectors of American society, was not exempt from the sacrifices demanded by war. The military draft cut deeply into team rosters, restrictions on fuel consumption forced teams to hold spring training near their home cities instead of in Florida, and during the regular season the number of road trips were also reduced. The level of play dropped significantly, and teams signed over-the-hill players or youngsters (Cincinnati signed 15-year-old Joe Nuxhall, the youngest player to appear in a big league game in 1944) to fill rosters that by 1945 had been decimated by nearly 60 percent.[4]

After the war, baseball was an altogether different game as well. African Americans, who were banned by the Major Leagues and other aspects of society by racial segregation laws, gained new freedoms and were given the opportunity to play baseball in the Major Leagues after Jackie Robinson broke the color barrier in 1947 with the Brooklyn Dodgers. Many of the older players who had gone to war returned to their teams and baseball would again capture the attention of the American public, as postwar prosperity and desegregation provided a new direction for life in the United States.

The War Years and After

The fortunes of the Reds took a new direction as well. It was astonishing, Lee Allen wrote, "the speed with which a world's champion ball club can disintegrate."[5] But that's what the Reds did — disintegrate. In 1941, Cincinnati had no more worlds to conquer and entered into the most challenging period for any champion, the year after they have won it all.

Billy Myers was the first casualty of McKechnie's and Giles's tinkering with the Reds following their rise to the top of the baseball world. Whether it was Myers's disappearing act during the final weeks of September or simply a belief that Eddie Joost would be a better choice at short was something only McKechnie and Giles knew for sure. It was probably a combination of both factors, but in the end it hardly mattered. Myers was gone — dealt to the Cubs for outfielder Jim Gleason, Bobby Mattick, and cash.

The trade helped neither team. Gleason hit .233 and .200 in his two seasons with the Reds and then was out of baseball. By 1942, Billy Myers was also out baseball. The Cubs had optioned Billy to the Milwaukee Brewers of the American Association, where he was paid a $12,000 stipend, believed to be the largest in the minor leagues that year. The following year, rather than accept a large cut in salary, Myers announced his retirement from the game. He made the announcement on February 25, and that night he went to work as an extra fireman on the railroad in Enola.

Myers said the size of the salary cut offered from Chicago was something he couldn't accept. One source put the figure at $4,500. "I'd take less money if I signed [the deal the Cubs offered] than when I broke into the majors," Myers said at the time. Instead, as a fireman, Myers earned between $6.88 and $8.34 for each day he worked.[6]

Other changes were occurring as well and not for the better. Though McKechnie (similar to his work with Vander Meer in 1938 and Gene Thompson in 1939) found another pitching prospect to turn into a phenom in Elmer Riddle, who went 19–4 in 1941, the Reds were headed in the wrong direction. Cincinnati won a respectable 88 games in 1941, but finished third, far out of contention in a two-team race between the Dodgers and Cardinals. Not a single member of the Reds starting lineup hit above .300 for the year. Mike McCormick led the hitters with a .287 average. Frank McCormick fell to .269, and Ernie Lombardi had the poorest season of his career, hitting .264.[7]

In 1942, after playing in the longest consecutive game streak since Lou Gehrig's streak ended, Frank McCormick caught his spikes in the first base bag while making a throw in practice, straining the ligaments in his back. He missed the next game against Pittsburgh, ending the streak at 652 games.[8]

After another monster season in 1944, where he hit .305 with 20 homers and 102 RBIs, his power numbers slipped significantly (10 HR and 81 RBI) and McCormick was sold to the Phillies.[9] He played the 1946 and part of the 1947 season for Philadelphia and then was released. He caught on with the Boston Braves and hit .354 for the remainder of 1947. The following year he was a part-time player with Boston and helped them win the pennant. Ever the iron man, from September 26, 1945, through September 23, Big Frank played 138 consecutive games without an error.

Though McCormick retired from baseball in 1948, he was never far from the game he loved. He managed in the minor leagues, coached, scouted, and was a television broadcaster for the Reds.[10] Eventually, he returned to his native New York, living on Long Island. He was hired by the Yankees in 1975 and worked as the director of group sales. He died of cancer in 1982 at the age of 70 at North Shore University Hospital in Manhasset.[11]

Tragedy After Triumph

The tragedy of Willard Hershberger's suicide cast a pall over the team in 1940, but other family tragedies followed members of the Reds through the years. In the Christmas season of 1941, Eddie Joost's infant son was in the hospital with a rare blood disease. The doctors told the Reds shortstop there was nothing they could do for the baby and that he and his wife could take the child home. The baby was discharged back to the care of his parents and died within a week. Later that year, when the Reds made 32 errors in 18 games during a frightful stretch at the beginning of the 1942 season, 17 of those errors belonged to the heartbroken Joost.

In spring 1942, a similar tragedy befell Reds starter Paul Derringer, who had just arrived in the north to start the season. As he "stepped off the plane, ... they told him his baby was dead back in Florida." Pneumonia was listed as the cause of death, which was all the more shocking to the Reds star because the Duke hadn't even known his child was sick."[12]

Through it all, Bill McKechnie, no stranger to tragedy with the Reds, managed through the individual heartaches and the inevitable slumps they produced. He had a way of touching the human side of those he managed and helped his players as people first and foremost. A perfect example was the case of Ernie Koy.

A new player on the 1941 squad, outfielder Ernie Koy was sold to the Reds by the St. Louis Cardinals in the 1941 season. He experienced the same tragedy that befell Derringer and Joost. Koy's two-year-old son had taken ill on a Friday in September 1941. McKechnie, told of the news during a game, immediately pulled Koy off the field in the middle of an inning, ushering him to the hospital. The boy's condition improved on Saturday but worsened during the night. Tragically, the child died the following morning.

When the outfielder returned to Cincinnati to pick up the pieces and begin play again in spring 1942, Koy and his wife could not stand to see the familiar sights and sounds of the city without their child. He went to McKechnie and begged for a trade. "Trade me Bill," Koy told the Deacon. "Any place but get us away from here."

Though the Deacon wanted to keep Koy, who he said "was a good outfielder" who could have helped the Reds "or a lot of other clubs in this league," McKechnie fulfilled Ernie's request and traded him to the Phillies. The change of scenery didn't help. It was Koy's final season in the Major Leagues.[13]

The Reds had experienced more than their fair share of heartache in the months preceding and following their world title. Yet further tragedy was still to come.

Jimmie Wilson

After the 1940 season, World Series star Jimmie Wilson left the Reds for another chance at managing, this time with the Chicago Cubs. He hit .353 (6 for 17) in the World Series and played in 16 games that final season due to the suicide of Hershberger and the injuries to Lombardi.

Wilson was a tested World Series veteran but, like Lombardi, had been known for a prized boneheaded play in a previous series contest. When Wilson was catching for the St. Louis Cardinals in the 1931 fall classic against Connie Mack's heavily favored Philadelphia Athletics, the Cardinals were ahead two to nothing in the ninth, when the Cards walked two Athletics. With two men on and two out, Cardinals pitcher Bill Hallahan had apparently struck out Jimmie Moore, who fanned on a low, sharp-breaking curve.

Wilson, who was catching, picked the ball out of the dirt and only had to throw the ball to first to complete the strikeout, but he blanked on what to do. When he snapped out of his momentary trance, he inexplicably threw the ball to third instead of first. He was too late to get the lead runner, and the bases were loaded.

Fortunately for Wilson, Max Bishop fouled out to Jim Bottomley to end the contest, preserving the Cardinals victory and saving his bonehead play from costing his team a World Series game.

After it was over, the reporters crowded around Wilson's locker and wanted to know what happened on that strikeout. Why had Wilson not thrown the ball to first base like he was supposed to?

Wilson offered no alibis. "I muffed the play, boys, and that's all there is to it," Wilson told the press corps. "You can call it the biggest blunder ever in a World Series game."[14] It hadn't cost his team a game, so the misplay was hardly the play that defined his career. Plus, thanks to the injury to Lombardi, Wilson had a chance at World Series redemption nearly a decade after his mistake. It was a chance for the eldest member of the Reds to shine, not only on the field but also in the eyes of his now grown son.

"The Busher"

Jimmie Wilson's son, Bob, was too young in 1931 to know about the blunder or about what a stand-up guy his father had been when grilled about the incident. But when he was older, Bob Wilson got a chance to watch his father on baseball's greatest stage.

Jimmie and Bob Wilson had a relationship that was probably no different than that of other fathers and sons. They used to call each other "Busher," a term that Jimmie first used when Bob was a mischievous little boy at his father's spring training camps. "Cut that out, you busher," Jimmie would tell his son when the boy would get into mischief. Gradually, the boy grew to call his father Busher, too, and it became a term of affection between them.

The younger Wilson aspired to be a catcher like his old man, the former Kensington mill worker who was discovered by a scout and left the mill to become a pretty good ballplayer. Jimmie Wilson beamed with a father's pride over his son's athletic success, but he was proudest of the boy's academic accomplishments—especially when his son was accepted at Princeton.

Jimmie told Ed Pollock how grateful he was for what baseball had done for him. It had helped make up for the formal schooling he never had, offered him an opportunity to give his family a comfortable life and his son the education he never had. "A busher from the mill in Kensington with a son at Princeton," he said. "Great ain't it?"[15]

Just as he was a standup guy with the media after his bonehead play in the 1931 World Series, Jimmie Wilson stood up again when he was a coach on Bill McKechnie's squad. McKechnie was lost as to what to do with a shortage behind the plate. It was a past-his-prime Wilson who volunteered to go on the active list.

"What'll we do?" McKechnie asked of his coach, not expecting that the 40-year-old Wilson would respond the way he did.

"I'll handle the job," Jimmie told the Deacon. "You call the managerial shots and I'll do the catching. And please Bill don't worry about [me]. It'll be my last shot but I'll give it a whirl."[16]

Though he volunteered for the assignment, he knew it wouldn't be easy. Wilson knew his body and he knew his legs were gone. "If I had your legs, Busher," he told his son, "I'd be okay."

Wilson was "forty years old, aching in every muscle, taped from stern to stem." He had helped inspire the Reds to the pennant, and now he was going to have to handle the bulk of the catching in the World's Series to help the Reds win the championship.[17]

Luckily for the Reds, Wilson saved his best for last. His .350 plus average in 17 at bats against Detroit was certainly impressive. But perhaps his most astonishing feat was swiping second base on those 40-year-old creaky legs in the series finale. It was the only stolen base of the fall classic.

After he had stolen the base, before the game ended, he was handed a telegram on the bench that read: "Why do you want my legs?" It was signed "Busher."[18]

Following the Reds championship win, Jimmie "Old Man" Wilson was given another chance to manage a big league club. After five years in purgatory at the helm of the Phillies and the two seasons he spent coaching championship clubs in Cincinnati, the Chicago Cubs wanted Wilson to be their new manager.

At first, Wilson resisted. He was happy in Cincinnati and got along famously with McKechnie. But Cubs owner P. K. Wrigley wouldn't take no for an answer, and Wilson weakened to the "write your own contract" offer the Cubs presented. He should have stuck to his original position and declined the job as Cubs field general. But after a while, the generosity of the offer and the lure of being a manager took over and he welcomed the opportunity to lead a team once again.

He didn't fare much better in Chicago than he had in Philadelphia, managing the Cubs to no higher than a fifth place finish during his four years there.[19] Though his teams were never great, Wilson was something less as a manager than he was as a player. A former player on his Phillie teams, Dick Bartell, even claimed that Wilson was "the worst manager I ever played for. I liked and respected him as a player, but not as a manager. He was like a wild man, just couldn't handle the players. He was on my back all the time no matter what I did."[20]

By 1944, tired of all the losing, Wilson suggested that the Cubs release him. After his team lost 10 games in a row, the Cubs took Jimmie's advice and fired him. He went back to coaching with his old friend Bill McKechnie in Cincinnati.

Ironically, just as Wilson's managing dreams came to an end, his son, the little busher, a promising ballplayer in his own right, had to put his baseball dreams on hold. Bob Wilson had enlisted in the Army Air Corps and was waiting for the call to active duty. Like his father, whose nickname was Ace, young Bob turned out to be an ace on his own merits—as an Air Corps pilot.

Bob Wilson's call to active duty came, and shortly after he arrived in India, his commanding officer asked for volunteers to go on a particularly dangerous mission. Like his old man, Bob Wilson did not hesitate. He stood up and volunteered to do what needed to be done.

Shortly thereafter, his father, coaching in his second go-round with the Reds, received the wire from Washington that said his son had been killed in the line of duty. The news absolutely devastated him. It was said that Jimmie was a man who loved life and enjoyed it more than anyone, but after his son died, the light went out of his eyes.[21]

The Philadelphia Sportswriters named Lieutenant Robert Wilson their most courageous athlete in 1944. Writer Ed Pollock recalled:

It was given posthumously to him and to all American athletes who had sacrificed their lives for their country during the war. We wanted Jimmie Wilson to have the plaque and I telephoned him at his home in Florida to ask if he would receive it in person. There was a long pause after I had told him why I called. "Thanks," he said finally. "Thanks a million ... but I can't do it ... I just ... can't take it."[22]

Though he returned as coach of Cincinnati, his heart was no longer in it. When McKechnie was dismissed at the end of the 1946 season, Wilson retired from the game to Florida. The following year, he died of a heart attack. He was 46 years old.

It was said of Jimmie Wilson that no one enjoyed life more than he did. He was never the same after his son was killed in World War II. The former Cincinnati catcher died of a heart attack at age 46.

Tragedy and heartache were not solely reserved for the players and their children. In addition to Lombardi's failed suicide attempt in 1953, Hershberger's friend Dan Cohen, who had found his lifeless body in the Copley Hotel in Boston after McKechnie had asked him to go and bring Hershberger to the field, also committed suicide in 1961.[23] Eerily, there were four suicides or attempted suicides of those somehow connected to the team — there was Hershberger, his father Claude before him, Lombardi (who survived), and finally Cohen.

As for Hershberger, his mother, Maude, collapsed in the Three Rivers, California, post office where she worked on hearing that her son, like her husband before him, had taken his own life. She eventually recovered from the news and after the Reds won the title, she was voted a winner's share of the World Series money by the team, $5,803.62. Maude Hershberger died seven years later.

The Reds, who had retired Hershberger's number five for the remainder of the 1940 season,[24] gave the number to Dick West the following year. The number was later permanently retired in 1984 in honor of Reds Hall of Fame catcher Johnny Bench.

Moving On

By 1942, Ernie Lombardi was sold to the Boston Braves and Billy Werber to the New York Giants. In the last year of the war, 1945, the team the Reds put on the field hardly resembled the championship squad it had been only five years earlier. Only Mike McCormick, Lonnie Frey, Johnny Vander Meer, Gene Thompson and Joe Beggs still wore the Reds uniform.

Eddie Joost, who had taken over the shortstop duties when Billy Myers was traded, was traded himself following the 1942 season, dealt to the Boston Braves along with pitcher Nate Andrews for Eddie Miller and $25,000.[25] It was the beginning of a second career for Joost though he could hardly tell from that first season in Boston.

"I was terrible in Boston," Joost freely admitted about his subpar play and anemic .185 average with the Braves in 1943. Rather than being on the verge of a personal renaissance in the game he loved, at first glance it looked as if Eddie Joost was through. He had fallen so far that he voluntarily retired from the game and spent the 1944 season working at a job in a meat-packing plant.[26]

After receiving a deferment from the draft in 1945, Joost came back to the Braves that season. He broke his wrist in a game, and though Joost said he was told by the team to return to his home in California, once he did, the team suspended him for leaving without permission. After futile attempts to straighten out the matter with Boston GM John Quinn and an appeal to Commissioner Landis, Eddie was eventually assigned to Rochester in 1946. He hit .276 and knocked in 101 runs. Philadelphia A's president Connie Mack took notice of Joost's play and for $15,000 and two players made him a member of the Philadelphia Athletics in 1947.[27]

Joost played for Philadelphia for the next eight seasons, including one as a player-manager, before his swan song with the Red Sox in 1955. He was named an all-star on two occasions in 1949 and 1952. The 1949 campaign was his best. Eddie hit .263, smacked 23 home runs, knocked in 81 runs, and had an on-base percentage of .429. On top of that, he helped turn 217 double plays. It was a season that still ranks among the best ever for a Major League shortstop.[28] He was a utility man no longer.

Bucky and the Duke

The two players who had so much to do with the team's rise from the second division to World Champions, the pitching tandem on which those Reds teams were built — Paul Derringer and Bucky Walters— began to wear down as the championship season passed further into history. For Derringer, the 1940 season was one of his last winning seasons as a big league pitcher. The Reds sold the Duke to the Cubs in 1943 after two successive losing seasons of 12–14 and 10–11. He had lost much of the velocity from his fastball and went 10–14, and 7–13 for Chicago, before posting a final winning tally, at the age of 38, going 16–11 and pitching 213 innings in 1945.

Derringer also managed to play in one final fall classic, pitching in relief in three games of the 1945 World Series against the Tigers. The Cubs lost that series to the Tigers, and Derringer was given his unconditional release following the season. The Duke pitched one more season for Indianapolis of the American Association and then retired from the game for good.

His post baseball life included jobs in real estate, life insurance, chemicals, a plastics company, and the electric sign business. His sign business failed in 1961, and Derringer fell on hard times. He relocated to Florida, by which time his weight swelled to 316 pounds and he barely resembled his former self.[29] He married three times, underwent surgery for prostate cancer, and recovered. By 1985, he had undergone various surgeries to replace knee and hip joints, and it was found that his cancer had reoccurred and spread to his lungs and his abdomen. A fighter all his life, the Duke lost his battle with cancer when he died one month after his eighty-first birthday.

Following the 1940 season, Derringer's mound-mate, Bucky Walters,

Bucky Walters won the MVP in 1939 and broke a World Series losing streak of five consecutive losses when he won Game 2 of the 1940 World Series. A former third baseman, Walters finished his career with 198 victories. He often joked that his two victories in the 1940 series made him "a 200-game winner."

had one more very good season and another truly dominant year in his career. In 1941, Bucky went 19–15, leading the National League with 27 complete games and 302 innings, a true workhorse. In 1944, he posted numbers reminiscent of his MVP year, going 23–8, pitching 285 innings with a 2.40 ERA. His last year with the Reds was 1948, when he was a player-manager. He managed the team and remained on its active roster to see if he could get two additional wins to give him 200 for his career. He never achieved that milestone, nor was he successful as a big league skipper.

He managed the Reds to a seventh-place finish that year and again in 1949. He was fired at the end of the second season, bringing an end to a brief managerial career, where he went 81–123.[30] Walters saw action in one game for the Braves in 1950, pitching four innings when he served as a coach for the franchise. Later, he also coached the New York Giants, from 1956–57, but left the game after they moved west because he did not like the travel.[31]

For a short time he worked in public relations for a custom machine company in his native Philadelphia.[32] The six-time All-Star died in 1991 at Abington Memorial Hospital in Pennsylvania in 1991 at the age of 82.

Bill and Warren and the Hall of Fame

After he left the Reds, McKechnie coached briefly with the Indians and then retired from baseball.

At the time of his departure from the Cincinnati dugout, Bill McKechnie had managed the Reds for longer than any other man — nine years. His ouster was forced by the fans, or so it was said, who had grown tired of McKechnie's old-fashioned style of managing. The defense and pitching that had won two pennants and one world championship in Cincinnati had grown stale to the fans who wanted more excitement. When GM Warren Giles let McKechnie go, he said bitterly, "Those fans just forced me to fire the best manager in baseball."

After his dismissal by the Reds, the Deacon was immediately hired to "assist" Lou Boudreau, the young player-manager of the Cleveland Indians.[33] He coached with Cleveland from 1947–49. In McKechnie's second year as a coach, the Indians won the pennant — an anomaly in a period of Yankee dominance in the American League. He moved on to one final stop, when he finished as a coach with the Red Sox from 1952–53.

Well off financially, having made smart investments in oil land and Florida citrus groves, Bill McKechnie retired to Bradenton, Florida, the following year. In his later years, his hair turned white, his features sharpened, and his already large ears seemed to grow even larger.[34] In 1962, he was elected to the National Baseball Hall of Fame. In his induction speech, he grew emotional, wiped his eyes, and said, "Anything that I have contributed to baseball, I have been repaid today seven times seven."

In the final analysis, McKechnie was a player's manager who got the best out of those who played for him with a kind word and encouragement. Sometimes the kindest thing he said was when he said nothing at all. He had accomplished much as a manager, and with the Hershberger episode, he had been tested like no other manager in baseball history and still managed to come out a winner.

He had said at the time of Hershberger's death that the night before the young catcher took his own life, Hershberger had told him what his problems were, that it was said in confidence, had nothing to do with anyone on the team and was "personal." "I will not utter it to anyone," the Deacon told reporters at the time. "I will take it with me to my grave."

Bill McKechnie died in October 1965, at his home in Bradenton, Florida, 20 years after that championship season. Though he was sometimes asked, the Deacon never told a soul about what he and Hershberger discussed. He protected Hershberger's confidence for more than 20 years after his former player's death.[35] It was as good an example as any of the kind of man he was.

For most of the Reds, being a part of a championship team was the pinnacle of their careers. For many who were associated with the team, it overshadowed all of the other accomplishments in their lives. Of the players themselves, it can be said that following their Reds careers Billy Werber, who became a millionaire, was the most successful from a financial perspective. In terms of accomplishments on the field, only Eddie Joost had a better playing career once he left Cincinnati than he ever had in a Reds uniform. For the rest of the team, 1940 remained the high point. Everything that came after paled by comparison.

However, the same could not be said so unequivocally for the man in the front office. Separate and apart from his years in Cincinnati, the Reds general manager Warren Giles left a lasting mark on the game as president of the National League that was far greater than what he accomplished for the Reds.

He almost became commissioner of Baseball in 1952, but he withdrew his name after a deadlock between him and Ford Frick (then National League president), the eventual commissioner, went to 17 ballots and needed to be broken. After Frick was named commissioner, Giles, in large part due to his magnanimous gesture, was appointed NL president. During his tenure as the senior circuit's top executive, Giles oversaw the move of the Giants and Dodgers to the West Coast — opening the Major Leagues to the entire country; approved expansion for new franchises in New York (the Mets) and Houston (baseball's first indoor stadium and the advent of Astroturf); and established Major League baseball outside the United States for the first time in Montreal. He was elected to the Baseball Hall of Fame posthumously, barely one month after he died in 1979 for his 50 years of service to the game.

For all that he did for baseball, and all the impact he had in expanding it and helping the National League grow, Giles wrote in a 1975 letter, long after he retired to become a fan again, that his greatest moment in baseball was in 1940. "I think the highlight of my satisfaction during my 50 years in baseball," Giles wrote, "was winning the World Championship in the Seventh Game of the World Series against Detroit in 1940 when I was General Manager of the Reds."[36]

Though he didn't say it in the letter, he could have added that he spoke for every member of that team.

Appendix A:
Where They
Played the Game:
Crosley Field

The boomerang at Western and Findlay streets had been a site for baseball games in Cincinnati since 1884 when it was known as the Cincinnati Base Ball Grounds and served as the host park of the American Association's Reds through 1889. The ballpark endured several incarnations from that date until its closing in 1970, but essentially what writer Lee Allen called the "history of baseball's cradle," hosted baseball games for 86 years in virtually the same location.

The stadiums that were built on that location in the angled streets of Cincinnati's West End were known as League Park (when it became a National League park), the Palace of the Fans (1902–1911) and Redland Field (1912–34). The name was changed to Crosley Field in 1934 and held that name until the Reds left for Riverfront Stadium midway through the 1970 campaign.

After the wooden Palace of the Fans burned down in 1911, Reds president August "Garry" Hermann was determined to bring Cincinnati's ball park into the modern era, and he replaced it with a concrete and steel design. For a cost of $225,000, Harry Hake was commissioned to build the new structure, and he subsequently made all of the additions and improvements to the park over the course of the next 40 years.

Hermann said Redland Field attracted "the wholesome and ordinary person. It evoked an America of fishing holes and masonic Lodges and strawberry socials. It was perfect for our town," he said. And so it was.

One of the charms of the park was that it had a clubhouse for home

Crosley Field, the home of the Cincinnati Reds.

and visiting players. "In most cities," Lee Allen said, "visiting players rode trolleys or buses to get to the game. They'd be heckled, taunted. In Cincinnati they dressed at the park." By extension, dressing in the clubhouse allowed visiting players to avoid the abuse of the more zealous hometown fans—at least until game time.

The capacity at Crosley Field rarely rose above 30,000 through all its variations, and during its last 10 years (1960–70), its maximum was 29,603.[7] One writer said that "partly because of [Crosley's] size, there are really no bad seats; only sun area is Sun Deck bleachers [called Moon Deck for night games]. Ticket prices are below average and ushers are efficient and polite.... Refreshment stands are adequate, prices reasonable, food good."[8]

So cozy was the atmosphere that back when it was still known as Redland Field," hardly anyone wanted to leave, including the ball. The park, whose original dimensions of 360 feet down each line and 420 feet to centerfield, was a pitcher's best friend. It took nine years before a ball actually left the stadium after the new steel and concrete construction was complete. Pat Duncan finally knocked one out, going beyond left field in 1921.[9]

By 1939, the ballpark's measurements were adjusted. The upper decks were extended into both corners, the plate was moved out another 20 feet, and the field was 328 feet to left, 387 to center, and 366 into the rightfield corner. Those measurements held for the championship season of 1940 as well.[10] On special occasions, such as opening day, which was akin to a national holiday in Cincinnati, the Reds put temporary stands on the left field terrace, even after the concrete stands were built.[11]

Famed for the inclined terrace in front of the left field wall and the Superior Towel and Linen Service, located behind left field, which had a large advertising sign that encouraged hitters to "Hit This and Win a Siebler Suit," Crosley Field played host to a number of historic feats.

Some were more glorious than others. One of the more inglorious events involved the naturally occurring inclined terrace (a deformity caused by an underground stream, as opposed to the purposeful throwback in Houston's Minute Maid Ballpark) and the great Babe Ruth who was playing out his career with the Boston Braves. The incline, which started 20 feet in front of the left field fence, gradually sloped upward, forming what was in essence a little hill in the outfield. Ruth, whose legs weren't what they had been, tripped when he was chasing down a fly. Embarrassed, he got up and walked off the field and said he would not return. True to his word, it was the last game the Bambino ever played.[12]

In 1929, the first radio broadcast of Major League baseball was made from Redland Field, a significant milestone because many of the owners of Major League clubs (erroneously) believed that people would stay home and listen to games rather than come out to the ballpark.[13] Radio broadcasts and of course later television broadcasts eventually became common.

Though the field was achieving its fair share of notoriety, all was not well with the team, and by 1933, Sid Weil, the team's owner, lost the club to bankruptcy. The bank hired Lee MacPhail to run the team, and MacPhail sold a majority interest in the club to Powel Crosley, a radio, refrigerator, and automobile manufacturer. Crosley named Lee MacPhail as his general manager, renamed Redland Field for himself, and allowed MacPhail to hire the legendary Red Barber as the team's radio voice for the 500,000 watt station WLW.[14]

The newly renamed Crosley Field played host to the first night game in 1935 when President Franklin Roosevelt threw a switch in the White House that lit the ballpark and night baseball was born. It had actually been born years earlier in 1909 when George Cahill erected five steel towers and strung lights for a game between the Elks Lodge of Cincinnati versus Newport, Kentucky, at Redland. Garry Herrman said of the event, "Night baseball had come to stay." Twenty-four years later, he was right. During that first season, night games were limited by agreement to seven

Powel Crosley, Jr., became owner of the Reds and hired Warren Giles to run the baseball operations. He renamed the park at Western and Findlay Street Crosley Field.

per season, one game against each of the National League clubs, so no club could claim it was unfairly penalized for having to play more games under the lights.

Later in 1935, the first woman to bat in a Major League game stepped up to the plate at Crosley Field. The St. Louis Cardinals were in town for the next-to-last night game of the season, and Lee Allen wrote that "the place was packed with people who came by train from Kentucky and Tennessee." Due to the overwhelming crowd, people spilled onto the field with ropes separating them from the fielders. A woman named Kitty Burke was not content to stay behind the ropes and as Reds GM Warren Giles recalled, she "rushed on the field, grabs Babe Herman's bat, and tells Paul Dean to pitch." He did and she grounded out.[15]

Two years later, the great Mill Creek flood submerged the entire field under water, so that the only thing visible from aerial photos was the roof of the stadium and the light towers. Two players got in a rowboat and paddled over the center field wall as wire service photographers captured the event for posterity.[16]

Crosley played host to the first of Vander Meer's back-to-back no-hitters, an All Star game in 1938 and also, during the 1940 season, actually cause of the Reds to lose a game against the Dodgers, when night game preparations weren't properly adjusted for a day game the following day.

What happened was that Powell Crosley had a canvas shield built behind Crosley's center field wall to protect batters' eyes from the street lights during night games. The canvas was traditionally taken down during the day, except for one game against Brooklyn. As it turned out, during the game against the Dodgers, Harry Craft hit the ball to the canvas in the ninth. The umpires ruled it a ground rule double as McKechnie fumed that it should have been a home run. But the umps' ruling held — reasoning that it was Cincinnati's park and Cincinnati's mistake. Craft didn't score, and Brooklyn won the game in extra innings.[17]

In addition to championship baseball on the field, Reds fans also thrilled to the antics of superfan Harry Thobe,[18] who dressed in a white suit with red stripes and wore one red shoe and one white one along with a straw hat with a red band and white parasol. He cheered the Reds on with impromptu Irish jigs and "12 gold teeth,"[19] and was as much a fixture at Crosley Field in the 1940s as the famed Siebler Suit sign.

Of all the historic moments, the most important moment for the Reds was undoubtedly Game 7 in 1940, the Reds World Series clinching victory. Though Crosley hosted another World Series (in 1961) and saw the emergence of the Big Red Machine in 1969–70, Cincinnati left Crosley Field midway through the 1970 season for Riverfront Stadium, the new cookie-cutter home of what would be the Reds' most dominant and legendary teams.

On the Reds' departure from the location on Findlay and Western Street, the city purchased Crosley Field from the club and for a while used it as a pound for illegally parked cars. Later the park, like many of the old ballparks, was torn down.

Appendix B:
The 1940 Cincinnati Reds
Game by Game

Date	Opponent	Result	Starter	Opposing Starter
April 16	v. CHI	W 2–1	Derringer	Lee
April 18	v. CHI	W 2–1	Thompson	Passeau
April 22	v. STL	W 6–1	Walters	McGee
April 25	@ CHI	L 2–4	Derringer	Dean
April 26	@ CHI	L 2–6	Thompson	Passeau
April 27	v. PIT	W 3–0	Walters	Bowman
April 28	v. PIT	W 8–2	Thompson	MacFayden
April 29	v. PIT	W 3–2	Derringer	Butcher
April 30	v. BRO	L 0–3	Turner	Carleton
May 1	v. BRO	W 9–2	Walters	Casey
May 4	v. PHI	W 3–2	Derringer	Higbe
May 5	v. NY	W 3–2	Walters	Schumacher
May 6	v. NY	W 9–1	Thompson	Gumbert
May 7	v. NY	W 7–6	Turner	Lohrman
May 8	v. BOS	L 4–10	Derringer	Posedel
May 9	v. BOS	W 4–1	Walters	Sullivan
May 11	@ STL	W 12–5	Thompson	Lanier
May 12 (1)	@ STL	W 7–1	Derringer	McGee
May 12 (2)	@ STL	W 13–4	Turner	Warneke
May 13	v. STL	T 8–8	Vander Meer	Cooper
May 14	@ BRO	L 5–6	Walters	Carleton
May 15	@ BRO	W 5–2	Thompson	Wyatt
May 17	@ PHI	W 7–2	Turner	Beck
May 18	@ PHI	L 3–8	Derringer	Mulcahy
May 19	@ BOS	W 8–4	Walters	Strincevich
May 20	@ BOS	L 4–13	Thompson	Errickson
May 22	@ NY	L 4–6	Derringer	Hubbell
May 25 (1)	v. STL	W 7–2	Walters	Warneke

Date	Opponent	Result	Starter	Opposing Starter
May 25 (2)	v. STL	L 1–5	Thompson	McGee
May 26	v. STL	W 4–0	Derringer	Cooper
May 27 (1)	@ PIT	W 2–1	Moore	Brown
May 27 (2)	@ PIT	W 7–3	Turner	Bauers
May 28	@ PIT	L 2–5	Thompson	Butcher
May 29	@ PIT	W 4–0	Walters	Bowman
May 30 (1)	@ CHI	W 4–2	Derringer	Lee
May 30 (2)	@ CHI	W 9–8	Moore	Root
June 1	v. BOS	W 3–2	Thompson	Posedel
June 2 (1)	v. BOS	W 11–1	Walters	Piechota
June 2 (2)	v. BOS	L 0–2	Turner	Errickson
June 3	v. BOS	W 3–2	Derringer	Sullivan
June 4	v. NY	L 4–5	Moore	Hubbell
June 5	v. NY	W 7–2	Thompson	Gumbert
June 7	v. BRO	L 2–4	Walters	Pressnell
June 8	v. BRO	W 23–2	Derringer	Fitzsimmons
June 9 (1)	v. BRO	L 1–9	Turner	Carleton
June 9 (2)	v. BRO	W 6–2	Thompson	Wyatt
June 11	v. PHI	L 1–4	Walters	Beck
June 12	v. PHI	W 2–1	Derringer	Higbe
June 14	@. BRO	L 0–2	Thompson	Hamlin
June 15	@ BRO	L 6–11	Walters	Carleton
June 16 (1)	@ BRO	W 1–0	Derringer	Wyatt
June 16 (2)	@ BRO	W 5–2	Turner	Davis
June 17	@ PHI	W 6–2	Vander Meer	Beck
June 18	@ PHI	L 1–3	Walters	Mulcahy
June 20	@ PHI	L 3–4	Thompson	Higbe
June 21	@ NY	L 3–4	Derringer	Gumbert
June 22	@ NY	W 3–1	Turner	Lohrman
June 23 (1)	@ NY	W 7–4	Walters	Hubbell
June 23 (2)	@ NY	W 2–0	Thompson	Dean
June 28	v. CHI	L 2–3	Derringer	Mooty
June 29	v. CHI	W 4–1	Turner	Passeau
June 30 (1)	v. CHI	W 7–4	Walters	French
June 30 (2)	v. CHI	W 7–6	Thompson	Root
July 1	@ STL	L 2–3	Moore	Warneke
July 2	@ STL	L 0–4	Derringer	McGee
July 4 (1)	v. PIT	W 9–1	Walters	Klinger
July 4 (2)	v. PIT	W 3–1	Thompson	Butcher
July 5	v. PIT	W 5–4	Turner	MacFayden
July 6	@ CHI	W 4–0	Derringer	Mooty
July 7	@ CHI	W 4–3	Hutchings	Lee
July 11	v. BRO	W 6–5	Walters	Wyatt
July 13 (1)	v. BRO	W 7–6	Derringer	Carleton
July 13 (2)	v. BRO	L 1–3	Thompson	Davis
July 14 (1)	v. PHI	W 3–2	Turner	Higbe
July14 (2)	v. PHI	W 7–1	Moore	Beck
July 15	v. PHI	W 3–2	Walters	Pearson

Date	Opponent	Result	Starter	Opposing Starter
July 17	v. BOS	W 4–3	Derringer	Salvo
July19	v. BOS	L 7–8	Thompson	Sullivan
July 20	v. NY	W 5–1	Walters	Lohrman
July 21(1)	v. NY	W 6–1	Derringer	Hudlin
July 21(2)	v. NY	W 4–2	Turner	Gumbert
July 23 (1)	@ BRO	W 4–3	Thompson	Wyatt
July 23 (2)	@ BRO	W 9–2	Moore	Davis
July 24	@ BRO	W 6–3	Walters	Carleton
July 26	@ PHI	W 9–5	Derringer	Higbe
July 27	@ PHI	L 3–5	Moore	Mulcahy
July 28 (1)	@ PHI	W 7–2	Turner	Beck
July 28 (2)	@ PHI	L 1–4	Walters	Blanton
July 29	@ NY	L 3–4	Hutchings	Hubbell
July 30	@ NY	W 6–3	Derringer	Schumacher
July 31	@ NY	L 4–5	Walters	Lohrman
August 2 (1)	@ BOS	L 3–10	Turner	Strincevich
August 2 (2)	@ BOS	L 3–4	Moore	Salvo
August 3 (1)	@ BOS	W 3–1	Derringer	Posedel
August 3 (2)	@ BOS	L 2–5	Hutchings	Piechota
August 4 (1)	@ BOS	L 3–5	Walters	Errickson
August 4 (2)	@ BOS	W 12–9	Beggs	Tobin
August 7	v. CHI	L 3–5	Derringer	Lee
August 8	v. CHI	W 3–1	Walters	French
August 9	v. STL	W 7–2	Thompson	McGee
August 10	v. STL	W 5–0	Moore	Bowman
August 11 (1)	v. STL	L 2–3	Derringer	Cooper
August 11 (2)	v. STL	L 1–3	Turner	Warneke
August 12	@ PIT	L 2–4	Walters	Butcher
August 13	@ PIT	W 4–3	Thompson	Bowman
August 15	@ CHI	L 0–1	Derringer	Passeau
August 16 (1)	@ CHI	W 9–4	Moore	Olsen
August 16 (2)	@ CHI	W 6–3	Thompson	Lee
August 18 (1)	@ STL	L 1–3	Walters	Cooper
August 18 (2)	@ STL	L 4–5	Turner	Doyle
August 19	v. NY	L 2–9	Derringer	Hubbell
August 20	v. NY	W 3–2	Thompson	Lohrman
August 21	v. NY	L 4–5	Moore	Schumacher
August 22	v. BOS	W 3–2	Walters	Strincevich
August 23	v. BOS	L 2–7	Derringer	Tobin
August 24	v. BOS	W 5–0	Thompson	Errickson
August 25 (1)	v. PHI	W 3–2	Turner	Beck
August 25 (2)	v. PHI	W 6–5	Moore	Mulcahy
August 26 (1)	v. PHI	W 3–2	Walters	Smoll
August 26 (2)	v. PHI	L 1–6	Moore	Johnson
August 29	v. BRO	W 9–3	Derringer	Wyatt
August 30	v. BRO	L 2–6	Thompson	Hamlin
August 31	v. CHI	W 5–4	Walters	Passeau
September 1(1)	v. CHI	W 6–5	Turner	Lee

Date	Opponent	Result	Starter	Opposing Starter
September 1 (2)	v CHI	W 2–1	Moore	French
September 2 (1)	v. STL	W 2–1	Derringer	Cooper
September 2 (2)	v. STL	L 4–7	Thompson	Warneke
September 3	v. STL	W 4–3	Hutchings	McGee
September 4	v. PIT	W 3–2	Walters	Butcher
September 5	v. PIT	W 6–3	Vander Meer	Lanning
September 7	@ CHI	W 7–6	Derringer	Root
September 8	@ CHI	L 1–3	Turner	Olsen
September 11 (1)	@ BOS	W 8–0	Walters	Salvo
September 11 (2)	@ BOS	W 3–1	Derringer	Strincevich
September 12	@ NY	W 9–4	Thompson	Lohrman
September 13	@ NY	W 5–2	Vander Meer	Hubbell
September 14	@ NY	W 3–2	Turner	Schumacher
September 15 (1)	@ BRO	W 13–3	Walters	Davis
September 15 (2)	@ BRO	T 1–1	Derringer	Hamlin
September 16	@ BRO	W 4–3	Thompson	Davis
September 17	@ PHI	W 2–1	Moore	Higbe
September 18	@ PHI	W 4–3	Vander Meer	Mulcahy
September 19	@ PHI	W 4–1	Derringer	Podgajny
September 21(1)	@ PIT	W 8–1	Walters	Butcher
September 21 (2)	@ PIT	L 7–8	Thompson	Dietz
September 22 (1)	@ PIT	W 2–1	Turner	Swigart
September 22 (2)	@ PIT	L 1–8	Vander Meer	Lanning
September 23	@ PIT	L 9–12	Derringer	Bowman
September 25 (1)	@ STL	W 5–0	Thompson	McGee
September 25 (2)	@ STL	L 3–4	Walters	Hutchinson
September 26 (1)	@ STL	W 4–3	Vander Meer	Doyle
September 26 (2)	@ STL	L 1–5	Riddle	Kimball
September 27	v. PIT	L 3–4	Derringer	Swigart
September 28	v. PIT	W 6–5	Turner	Dietz
September 29	v. PIT	W 11–3	Walters	Rambert

Appendix C:
Final Major League
Standings, 1940

National League

Team	GP	W	L	PCT.	GB	RS	RA
Cincinnati Reds	155	100	53	.653	—	707	528
Brooklyn Dodgers	156	88	65	.575	12.0	697	621
St. Louis Cardinals	156	84	69	.549	16.0	747	699
Pittsburgh Pirates	156	78	76	.506	22.5	809	783
Chicago Cubs	154	75	79	.487	25.5	681	636
New York Giants	152	72	80	.473	27.5	663	659
Boston Bees	152	65	87	.427	34.5	623	745
Philadelphia Phillies	153	50	103	.326	50.0	494	750

American League

Team	GP	W	L	PCT	GB	RS	RA
Detroit Tigers	155	90	64	.584	—	888	717
Cleveland Indians	155	89	65	.577	1.0	710	637
New York Yankees	155	88	66	.571	2.0	817	671
Boston Red Sox	154	82	72	.532	8.0	872	825
Chicago White Sox	155	82	72	.532	8.0	735	672
St. Louis Browns	156	67	87	.435	23.0	757	882
Washington Senators	154	64	90	.415	26.0	665	811
Philadelphia Athletics	154	54	100	.350	36.0	703	932

Appendix D:
Cincinnati Reds Final
Batting Statistics, 1940

Player	G	AB	R	H	2B	3B	HR	RBI	BB	SO	BA	OBP
Ernie Lombardi	109	376	50	120	22	0	14	74	31	141	.319	.382
Frank McCormick	155	618	93	191	44	3	19	127	52	26	.309	.367
Lonny Frey	150	563	102	150	23	6	8	54	80	48	.266	.361
Billy Werber	143	584	105	162	35	5	12	48	68	40	.277	.361
Billy Myers	90	282	33	57	14	2	5	30	30	56	.202	.283
Ival Goodman	136	519	78	134	20	6	12	63	60	54	.258	.335
Harry Craft	115	422	47	103	18	5	6	48	17	46	.244	.277
Mick McCormick	110	417	48	125	20	0	1	30	13	36	.300	.326
Eddie Joost	88	278	24	60	7	2	1	24	32	40	.216	.301
Morrie Arnovich	62	211	17	60	10	2	0	21	13	10	.284	.326
Willard Hershberger	48	123	6	38	4	2	0	26	6	6	.309	.351
Johnny Rizzo	31	110	17	31	6	0	4	17	14	14	.282	.363
Jimmy Ripple	32	101	15	31	10	0	4	20	13	5	.307	.397
Lew Riggs	41	72	8	21	7	1	1	9	2	4	.292	.311
Bill Baker	27	69	5	15	1	1	0	7	4	8	.217	.260
Lee Gamble	38	42	12	6	1	0	0	0	0	1	.143	.143
Jimmie Wilson	16	37	2	9	2	0	0	3	2	1	.243	.282
Dick West	7	28	4	11	2	0	1	6	0	2	.393	.393
Mike Dejan	12	16	1	3	0	1	0	2	3	3	.187	.316
Vince DiMaggio	2	4	2	1	0	0	0	0	1	0	.250	.400
Wally Berger	2	2	0	0	0	0	0	0	0	1	.000	.000

Appendix E: Cincinnati Reds Team Pitching, 1940

Player	G	ERA	W	L	SV	GS	GF	CG	SHO	IP	H	R
Paul Derringer	37	3.06	20	12	0	37	0	26	3	296.7	280	110
Bucky Walters	36	2.48	22	10	0	36	0	29	3	305.0	241	95
Junior Thompson	33	3.32	16	9	0	31	1	17	3	225.3	197	90
Jim Turner	24	2.89	14	7	0	23	1	11	0	187.0	187	70
Whitey Moore	25	3.63	8	8	1	15	7	5	1	116.7	100	48
Joe Beggs	37	2.00	12	3	7	1	27	0	0	76.7	68	19
Milt Shoffner	20	5.63	1	0	0	0	5	0	0	54.3	56	35
Johnny Hutchings	19	3.50	2	1	0	4	9	0	0	54.0	53	21
Elmer Riddle	15	1.87	1	2	2	1	12	1	0	33.7	30	12
Johnny Vander Meer	10	3.75	3	1	1	7	2	2	0	48.0	38	24
Lefty Guise	2	1.17	0	0	0	0	0	0	0	7.7	8	2
Red Barrett	3	6.75	1	0	0	0	0	0	0	2.7	5	2

Appendix F:
1940 World Series
Line Scores

Game 1, Wednesday, October 2, at Crosley Field, Cincinnati

	1	2	3	4	5	6	7	8	9	R	H	E
Detroit Tigers	0	5	0	0	2	0	0	0	0	7	10	1
Cincinnati Reds	0	0	0	1	0	0	0	1	0	2	8	3

Pitchers Det **Bobo Newsom** (W, 1–0), IP 9, H 8, R 2, ER 2, BB 1, SO 4.
           Cin **Paul Derringer** (L, 0–1), IP 1 1/3, H 5, R 5, ER 5, BB 1, SO 1; **Whitey Moore**, IP 6 2/3, H 5, R 2, ER 2, BB 4, SO 7; **Elmer Riddle**, IP 1, H 0, R 0, ER 0, BB 0, SO 2.

Top Hitters
           Det **Bruce Campbell**, 2 for 3, 1 R, 2 RBI, 1 BB; **Rudy York**, 2 for 4, 2R, 1 BB
           Cin **Ival Goodman**, 2 for 4, 1 R, 1 RBI; **Eddie Joost**, 2 for 4.

2B—Cin/Goodman, M. McCormick, Werber. 3B—Det/York. **HR**—Det/Campbell. **Time** 2:09. **Attendance** 31,793.

Game 2, Thursday, October 3, at Crosley Field, Cincinnati

	1	2	3	4	5	6	7	8	9	R	H	E
Detroit Tigers	2	0	0	0	0	1	0	0	0	3	3	1
Cincinnati Reds	0	2	2	1	0	0	0	0	x	5	9	0

Pitchers Det **Schoolboy Rowe** (L, 0–1), IP 3 1/3, H 8, R 5, ER 5, BB 1, SO 1; **Johnny Gorsica**, IP 4 2/3, H 1, R 0, ER 0, BB 0, SO 1.
           Cin **Bucky Walters** (W, 1–0) IP 9, H 3, R 3, ER 3, BB 4, SO 4.

Top Hitters
           Cin **Bill Werber**, 1 for 3 1 RBI, 1 BB; **Jimmie Wilson**, 2 for 4, 1 R

2B—Det/Greenberg, Higgins; Cin/Walters, Werber. HR—Cin/Ripple. **Time:** 1:54. **Attendance:** 30,640.

Game 3, Friday, October 4, at Briggs Stadium, Detroit

	1	2	3	4	5	6	7	8	9	R	H	E
Cincinnati Reds	1	0	0	0	0	0	0	1	2	4	10	1
Detroit Tigers	0	0	0	1	0	0	4	2	x	7	13	1

Pitchers Cin **Jim Turner** (L, 0–1), IP 6, H 8, R 5, BB 0, SO 4; **Whitey Moore**, IP 1, H 2, R 0, ER 0, BB 0, SO 0; **Joe Beggs** IP 1, H3, R 2, ER 2, BB 0, SO 1.

Det **Tommy Bridges** (W, 1–0) IP 9, H 10, R 4, ER 3, BB 1, SO 5.

Top Hitters

Cin **Mike McCormick**, 2 for 5, 1 RBI; **Bill Werber**, 3 for 4, 1 R, 1 RBI, 1 BB

Det **Bruce Campbell**, 3 for 4, 2 R, 1 RBI; **Mike Higgins**, 2 for 4, 1 R, 3 RBI

2B—Cin/Lombardi, Werber; Det/Campbell, Higgins, McCosky, 3B—Det/Greenberg. HR—Det/Higgins, York. **Time:** 2:08. **Attendance:** 52,877.

Game 4, Saturday, October 5, at Briggs Stadium, Detroit

	1	2	3	4	5	6	7	8	9	R	H	E
Cincinnati Reds	2	0	1	1	0	0	0	1	0	5	11	1
Detroit Tigers	0	0	1	0	0	1	0	0	0	2	5	1

Pitchers Cin **Paul Derringer** (W, 1–1), IP 9, H 5, R 2, ER 2, BB 6, SO 4.

Det **Dizzy Trout** (L, 0–1), IP 2, H 6, R 3, ER 2, BB 1, SO 1; **Clay Smith**, IP 4, H1, R 1, ER 1, BB 3, SO 1; **Archie McKain**, IP 3, H 4, R 1, ER 1, BB 0, SO, 0.

Top Hitters

Cin **Ival Goodman**, 2 for 5, 2 R, 2 RBI; **Bill Werber**, 2 for 3, 2 R, 2 BB.

Det **Mike Higgins**, 2 for 4, 1 RBI; **Barney McCoskey**, 1 for 2, 1 R, 2 BB.

2B—Cin/Goodman, M. McCormick, Ripple; Det/Greenberg. 3B—Det/Higgins. **Time:** 2:06. **Attendance:** 54,093.

Game 5, Sunday, October 6, at Briggs Stadium, Detroit

	1	2	3	4	5	6	7	8	9	R	H	E
Cincinnati Reds	0	0	0	0	0	0	0	0	0	0	3	0
Detroit Tigers	0	0	3	4	0	0	0	1	x	8	13	0

Pitchers Cin **Junior Thompson** (l, 0–1), IP 3 1/3, H 8, R 6 ER 6, BB 4, SO 2; **Whitey Moore**, IP 2/3, H 1, R 1, ER 1, BB 2, SO 0; **Johnny Vander Meer**, IP 3, H2, R 0, ER 0, BB 3, SO 2; **Johnny Hutchings**, IP 1, H 2, R 1, ER 1, BB 1, SO 0

          Det **BoBo Newsom** (W 2–0), IP 9, H 3, R 0, ER 0, BB 2, SO 7

Top Hitters

          Det **Hank Greenberg**, 3 for 5, 2 R 4 RBI; **Barney McCoskey**, 2 for 3, 2 R, 2 BB

2B—Det/Bartell; Cin/Werber. HR—Det/Greenberg **Time:** 2:26 **Attendance:** 55,189

Game 6, Monday, October 7, at Crosley Field, Cincinnati

	1	2	3	4	5	6	7	8	9	R	H	E
Detroit Tigers	0	0	0	0	0	0	0	0	0	0	5	0
Cincinnati Reds	2	0	0	0	0	1	0	1	x	4	10	2

Pitchers Det **Schoolboy Rowe** (L, 0–2), IP 1/3, H 4, R2, ER 2, BB 0, SO 0; **Johnny Gorsica**, IP 6 2/3, H 5, R 1, ER 1, BB 4, SO 3; **Fred Hutchinson**, IP 1, H 1, R 1, ER, 1, BB, 1, SO 1

          Cin **Bucky Walters** (W, 2–0), IP 9, H 5, R 0, ER 0, BB 2, S0 2

Top Hitters

          Det **Dick Bartell**, 2 for 3; **Rudy York** 2 for 4

          Cin **Ival Goodman**, 2 for 4, 1 R 1 RBI; **Jimmy Ripple**, 2 for 2, 1 RBI 2 BB

2B—Det/Bartell; Cin/Werber. HR—Cin/Walters. **Time:** 2:01 **Attendance:** 30,481.

Game 7, Tuesday, October 8, at Crosley Field, Cincinnati

	1	2	3	4	5	6	7	8	9	R	H	E
Detroit Tigers	0	0	1	0	0	0	0	0	0	1	7	0
Cincinnati Reds	0	0	0	0	0	0	2	0	x	2	7	1

Pitchers Det **Bobo Newsom** (L 2–1), IP 8, H 7, R 2, ER 2, BB 1, SO 6

          Cin **Paul Derringer** (W, 2–1), IP 9, H 7, R 1, ER 0, BB 3, SO 1

Top Hitters

          Det **Charlie Gehringer**, 2 for 4; **Hank Greenberg** 2 for 4

          Cin **Jimmy Ripple**, 1 for 3, 1 R, 1 RBI; **Jimmie Wilson**, 2 for 2

2B—Det/Higgins; Cin/F. McCormick, M. McCormick, Ripple. SB—Wilson. **Time:** 1: 47. **Attendance:** 26,854

Appendix G:
Cincinnati Reds 1940 World Series Composite Stats

Hitting

Name	Pos	G	AB	H	2B	3B	HR	R	RBI	AVG	BB	SO
Arnovich, M.	OF	1	1	0	0	0	0	0	0	.000	0	0
Baker, B.	C	3	4	1	0	0	0	1	0	.250	0	1
Beggs, J	P	1	0	0	0	0	0	0	0	.000	0	0
Craft, H.	PH	1	1	0	0	0	0	0	0	.000	0	0
Derringer, P.	P	3	7	0	0	0	0	0	0	.000	0	1
Frey, L.	PH	3	2	0	0	0	0	0	0	.000	0	0
Goodman, I.	OF	7	29	8	2	0	0	5	5	.276	0	3
Hutchings, J.	P	1	0	0	0	0	0	0	0	.000	0	0
Joost, E.	2B	7	25	5	0	0	0	0	2	.200	1	2
Lombardi, E.	C-1	2	3	1	1	0	0	0	0	.333	1	0
McCormick, F	1B	7	28	6	1	0	0	2	0	.214	1	1
McCormick, M	OF	7	29	9	3	0	0	1	2	.310	1	6
Moore, W.	P	3	2	0	0	0	0	0	0	.000	0	1
Myers, B.	SS	7	23	3	0	0	0	0	2	.130	2	5
Riddle, E.	P	1	0	0	0	0	0	0	0	.000	0	0
Riggs, L.	PH	3	3	0	0	0	0	1	0	.000	0	2
Ripple, J.	OF	7	21	7	2	0	1	3	6	.333	4	2
Thompson, J.	P	1	1	0	0	0	0	0	0	.000	0	1
Turner, J.	P	1	2	0	0	0	0	0	0	.000	0	0
Vander Meer, J.	P	1	0	0	0	0	0	0	0	.000	0	0
Walters, B.	P	2	7	2	1	0	1	2	2	.286	0	1
Werber, B.	3B	7	27	10	4	0	0	5	2	.370	4	2
Wilson, J.	C	6	17	6	0	0	0	2	0	.353	1	2
Totals	—	—	232	58	14	0	2	22	21	.250	15	30

Pitching

Name	W	L	G	CG	S	Sh	IP	ERA	H	SO	ER	BB
Beggs	0	0	1	0	0	0	1.0	9.00	3	1	1	0
Derringer	2	1	3	2	0	0	19.1	2.79	17	6	6	10
Hutchings	0	0	1	0	0	0	0	9.00	2	0	1	1
Moore	0	0	3	0	0	0	8.1	3.24	8	7	3	6
Riddle	0	0	1	0	0	0	1.0	0.00	0	2	0	0
Thompson	0	1	1	0	0	0	3.1	16.20	8	2	6	4
Turner	0	1	1	0	0	0	6.0	7.50	8	4	5	0
Vander Meer	0	0	1	0	0	0	3.0	0.00	2	2	0	3
Walters	2	0	2	2	0	1	18.0	1.50	8	6	3	6
Totals	4	3	14	4	0	1	61.0	3.69	56	30	25	30

Appendix H:
Transactions for the
1940 Cincinnati Reds

January 4, 1940

Lost Johnny Niggeling to St. Louis Browns on waivers.
Traded Lee Grissom to New York Yankees in exchange for Joe Beggs.

May 8, 1940

Traded Vince DiMaggio to Pittsburgh Pirates in exchange for Johnny Rizzo.

June 15, 1940

Traded Johnny Rizzo to Philadelphia Phillies in exchange for Morrie Arnovich.

August 23, 1940

Claimed Jimmy Ripple from Brooklyn Dodgers on waivers.

September 10, 1940

Claimed Woody Williams from Brooklyn Dodgers on waivers.

December 4, 1940

Traded Billy Myers to Chicago Cubs in exchange for Jim Gleeson and Bobby Mattick.

December 9, 1940

Traded Lew Riggs to Brooklyn Dodgers in exchange for Pep Young.

December 10, 1940

Sold Morrie Arnovich to New York Giants.

December 16, 1940

Purchased Tot Pressnell from St. Louis Cardinals.

December 30, 1940

Traded Don Lang and $20,000 to New York Yankees in exchange for Monte Pearson.

Chapter Notes

The following abbreviations are used in the endnotes: *CE: Cincinnati Enquirer, NYT: New York Times, WT: World Telegram, HOF: National Baseball Hall of Fame, TSN: The Sporting News.*

Chapter 1

1. Richard Tofel, *The 1939 New York Yankees: A Legend in the Making*, Chicago: Ivan R. Dee, 2004, p. 198.
2. Gene Schorr, *The History of the World Series*, New York: William Morrow, 1998, pp. 174–175.
3. Tofel, p. 199.
4. John Drebinger, "Yankees Top Reds by 2 to 1 in Opener of World Series," *NYT*, October 5, 1939, p. 1.
5. Tofel, p. 201.
6. James P. Dawson, "Yankees Take World Series Opener from Reds on Single by Dickey in Ninth," *NYT*, October 5, 1939, p. 28.
7. Tofel, p. 202.
8. Ibid., p. 202.
9. John Drebinger, "Pearson Shuts Out Reds with 2 Hits as Yanks Win, 4–0," *NYT*, October 6, 1939, p. 1.
10. Ibid., p. 32.
11. Ibid., p. 1.
12. John Drebinger, "Keller Drives Two," *NYT*, October 8, 1939, p. 1.
13. Tofel, p. 207.
14. Drebinger, "Keller Drives Two," p. 8.
15. John Drebinger, "Yankees Beat Reds by 7–4 in the Tenth to Win Series, 4–0," *NYT*, October 9, 1939, p. 1.
16. Ibid., p. 22.
17. Joe Williams, "Deacon Bill McKechnie," *Saturday Evening Post*, September 14, 1940, pp. 41–44.
18. Tofel, p. 207.
19. *NYT*, October 9, 1939.

Chapter 2

1. William Nack, "The Razor's Edge," *Sports Illustrated*, May 6, 1991, p. 55.
2. Fullerton Union High School Web site; FUHS alumni/fuhswall.htm.
3. Ibid.
4. Nack, p. 56.
5. Ibid., p. 56.
6. Ibid., p. 56.
7. James Barbour, "The Death of Willard Hershberger," *The National Pastime*, Society for American Baseball Research (SABR), Winter 1987, p. 65.
8. Nack, p. 56.
9. Ibid., p. 58.
10. Cincinnati Reds Team Press Release, Willard Hershberger Baseball Hall of Fame (HOF) bio file, Cooperstown, NY.
11. Ronald A. Mayer, *The 1937 Newark Bears: A Baseball Legend*, New Brunswick: Rutgers University Press, 1994, p. 125.
12. Barbour, p. 63.
13. Nack, p. 58.
14. Cincinnati Reds Team Press Release, Hershberger HOF bio file.
15. Ibid.
16. Nack, p. 58.
17. Ibid., p. 58.
18. Barbour, p. 63.
19. Willard Hershberger, HOF bio file.
20. Nack, p. 58.
21. Mayer, pp. 230–285.
22. Ibid., p. 126.

Chapter 3

1. Joe Williams, "Deacon Bill McKechnie," *Saturday Evening Post*, September 14, 1940, p. 39.

2. Staff Correspondent, "DiMaggio's Base-Running Is Praised as Yanks Celebrate," *NYT*, October 9, 1939, p. 26.

3. Ibid., p. 26.

4. Ibid., p. 26.

5. Williams, p. 39.

6. Ibid., p. 39.

7. Ibid., p. 41

8. Ibid., p. 41.

9. Frank Graham, "Another Pennant for McKechnie? Winner of Four Flags in Three Cities, He Is Picked by Many to Win Again with the Reds this Year," *Look*, April 14, 1944, p. 42.

10. Thomas Swope, "On the Pennant Path: Bill, the Leader: A Quiet Gentleman with a Working Sense of Humor," *Cincinnati Post*, August 16, 1939, p. 15.

11. Graham, p. 44.

12. Edwin Pope, *Baseball's Greatest Managers*, New York: Doubleday, 1960, p. 184.

13. Williams, p. 88.

14. Ibid., p. 88.

15. Ibid., p. 88.

16. Ibid., p. 88.

17. Graham, p. 44.

18. Williams, p. 87.

19. Ibid., p. 89.

20. Tom Meany, "Bill McKechnie of Cincinnati; He Doesn't Mind the $30,000 a Year, but He Dislikes the Spotlight," *Look*, June 20, 1939, p. 40.

21. Williams, p. 89.

22. Ibid., p. 89.

23. Bill McKechnie, HOF bio file, "Application of Common Sense Methods."

24. Meany, p. 41.

25. Gene Thompson, phone interview, April 22, 2001.

Other Sources

Associated Press, "Bill McKechnie Is Dead at 78; Ex-Manager in National League," *NYT*, October 30, 1965.

"Bill McKechnie Quits Baseball After 43 Years to be a Farmer," *WT*, December 3, 1949.

Cincinnati Reds Biographical News Release, "Manager Bill McKechnie," Bill McKechnie HOF bio file.

James, Bill, *The Bill James Guide to Baseball Managers from 1870 to Today*, New York: Scribners, 1997, pp. 72–78.

Lieb, Frederick G., "McKechnie, Flag-Winner in 3 Cities, Dead," *TSN*, November 13, 1965, p. 25.

Chapter 4

1. Thomas Swope, "Red-Letter Season for Cincy Fielders," *TSN*, December 26, 1940, p. 3.

2. Bill James, *The Bill James Historical Baseball Abstract*, Free Press, 2001, p. 505.

3. Bill Werber interview, *Sports Collector's Digest*, June 17, 1994, p. 187.

4. Ibid., p. 187.

5. Ibid., p. 187.

6. Edgar G. Brands, "F. McCormick Named N.L.'s Most Valuable, Third Red in Three Years," *TSN*, November 14. 1940, p. 1.

7. Microsoft Complete Baseball 1994, Frank McCormick bio.

8. James, p. 452.

9. Ibid., p. 452.

10. Microsoft Complete Baseball, McCormick bio.

11. Brands, p. 1.

12. Ibid., p. 1.

13. Microsoft Complete Baseball.

14. Brands, p. 1.

15. Microsoft Complete Baseball.

16. Ibid.

17. Brands, p. 1.

18. Ibid., p. 1

19. Ibid., p. 2.

20. John Thorn, Pete Palmer, Michael Gershman, and David Pietrusza, *Total Baseball*, 6th ed., Total Sports, 1999, p. 1078.

21. Frank McCormick HOF bio file.

22. Microsoft Complete Baseball.

23. Thorn et al., p. 356.

24. Brands, p. 4.

25. Ibid., p. 4.

26. Thorn et al., p. 2151.

27. Brands, p. 4.

28. Ibid., p. 1.

29. George Kirksey, "Bill Werber Turned His 'Lawyer' Rap from A.L. Days Into Rep with the Reds as Best Third Sacker in N.L," *TSN*, May 1, 1941, p. 3.

30. Thorn et al., *TB*, p. 1350.

31. Kirksey, p. 3.

32. James, p. 580.

33. Kirksey, p. 3.

34. Jack Murray, "Billy Werber Millionaire Who Still Follows Baseball," *CE*, June 26, 1976, p. C-9.

35. Kirksey, p. 3.

36. Ibid., p. 3.

37. Thorn et al., p. 1350.

38. "Reds' Spearhead Off to a Flying Start," May 1939, NL Service Bureau press release, Bill Werber HOF bio file.

39. *Sports Collector's Digest*, p. 187.

40. Ibid., p. 187.

41. Murray, p. C-9.

42. Ibid., p. C-9.

43. Bill Werber, "A Ballplayer Boos Back," *Magazine Sigma Chi*, July-August 1943 p. 21.

44. Ibid., p. 21.

45. Kirksey, p. 3.

46. Ibid., p. 3.

47. James, p. 580.

48. Kirksey, p. 3.

49. Gabe Paul, Cincinnati Reds press release, March 1939, Bill Werber HOF bio file.

50. Tom Meany, *WT*, 1939.

51. Charles E. Parker, "Fans Rate Frey Standout Shortstop of New Season," *WT*, April 25, 1933.

52. Lonnie Frey HOF bio file.

53. Jack Murray, "Lonnie Frey from Snohomish, Laughter Now at Oh-for-October," *Cincinnati Enquirer*, July 25, 1976, p. C-9.

54. Bill McCullough, "Dodgers' Captain Unable to Stand Riding from Fans," Lonnie Frey HOF bio file, May 25, 1936.

55. Lonnie Frey HOF bio file.

56. "Frey Problem Child," HOF bio file.

57. Edward T. Murphy, "Stengel Tries Fry as Fly Chaser," Lonnie Frey HOF bio file, May 27, 1936.

58. Paul, Gabe, Cincinnati Reds Press Release, Lonnie Frey HOF Bio File.

59. Arthur E. Patterson, "Frey Credits Jump to Stardom to McKechnie's Faith in Him," Lonnie Frey HOF bio file.

60. Murray, p. C-9.

61. Gabe Paul, Lonnie Frey player release 1941, HOF bio file.

62. Patterson, Frey HOF bio file.

63. Ibid.

64. Murray, p. C-9.

65. James, p. 505.

66. Werber, p. 21.

67. Gary Schumacher, "Billy Teams Nicely with Frey Around Keystone Sector," July 13, 1938, Billy Myers HOF bio file.

68. "Red Thumbnail Sketches," June 14, 1935, Billy Myers HOF bio file.

69. "Wins Captain's Stripes Early — William Harrison Myers," Billy Myers HOF bio file.

70. "Red Thumbnail Sketches."

71. Bill Braucher, "Billy Myers Saw First Major Game at Start of Season; Captained Reds Before It Closed," February 11, 1936, Billy Myers HOF bio file.

72. Lee Allen, *The Cincinnati Reds*, Van Rees Press, 1948, p. 282.

73. Ibid., p. 283.

74. Gabe Paul, Cincinnati Reds press release, Eddie Joost HOF bio file, 1940.

75. Rich Marazzi, "Joost Spins a Tale of Two Careers," *Sports Collector's Digest*, July 2, 1999, p. 70.

76. Art Morrow, "Joost Rules A.L. Roost at Short, Philly Claims," *TSN*, June 22, 1949, p. 5.

77. Marazzi, p. 70.

78. Cincinnati Reds press release, Eddie Joost HOF bio file.

79. Marazzi, p. 71.

80. Stan Gosshandler, "Eddie Joost: He was an Ideal Lead off Hitter," *Baseball Digest*, February 1992, p. 39.

81. Eddie Joost HOF bio file.

82. Marazzi, p. 70.

83. Ibid., p. 70.

84. Gosshandler, p. 40.

85. Marazzi, p. 71.

Chapter 5

1. Letter from Warren Giles to Bill McKechnie, Bill McKechnie HOF bio file, October 19, 1937.

2. Ibid.

3. Paul Derringer, HOF bio file.

4. Paul Derringer obituary, Paul Derringer HOF bio file, November 30, 1987.

5. John Thorn, Pete Palmer, Michael Gershman, and David Pietrusza, *Total Baseball*, Total Sports, 1999, p. 1498.

6. George Kirksey, "Derringer Whose Career Resembles His Own Curves Credits 'McKechnie Influence' for Rise to Real Stardom," *TSN*, September 26, 1940, p. 3.

7. Ibid., p. 3.

8. Derringer obituary, 1987.

9. Kirksey, p. 3.

10. Thorn et al., *TB*, p. 1498.

11. Derringer, HOF bio file.

12. Kirksey, p. 3.

13. Derringer, HOF bio file.

14. Kirksey, p. 3.

15. Tom Meany, "Reds' Pilot Puts Paul Derringer on Block When Star Pitcher Fails to Slide Home," *WT*, May 4, 1938.

16. Thomas Swope, "Cincy Tongues Wag Over Derringer Ban," Paul Derringer HOF bio file.

17. Kirksey, p. 3.

18. Ibid., p. 3.

19. Bill James, *The Bill James Historical Baseball Abstract*, Free Press, 2001, p. 412.

20. Jack Murray, "Thou Fine with Bucky," *CE*, October 17, 1976, p. C-12.

21. Ibid., p. C-12.

22. Bucky Walters Cincinnati Reds press release, HOF bio file.

23. Murray, p. C-12.

24. Thorn et al., p. 1870.

25. "Heats Up Hot Corner," Bucky Walters HOF bio file.

26. Thorn et al., p. 1330.

27. Murray, p. C-12.
28. Ibid., p. C-12.
29. Bucky Walters press release, HOF bio file.
30. Thorn et al., p. 1870.
31. Bucky Walters press release, HOF bio file.
32. Murray, p. C-12.
33. Bucky Walters press release, HOF bio file.
34. "Reds Formula: Versatility Plus a Brain Trust, Added to a Brilliant Array of Pitching Talent," *Newsweek*, p. 44.
35. Dan Daniel, "Cards Best Says Casey: Two Men Carry Reds Derringer Walters Make Difference," *WT*, August 9, 1939.
36. Roscoe McGowan, "Walters Tops Poll in National League: Reds' 27-Game Winner Named Most Valuable with 303 of Possible 336 Points," *NYT*, October 18, 1939.
37. Ibid.
38. Instituted in 1922, the MVP Award was confined to the American League for two seasons, being awarded to George Sisler in 1922 and Babe Ruth in 1923. In 1924, the National League also instituted an MVP Award. Subsequent selections were made by the NL from 1925 until 1929, when the senior circuit discontinued making the award. The AL named MVPs from 1924–1928 and then discontinued the practice. In 1929, *The Sporting News* named the AL MVP and then made the MVP selections for both leagues from 1930 to 1937. The Baseball Writers Association had been simultaneously making its own selections. Beginning in 1938, the BBWA and *The Sporting News* combined their selections with only one set of awards being given.
39. McGowan, October 8, 1939.
40. Cincinnati Reds news release, Bucky Walters HOF bio file.
41. Murray, p. C-12.
42. Ibid., p. C-12.
43. Tom Swope, "Styled by McKechnie and Grove, Johnny Vander Meer Fashions Pennant Hopes for Reds with Model Games," *TSN*, June 23, 1938, p. 3.
44. Joseph Wallace, Neil Hamilton, and Marty Appel, *Baseball: 100 Classic Moments in the History of the Game*, Dorling Kindersley, pp. 82–83.
45. Ibid., pp. 82–83.
46. Swope, p. 3.
47. Ibid., p. 3.
48. Ibid., p. 3.
49. Eddie Joost, phone interview, April 22, 2001.
50. Swope, p. 3.
51. Ibid., p. 3.
52. Ibid., p. 3.
53. Ibid., p. 3.
54. Tommy Holmes, "Everybody Follows the Ball but Dodgers as MacPhail Sells Brooklyn on Night Game," *TSN*, June 23, 1938, p. 5.
55. Ibid., p. 5.
56. Ibid., p. 5.
57. Ibid., p. 5.
58. Wallace et al., pp. 82–83.
59. Ibid., p. 82.
60. Swope, p. 3.
61. Ibid., p. 3.
62. Ibid., p. 3.
63. Junior Thompson, phone interview, April 22, 2001.
64. "Scribbled by Scribe," *TSN*, July 11, 1940, p. 4.
65. Ibid., p. 4.
66. Ibid.
67. Joost was mistaken in his recollection. Vander Meer pitched one inning in Game 5 of the 1940 World Series. *Total Baseball*, p. 357.
68. The winning player's World Series share in 1940 was $5,804. Josh Leventhal, *The World Series*, p. 108.
69. Joost phone interview.
70. Thompson phone interview.
71. Thorn et al., p. 1857.
72. Thompson phone interview.
73. George Kirksey, "Dad Turned Gene Thompson Into Pitcher at Age of 12 to Keep His Face from Being Bashed in as Backstop," *TSN*, December 19, 1940, p. 3.
74. Ibid., p. 3.
75. Ibid., p. 3.
76. Ibid., p. 3.
77. Ibid., p. 3.
78. Ibid., p. 3.
79. Thompson phone interview.
80. Kirksey, p. 3.
81. Thompson interview.
82. Ibid.
83. Kirksey, p. 3.
84. Ibid., p. 3.
85. Dan Daniel, "Rambling Round the Circuit with Pitcher Snorter Casey," *TSN*, December 30, 1937, p. 4.
86. Two other pitchers Cliff Melton of the New York Giants and Turner's teammate Lou Fette also won 20 games in the National League in 1937.
87. Thorn et al., p. 2139.
88. Paul Shannon, "Jim Turner, 20-Game Winner for the Bees, Credits Success to 'Cutting Corners' and Expects to Repeat," *Boston Post*, March 10, 1938, p. 5.
89. Ibid., p. 5.
90. Ibid., p. 5.
91. Tom Swope, "Reds Expect Good Turn from Turner," *TSN*, December 14, 1939, p. 5.
92. Ibid., p. 5.

93. Ibid., p. 5.
94. Ibid., p. 5.
95. Thorn et al., p. 1413.
96. Ronald Mayer, *The 1937 Newark Bears: A Baseball Legend*, New Brunswick: Rutgers University Press, 1994, p. 133.
97. Ibid., p. 133.
98. Thorn et al., p. 1413.
99. Mayer, p. 135.
100. "Yankees Laugh at Trading Ban in Slipping Over Grissom Deal," *TSN*, January 11, 1940, p. 1.
101. Mayer, p. 135.
102. Thomas Swope, "Giles Goes to Town on Red Autographs," *TSN*, January 11, 1940, p. 2.
103. Ibid., p. 2.
104. Ibid., p. 2.
105. Mayer, p. 135.

Chapter 6

1. Tom Swope, "Redland Guessing on What Reds Want," *TSN*, November 30, 1939, p. 3.
2. Lee Allen, *The Cincinnati Reds*, Van Rees Press, 1948, p. 276.
3. "Cincinnati Loyalty Unshaken: Opener Already Sellout," *TSN*, December 21, 1939, p. 1.
4. Warren Crandall Giles, HOF bio file.
5. J. G. Taylor Spink, "Warren Giles—Who Glued Together a Pennant Club," October 5, 1939.
6. Ibid.
7. Hal Leibovitz, "Does Honesty Pay?" Warren Giles HOF bio file.
8. Broeg, Bob, "Honestly, Warren Giles Became a National Treasure," *St. Louis Post Dispatch*, February 11, 1979, p. 8E.
9. Ibid., p. 8E.
10. Leibovitz, HOF bio file.
11. Spink, October 5, 1939.
12. Ibid.
13. Warren Crandall Giles, HOF bio file.
14. Spink, October 5, 1939.
15. Ibid.
16. Allen, p. 257.
17. Ibid., p. 258.
18. Tom Swope, "Reds Promise to Stay in Pink with Replacements Coming Up from Farms," *TSN*, January 25, 1940, p. 1.
19. Edgar G. Brands, "Scribes Pick Yanks, Cards to Resume '28 Series Battle," *TSN*, April 25, 1940.
20. Tom Swope, "Two of Tiger Purge Pick-Ups Leave Reds," *TSN*, April 4, 1940, p. 2.
21. Tom Swope, "Reds Hear Three Games in Havana May Draw 100,000," *TSN*, February 29, 1940, p. 1.
22. Allen, p. 277.
23. John Thorn, Pete Palmer, Michael Gershman, and David Pietrusza, *Total Baseball*, 6th ed., Total Sports, 1999, p. 792.
24. Ibid., p. 899.
25. Ibid., p. 899.
26. Tom Swope, "A Good Man in Right Is Cincinnati's Ival Goodman," *TSN*, June 15, 1939.
27. Ival Goodman obituary, *TSN*, December 10, 1984, p. 57.
28. Thorn et al., p. 899.
29. Swope, June 15, 1939, p. 3.
30. *TSN*, December 10, 1984, p. 57.
31. Frederick G. Lieb, "It's Crafty Fielding That Makes Craft Valuable to Reds," *TSN*, September 21, 1939, p. 3.
32. Ibid., p. 3.
33. James, *The Bill James Historical Baseball Abstract*, p. 382.
34. Lieb, p. 3.
35. Allen, p. 277.
36. Tom Swope, "Mike McCormick Born Where Gold Rush Started in '49, Looks Like 'Pay Dirt' as Left Fielder for Cincinnati," *TSN*, April 25, 1940, p. 3.
37. Ibid., p. 3.
38. Tom Swope, "Reds Slip Into High, Proving McKechnie's Patience Warranted," *TSN*, April 11, 1940, p. 1.
39. Tom Swope, "Cincinnati Express Ahead of Schedule," *TSN*, May 16, 1940.
40. Retrosheet.org, "1940 Cincinnati Reds Game Log."
41. National Baseball Hall of Fame Web Site, "Baseball's Opening Day," April 6, 2004.
42. Swope, May 16, 1940, p. 3.
43. Allen, p. 277.
44. Swope, May 16, 1940, p. 3.
45. Retrosheet.org.
46. Ibid.
47. Tom Swope, "Reds High in Polish Despite Their Drop in Luster Entries," *TSN*, July 4, 1940, p. 1.
48. Ibid., p. 2.
49. Retrosheet.org.
50. Swope, July 4, 1940, p. 2.
51. Tom Swope, "Reds Hot Sunday Team, If Not All-Star Gang," *TSN*, July 4, 1940, p. 3.
52. Retrosheet.org.
53. Dan Daniel, "Grissom to Get Chance in New MacPhail Shakeup," *WT*, July 24, 1940.
54. George Kirksey, "Ripple, Cincinnati's Wave of Fury in World Series, a $7,500 Hunch That Delivered Million Dollar Punch," *TSN*, October 20, 1940, p. 3.
55. Ibid., p. 3.
56. Ibid., p. 3.
57. Thorn et al., p. 2139.
58. Kirksey, p. 3.
59. Ibid., p. 3.

Chapter 7

1. Tom Swope, "Hershberger Suicide No Unpremeditated Act, Told McKechnie: 'My Father Did It and I'm Going to Do It Too,'" *TSN*, August 8, 1940, p. 8.

2. Ibid., p. 8.

3. Ibid., p. 8.

4. William Nack, "The Razor's Edge," *Sports Illustrated*, May 6, 1991, p. 61.

5. Swope, p. 8.

6. James Barbour, "The Death of Willard Hershberger," *The National Pastime*, SABR, Winter 1987, p. 62.

7. Nack, p. 61.

8. Swope, p. 8.

9. Swope, p. 8, and Nack, p. 61.

10. Nack, p. 61.

11. Eddie Joost, phone interview, April 22, 2001.

12. Nack, p. 61.

13. Barbour, p. 64.

14. "The Fans Speak Out," Letter to the Editor, *Baseball Digest*, June 2004, p. 13.

15. Nack, p. 61.

16. Bill Werber, "A Ballplayer Boos Back," *Magazine Sigma Chi*, July-August 1943, p. 22.

17. Barbour, p. 64.

18. Nack, p. 62.

19. Ibid., p. 62.

20. Barbour, p. 64.

21. Ibid., p. 64.

22. Swope, p. 8.

23. Ibid., p. 8.

24. Nack, p. 60.

25. Swope, p. 8.

26. Ibid., p. 8.

27. Nack, p. 62.

28. Swope, p. 8.

29. Nack, p. 62.

30. Ibid., p. 62.

31. Joost phone interview.

32. Joe Williams, "Deacon Bill McKechnie," *Saturday Evening Post*, September 14, 1940, p. 88.

33. Gene Thompson, phone interview, April 22, 2001.

34. Dan Daniel, "Daniel's Dope," *WT*, August 5, 1940.

35. Ibid.

36. Swope, p. 8.

37. Williams, p. 88.

38. Werber, p. 23.

Other Sources

"Fans Shocked and Puzzled by Hershberger's Death," *Brooklyn Eagle*, August 4, 1940.

Paul, Gabe, Willard Hershberger news release, Willard Hershberger HOF bio file.

Ripp, Bart, "Why Willard? UNM Prof Researches Suicide of Ballplayer 46 Summers Ago," *Albuquerque Tribune*, May 12, 1986, pp. D8–D20.

Chapter 8

1. "Ex-Dodger Catcher Cuts Throat in Suicide Attempt," *Brooklyn Eagle*, April 9, 1953.

2. "Ernie Lombardi Throat Slashed Is Near Death," *Sacramento Bee*, April 9, 1953, p. 27.

3. Jay Mariotti, "At Last Honor, Fascinating Ex-Red Lombardi Will Finally Enter Hall," *Cincinnati Post*, July 30, 1986.

4. Jack Zanger, *Great Catchers of the Major Leagues*, Random House, New York, 1970, p. 127.

5. Ibid., p. 127.

6. "Lombardi May Become Mound Ace for Robbie," *WT*, September 17, 1937.

7. Zanger, p. 129.

8. Ibid., p. 130.

9. Ibid., p. 130.

10. Wells Twombly, "He'd Reject Shrine: Lombardi's Bitterness Overflows," Ernie Lombardi, Baseball HOF bio file, July 6, 1974.

11. Ibid.

12. Zanger, p. 131.

13. Ibid., p. 124.

14. Joseph Wallace, Neil Hamilton, and Marty Appel, *Baseball: 100 Classic Moments in the History of the Game*, Dorling Kindersley, p. 83.

15. Zanger, pp. 131–132.

16. Ernie Lombardi obituary, Lombardi, Baseball HOF bio file, October 15, 1977.

17. Joe Williams, "Deacon Bill McKechnie," *Saturday Evening Post*, September 14, 1940.

18. Eddie Joost, phone interview, April 22, 2001.

19. Williams.

20. Ben Swesey, "Schnozz Lombardi Recalls the Homer He Hit 40 Miles," *Sacramento Bee*, August 19, 1974, p. C-1.

21. Will Grimsley, "Will No One Rescue Sleeping Beauty?" *San Francisco Examiner*, February 1, 1977.

22. Zanger, p. 134.

23. Ibid., p. 134.

24. Mariotti, "At Last, Honor."

25. Zanger, p. 135.

26. Tom Callahan, "Ernie Lombardi: Baseball's Forgotten Man," *Baseball Digest*, vol. 31. October 1972, pp. 75–77.

27. Twombly, "He'd Reject Shrine."

28. Callahan, p. 77.

29. Ernie Lombardi obituary, October 15, 1977.

30. Mariotti, p. 4D.

31. Ibid., p. 4D.

Chapter 9

1. John Thorn, Pete Palmer, Michael Gershman, and David Pietrusza, *Total Baseball*, 6th ed., Total Sports, p. 2153.
2. Roy J. Stockton, "Big Bats of Tiger Players Conceded to Be Only Detroit Advantage," *Cincinnati Enquirer*, October 2, 1940.
3. "Berlin Has Five Hour Raid; Night Fighters Aid London," *CE*, October 1, 1940, p. 1.
4. "Little Betting on Series," *NYT*, October 1, 1940.
5. Bob Considine, "Yanks Are Dead Is General View of Fans, Who Pick Deacon's Lads to Win Series," *CE*, October 2, 1940.
6. *NYT*, October 1, 1940, p. 33.
7. "World Series Rush Is On; Hotels Booked to Limit," *CE*, October 1, 1940, p. 16.
8. Dawson Jones, "Tigers Hit Successive Homers to Show They Are Ready," *NYT*, October 1, 1940.
9. "Little Betting on Series," *NYT*.
10. Lou Smith, "Two Cripples May Not Start," *CE*, October 2, 1940, p. 1.
11. Lou Smith, "First Tilt Taken by Tigers," *CE*, October 3, 1940, p. 1.
12. Smith, "Two Cripples," p. 6.
13. Charles Doyle, "'Smoothies' Is Term Given Reds Because They Outsmart Other Outfits," *CE*, October 2, 1940.
14. John Drebinger, "Tigers in Second Crush Reds 7 to 2, as Series Starts," *NYT*, October 3, 1940, p. 1.
15. George Kirksey, "In Silence Redleg Fans Suffer," *CE*, October 3, 1940, p. 16.
16. Smith, "First Tilt," p. 2.
17. Ibid., p. 2.
18. Ibid., p. 2.
19. Drebinger, p. 33.
20. Ibid., p. 33.
21. Henry McLemore, "'Wanted to Win for Deacon,' Says Paul; 'Different Story Next Time,' He Declares,'" *CE*, October 3, 1940, p. 16.
22. Smith, "First Tilt," p. 2.
23. Bob Bohne, "Newsom Is Hero as Tigers Whoop Up on Reds," *CE*, October 3, 1940, p. 17.
24. Bob Saxton, "Betting Odds Are All Against 'Em," *CE*, October 3, 1940, p. 16.
25. Joseph Garretson, Jr., "Reds Confident of Evening Series; Tiger Bats Too Hot in First Game," *CE*, October 3, 1940, p. 2.
26. "Newsom's Dad Dies at Hotel; Buck Is to Stay with Team," *CE*, October 4, 1940.
27. "Newsom's Father Dies in Cincinnati, Pitcher Attends Service While Teammates Play," *NYT*, October 4, 1940.
28. "Newsom's Dad Dies," *CE*.

29. John Drebinger, "30,640 Watch Reds Defeat Tigers 5–3 Tying Series at 1–1," *NYT*, October 4, 1940, p. 1.
30. "Scalpers Fare Poorly, Numbers Are Unlikely to Show Profit Officials Say," *CE*, October 4, 1940, p. 2.
31. Raymond J. Kelly, "Play-by-Play," *NYT*, October 4, 1940, p. 30.
32. Judon Bailey, "Wild Start Redeemed by Bucky," *CE*, October 4, 1940, p. 15.
33. "Second Game Play-by-Play," *CE*, October 4, 1940, p. 16.
34. Kelly, p. 30.
35. Joseph, Garretson, Jr. "Taste of Glory Sets World Right for Reds After Wait of 21 Years," *CE*, October 4, 1940, p. 1.
36. George Kirksey, "Number 7 Haunts Reds Again," *CE*, October 5, 1940, p. 15.
37. Staff Correspondent, "Tigers Intersperse Homers by York and Higgins with Singles in Big Seventh; Play-by-Play of Third Game," *NYT*, October 5, 1940.
38. Ibid.
39. Kirksey, p. 15.
40. Ibid., p. 15.
41. Staff Correspondent, "Tigers Intersperse Homers."
42. James, P. Dawson, "Bridges Is Hailed by Joyful Tigers," *NYT*, October 5, 1940, p. 9.
43. Ibid., p. 9.
44. Lou Smith, "Load Placed on Young Hurler," *CE*, October 5, 1940, p. 1.
45. Lou Smith, "Series Even. Paul Comes Back," *CE*, October 6, 1940, p. 1.
46. Judson Bailey, "Thunder Stolen from Tigers," *CE*, October 6, 1940.
47. McLemore, Henry, "Baker Strategy Called Daring, as Riegel's Wrong Way Run," *CE*, October 6, 1940, p. 19.
48. Smith, "Series Even," p. 1.
49. McLemore, p. 19.
50. Ibid., p. 19.
51. Charles Dunkley, "Reds Spunky, Tigers Droop in Clubhouse After Game," *CE*, October 6, 1940.
52. "Denial Issued by Deacon of Reported Cleveland Bid to Replace Oscar Vitt," *CE*, October 6, 1940, p. 30.
53. Judson Bailey, "31 Batters All That Face Newsom," *CE*, October 7, 1940.
54. Lou Smith, "Masterpiece Is Spun by Newsom," *CE*, October 7, 1940, p. 13.
55. Bailey, "31 Batters."
56. Associated Press, "Tears Fill Eyes of Newsom in Clubhouse After Game. Boys Move About Silently," *CE*, October 7, 1940.
57. *E*, October 8, 1940, p. 15.
58. Joseph, Garretson, Jr., "Reds Dispel Pessimism of Fans in First Inning When Werber Starts Rally," *CE*, October 8, 1940, p. 1.

59. John Drebinger, "Reds Even Series Beating Tigers Again, 4–0," *NYT*, October 8, 1940, p. 32.

60. Ibid., p. 32.

61. "Poor Start Proves Costly to Detroit," *NYT*, October 8, 1940, p. 32.

62. Lou Smith, "Sixth Tilt to Walters 4–0," *CE*, October 8, 1940, p. 1.

63. Sue Goodwin, "Skirting the Field," *CE*, October 8, 1940, p. 15.

64. Ibid., p. 15.

65. Smith, p. 15.

66. Ibid., p. 1.

67. George Kirksey, "Pot of Gold Is at Rainbow's End, Redlegs Greatest One-Run Champs," *CE*, October 9, 1940, p. 26.

68. Ibid., p. 26.

69. "Play-by-Play," *CE*, October 9, 1940, p. 26.

70. Henry McLemore, "Cincinnati Proves to Be City Without Reason Is Way UPI Correspondent Describes It," *CE*, October 9, 1940, p. 26.

71. Joe Cronin, "Reds Are World Champions. Paper Blizzard Falls in Financial Area; Traffic Tied Up," *CE*, October 9, 1940, p. 1.

72. Joseph Garretson, Jr., "Derringer Toast of Town as Reds Come Back with Fighting Hearts to Become World Champions," *CE*, October 9, 1940, p. 1.

73. Ibid., p. 1.

Other Sources

Falls, Joe, *The Detroit Tigers: An Illustrated History*, New York: Walker, 1989.

Hoppel, Joe, *The Series: An Illustrated History of Baseball's Postseason Showcase*, Sporting News, 1989.

Leventhal, Joseph, *The World Series: An Illustrated Encyclopedia of the Fall Classic*, New York: Black Dog and Leventhal, 2002.

Chapter 10

1. Lou Smith, "Reds Outshine Foe in All Departments," *CE*, October 9, 1940, p. 16.

2. Joseph Wallace, Neil Hamilton, and Marty Appel, *Baseball 100 Classic Moments in the History of the Game*, Dorling Kindersley, p. 94.

3. Ibid., p. 100.

4. Ibid., p. 100.

5. Lee Allen, *The Cincinnati Reds*, Van Rees Press, 1948, p. 288.

6. Izzy Katzman, "He's Working on the Railroad Now," Billy Myers HOF bio file, March 5, 1942.

7. Allen, p. 290.

8. Ibid., p. 291.

9. David L. Porter, ed., *Biographical Dictionary of American Sports*, Frank McCormick HOF bio file.

10. Ibid.

11. "Buck McCormick Dies, Was N.L. MVP in 1940," *Sports Collectors' Digest*, December 24, 1982.

12. Eddie Joost HOF bio file, May 13, 1942.

13. Ibid.

14. Sid Keener, "Series Boner Tagged Jimmie a Regular Guy," *TSN*, June 11, 1947, p. 16.

15. Ed Pollock, "Playing the Game," *TSN*, June 11, 1947, p. 15.

16. Keener, p. 16.

17. Stan Baumgartner, "Wilson, Former Catcher and Manager Stricken in Florida Home at Age of 46," *TSN*, June 11, 1947, p. 16.

18. Pollock, p. 15.

19. John Thorn, Pete Palmer, Michael Gershman, and David Pietrusza, *Total Baseball*, 6th ed., Total Sports, 1999, p. 2476.

20. Bill James, *The Bill James Historical Abstract*, Free Press, 2001, p. 412.

21. Ibid., p. 412.

22. Pollock, p. 15.

23. William Nack, "The Razor's Edge," *Sports Illustrated*, May 6, 1991, p. 63.

24. "Hershberger's Number Retired," *WT*, August 6, 1940.

25. Art Morrow, "Joost Rules A.L. Roost at Short, Philly Claims," *TSN*, June 22, 1949, p. 5.

26. James, p. 625.

27. Morrow, p. 5.

28. James, p. 626.

29. Paul Derringer obituary, Paul Derringer HOF bio file, November 30, 1987.

30. Jack Murray, "Thou Fine with Bucky," *CE*, October 17, 1976, p. C-12.

31. Thorn et al., p. 2485.

32. Murray, p. C-12.

33. Associated Press, "Bill McKechnie Is Dead at 78; Ex Manager in National League," *NYT*, October 30, 1965.

34. Ibid.

35. Nack, p. 63.

36. Giles, Warren C., Warren Giles Letter to Mr. Krosula, April 8, 1975.

Appendix A

1. Curt Smith, *Storied Stadiums: Baseball's History Through Its Ballparks*, Carroll & Graf, 2001, p. 84.

2. Ron Smith, *The Ballpark Book*, TSN, 2000, p. 223.

3. C. Smith, p. 78.

4. Bill Shannon, *The Ballparks*, Hawthorn Books, 1975, p. 78.

5. John Thorn, Pete Palmer, Michael Gershman, and David Pietrusza, *Total* Baseball, 6th ed., Total Sports, 1999, p. 91.
6. C. Smith, p. 85.
7. Shannon, p. 81.
8. C. Smith, p. 91.
9. Shannon, p. 78.
10. Ibid., p. 81.
11. Ibid., p. 78.
12. R. Smith, p. 222.
13. Shannon, p. 78.
14. C. Smith, p. 86.
15. Ibid., p. 87.
16. Shannon, p. 78.
17. C. Smith, p. 89.
18. R. Smith. p. 225.
19. C. Smith, p. 90.

Bibliography

Allen, Lee. *The Cincinnati Reds*. New York: Van Rees Press, 1948.

Falls, Joe. *The Detroit Tigers: An Illustrated History*. New York: Wallace, 1989.

Hoppel, Joe. *The Series: An Illustrated History of Baseball's Postseason Showcase*. 1989.

James, Bill. *The Bill James Guide to Baseball Managers from 1870 to Today*. New York: Scribners, 1997

_____. *The New Bill James Historical Baseball Abstract*. New York: Free Press, 2001.

Leventhal, Josh. *The World Series: An Illustrated Encyclopedia of the Fall Classic*. New York: Black Dog & Leventhal, 2002.

Mayer, Ronald A. *The 1937 Newark Bears: A Baseball Legend*. Princeton, N.J.: Rutgers University Press, 1994.

McCabe, Neal, and Constance McCabe. *Baseball's Golden Age: The Photographs of Charles M. Conlon*. St. Louis: Harry N. Abrams, 1993.

Pope, Edwin. *Baseball's Greatest Managers*. Garden City, N.Y.: Doubleday, 1960.

Schorr, Gene. *The History of the World Series*. New York: William Morrow, 1998.

Sherman, Bill. *The Ballparks*. New York: Hawthorn, 1975.

Smith, Curt. *Storied Stadiums: Baseball's History through its Ballparks*. New York: Carroll & Graf, 2001.

Smith, Ron. *The Ballpark Book*. St. Louis: Sporting News, 2000.

Thorn, John; Pete Palmer; Michael Gershman; and David Pietrusza. Kingston, N.Y.: *Total Baseball: Sixth Edition*, Total Sports, 1999.

Tofel, Richard. *The 1939 New York Yankees: A Legend in the Making*. Chicago: Ivan R. Dee, 2004.

Wallace, Joseph; Hamilton, Neil; and Appel, Marty. Baseball: *100 Classic Moments in the History of the Game*. New York: Dorling Kindersley, 2000.

Zanger, Jack. *Great Catchers of the Major Leagues*, New York: Random House, 1970.

Newspapers, Magazines and Websites

Albuquerque Tribune
Baseball-Almanac.com
Baseball Digest
Brooklyn Eagle
Cincinnati Enquirer
Cincinnati Post
Look Magazine
Microsoft Complete Baseball
The National Pastime
The New York Times
Newsweek
Retrosheet.org

Bibliography

Sacramento Bee
The Saturday Evening Post
The Sporting News
Sports Collector's Digest

Sports Illustrated
St. Louis Post-Dispatch
The World Telegram

Index

215

Index